P

LIKE EVERY FORM OF LOVE

"Padma Viswanathan . . . evokes an impressive mix of memory, friendship, true crime—and a detective story where her own skills play an important role. . . . The resulting memoir is painstakingly honest, always complex, sometimes strange." —*Toronto Star*

"Viswanathan's struggle is fascinating and humanizing. . . . A thought-provoking and personal examination of a difficult friendship and what sometimes gets sacrificed when a writer is determined to see a project through to its conclusion." —*Winnipeg Free Press*

"...a book both intimate and universal in its exploration of writing, friendship, and the human desire for closure that remains stubbornly out of reach...Viswanathan may not have all the answers, but she poses the questions beautifully in this achingly honest book that stimulates the heart and mind at all levels." —*Montreal Review of Books*

"*Like Every Form of Love* is a rich hybrid of biography, autobiography, fairy tale and detective work. In moments of lyric intensity, Viswanathan searches others' minds, others' memories and discovers how fluid and fragmentary identity is. A potent meditation on what it means to turn others into story." —**Rosemary Sullivan, author of *The Betrayal of Anne Frank: A Cold Case Investigation***

"Everyone knows that the teller tells the tale, but master tellers also know how the tale tells them, exacting a toll. Padma Viswanathan is a born teller, a master reporter, a master senser, and indeed this may be her masterpiece. The tale she tells is a doozie, but so has been its toll, and her reader will experience the rare, sometimes heartrending privilege of partaking in both."
—**Lawrence Weschler, *Mr. Wilson's Cabinet of Love* and *Seeing is Forgetting the Name of the Thing One Sees***

"As Padma Viswanathan's unlikely friendship with a stranger develops over twenty years, the two uncover his perilous childhood, his loving and dangerous stepmother, an unsolved murder and a thousand shards from his mysterious past. This is the searching story of how digging for the truth tests the boundaries of a passionate friendship." **—Linda Spalding, author of *Who Named the Knife* and *The Purchase***

PRAISE FOR *THE TOSS OF A LEMON*

"...altogether a pleasure."
—*Kirkus Reviews (starred review)*

"She makes a vanished world feel completely authentic. Superbly done."
—*Booklist*

"A brilliant tour de force."
—*India Today*

PRAISE FOR *THE EVER AFTER OF ASHWIN RAO*

"Viswanathan's intricate and empathetic tale deftly reveals the cultural rifts of immigration, post-9/11 politics, and conflicts of faith..."
—*Booklist*

"This new book is the best kind of political novel: the kind that doesn't force you to constantly notice it's a political novel...."
—*The Globe and Mail*

LIKE EVERY FORM OF LOVE

by

Padma Viswanathan

7.13 Books

ALSO BY PADMA VISWANATHAN

The Toss of A Lemon
The Ever After of Ashwin Rao

For C.L.

All right! Let's start the story. When we come to the end, we'll know more than we do now.
—Hans Christian Andersen, *"The Snow Queen"*

The art of writing stories lies in being able to draw, from what little you've understood of life, all the rest, but at the end of the page life resumes and you realize that what you knew was nothing at all.
—Italo Calvino, *The Nonexistent Knight*

Printed in the United States of America

Second Edition
Originally published by Random House Canada in 2023
1 2 3 4 5 6 7 8 9

Cover art by Gigi Little

Library of Congress Cataloging-in-Publication Data

ISBN (paperback): 979-8-9891214-4-1
ISBN (eBook): 979-8-9891214-5-8

CONTENTS

A COMPLICATED BUSINESS

In September 1997, I went to stay on a chunky decommissioned tugboat moored in Genoa Bay, a tiny marina on Vancouver Island. My plan was to spend a couple of weeks writing, alone.

Instead, I made a friend.

On arrival, I'd quickly drawn the attention of my neighbours, people who lived on their boats and spent any spare time or money grooming them, who made their living restoring antique wooden boats, even a woman who had sailed the entire southern hemisphere with her young kids. When I mentioned that my husband was coming out from Edmonton to Victoria for a visit, and that I needed to go see him, they introduced me to Phillip, a fellow land-lubber, who was occupying a friend's boathouse for a few months. He was going to the city for a haircut and could take a passenger.

The marina's permanent residents gave off some snide energy when they mentioned Phillip, but the Genoa Bayers were all characters of towering eccentricity and outsized opinions. Rumours and slights darted between the piers like schools of tiny fish; cliques formed and exploded with the predictability of a lava lamp. Innuendo wasn't to be taken too seriously. My own membership in Genoa Bay society was practically affirmed by a couple of snarky comments about the derelict condition of my tugboat, property of my husband's family.

Phillip was buff, with hollow cheeks and expressive blue eyes: flinty or inquisitive or fonts of loving kindness by turns. There was nothing femmy or camp about him, yet he affected a performative masculinity in public, brusquely calling security guards and checkout clerks "man" and "bud." In private, he unloosed throaty, symphonic laughs, blasts from a rogue angel's trumpet. (God, I loved his laugh.) He'd locked that hard body around a tender heart.

His defences dropped quickly; after that trip to the city, he pursued my friendship. My other project in this time, though, was a three-day fast (either confronting or avoiding my then-life's most urgent subject, my disastrous marriage—I'm still not sure). And as my mother had told me, a food fast is traditionally done with a social fast. She used a Sanskrit word for it, maunam, silence.

Phillip didn't believe in it, not like the fast conflicted with his beliefs, but like he couldn't absorb the fact of its existence. He wanted me to come thrifting with him; he wanted me to taste a delicious cookie he'd bought. I caved on all counts. I had only a few days left in Genoa Bay and was charmed and intrigued. He was so different from my other friends. His courtly manners, opening doors for me and making me walk on the side of the street away from the curb; the way he spoke, in a thick BC lilt, his speech peppered with "fuck" the way others use "like" or "um," using colourful, unfamiliar idioms I'd repeat to myself and write down later. I heard the *stern, brass-knuckled poetry of the dangerous classes* in his waxings-on about his main topic, the pursuit of rough sex, "the game, the gay game," as he put it.

After his haircut in Victoria on our first time out together, he ran a hand along his new fade and mused, "Maybe I'll find me a long-haired motorcycle dude, with my soldier's buzz cut." He told me he hadn't been sure how I would "take the whole homosexuality thing, being straight . . ."

"And Indian?" I guessed.

"Well, yeah," he admitted, "of the culture. But I used to work at a pulp mill, and all the guys there"—Sikhs, I supposed, since they'd been stalwarts in BC's lumber industry for generations—"they'd be having sex with women, men, everyone. I'd get to know these guys and get to know their dads and go to bed with them."

Stories: he had a million of 'em.

On my last afternoon, he invited me for tea at the boathouse where he was living, a floating bungalow with walls of some honey-coloured wood, maybe pine. To one side, its windows showed a low black cliff like a side-hugging arm around the bay; to the front, open water. I'd recorded in my journal that week a series of seal sightings over successive dawns, and also birds: black oystercatcher, mountain bluebird, mute swan, hairy woodpecker, belted kingfisher, and a great blue heron I saw daily from my writing desk, the tugboat's helm. Once, I took my seat to find my eyes level with its scaly feet on the pier beside me.

As Phillip fixed our tea, we chatted idly about desserts. He mentioned a delicious coconut pudding he'd sampled in Cuba and never forgotten.

Cuba? What was he doing there?

It turned out to be the only topic that day: a single story, it took up the entire afternoon.

When Phillip was eleven, his father, Harvey Totten, a single parent in Chilliwack, BC, placed an ad: *Help wanted, three boys.* Two women came and left, third time was the charm: Delia Pilon, petite and sassy, with a narrow, calculating face and an air of glamour. Glossy light-brown hair; blouses tied at the waist. Later, when they lived up north for a time, she liked to smoke a cigar while browsing the aisles at Safeway, "just to shock the shit out of everybody," as Phillip put it. It was her way.

"I told everyone at school that we had a new house keeper." It still made him dreamy to recall it. Del integrated quickly, into the Totten household and into Harvey's bed. Phillip was enraptured.

His mother had been in and out of hospital when he was tiny and gone back east when he was about six. Harvey kept the boys; they'd moved every year since, the main constant being Harvey's severe regimen of chores (corporal punishment always available as an alternative).

In fairy tales the coming of a stepmother is never regarded as anything but a misfortune, but picture Phillip: a tender boy, living in a house of men, when in waltzes this wisecracking lady, smelling good and with soft arms open. What he called the "negative pressure" of the years before, of all his life, really, or all he could remember, he could feel it releasing. When he came home from school, he'd find Del at the kitchen table; he'd natter on about his day as she poured him a glass of milk and filed her nails, a ribbon of smoke fraying from her cigarette.

And after school let out for the year (the Fraser Valley brimming with scents of mud, manure, wild rose, and yarrow), he came home one afternoon to find Del and Harvey packing the car. A holiday. They'd never taken a holiday.

His eldest brother Ben, who was eighteen, was AWOL by then—he'd been running away from home for a few years and eventually did a stint in prison—but Phillip, his brother Rob, Del and Harvey headed south, taking the coastal route into California. Occasionally, Harvey would pull over so he and Del could consult maps; sometimes, they would leave the car and walk into a field or send the boys out of earshot while they had mysterious, intense discussions.

L.A., San Diego, Tijuana. When they attempted to cross the border into Mexico, they were stopped: Del had no ID.They backed up, conferred. Del took the wheel and "stuck a fifty in her tits." Phillip heard her speaking Spanish with the border guard, but as she extracted the money from her cleavage, the guard shook his head. They tried one last time, with Harvey tucking another fifty-dollar bill into his passport along with her warmly creased one.

"No. They turned us around."

Back in San Diego, Del and Harvey explained that the boys would take a Greyhound with him, while Del would take "the midnight express, what criminals took to get to Mexico. The driver would bribe the guards—no stops, no questions."

Once they were reunited in Mexico City, Del had a talk with the kids. "So, listen, guys," she said, as matter-of-fact and maternal as a mother in a TV show, "you have to know something." The boys cocked their heads. "I'm not 'Delia Pilon.' My name is Mary Lloyd and I'm a bank robber. I was paroled, but the conditions stipulated I was supposed to stay in Prince George, ass end of nowhere, nothing and no one. So I broke parole and came down south to be closer to my mum. I'm on the lam." The afternoon light must have been shifting around Phillip as he talked. There are things we can't remember but whose truth we take for granted.

I remember the boathouse as having many windows.

I remember that the tea—regular black tea with milk, probably Red Rose (*only in Canada*)—tasted salty to me, but that when I asked Phillip, he said his tasted fine. (In a nostalgic conversation a couple of years later, I mentioned that strange detail and he confessed he'd mistakenly used water he'd salted for pasta. Why did I still remember it? Because it was strange. Why did he? Because he lied.)

I don't remember that we got on to his family story out of idle chit-chat about desserts: that was in my journal.

I don't remember exactly how Phillip told the story.

I typed it into my computer when I got back to my boat that night, but I've since lost the file. I don't even remember which computer it was. It doesn't matter, because Phillip repeated it many times over the years and because it's not important how he said it but how I heard it, which was how most people hear it: they hear "woman bank robber travelling under an alias," and they're hooked.

In the course of their developing intimacy, Harvey and Del had learned that they had shared political convictions: Harvey was a long-committed leftist, insisting his kids read Marx and sing along to old union songs; Del had gotten to know Fidel Castro and Che Guevara back when those compañeros were planning the Cuban Revolution. She and her late husband, Lew, her former partner in crime, had donated some ill-gotten proceeds to the cause.

"Harvey was a pipefitter," Phillip said, "had his steam ticket, knew carpentry. It was my understanding that we were going down to Cuba to help them rebuild." Del, meantime, was looking forward to a reunion with Fidel.

Now they were stuck in Mexico City because she had no passport. Fortunately, she and Harvey had a "concoction"—Phillip's term—inspired by her having fainted in the crowded exit corridor of a bullfighting arena. They would go to the Canadian embassy and say that in the confusion, her purse, containing her passport, had been stolen.

As the boys tried to keep up with what was genuine and what invented, Del explained what they needed to do to help make sure their fledgling family stayed together. Harvey, with great foresight, had brought along various papers related to the boys' biological mother, Lucille, including their marriage certificate. The idea was that Del would pretend to be her.

"And so," Del asked, all business, "can you guys make it look like I'm your mum?"

Sure, said the boys. *No problem.* Lucille had been gone almost half their life; Del was the closest thing they had to a mother. It wouldn't even really be pretending.

Del went out the next day and bought new clothes—a mid-calf-length dress and jacket, and a hat with a veil that swooped down over one eye. "She looked beautiful, very elegant," Phillip recalled. "Just before we went inside the embassy, she stops, does a look around, to see if anyone's watching." I thought this was vanity, but Phillip clarified: she was "a bit on the paranoid side."

And then, "In the embassy, we boys were all *Mum this* and *Mum that*. We played it to the hilt. Harvey filled out the application, with my real mum's maiden name, her sister's name, her brothers' names, the whole deal. And Del walked out of there with a passport."

"A book should be written."

At some point, Phillip said this. I know he did because I wrote it down in my journal. It's not actually attributed, but it's on a page with other quotes from Phillip. Unless I said it? Unlikely: I'm not inclined to the passive voice. Anyway, I've thought about it so many times now that I can hear him saying it, just as if he did.

Was it a throwaway phrase, a cliché to underline the story's outrageousness?

Or was it calculated to plant a seed, because he knew I was a writer?

It doesn't matter unless we need to decide who to credit or blame for starting this whole mess.

It doesn't matter because as soon as I heard the story, I wanted to write a book, a book about Del—ballsy, beguiling Del.

They landed in Cuba on July 26, 1965. "The Cuban national holiday—we just happened to arrive that day. There was music and gaiety." The streets thronged with people dancing, vibrated with sounds, a *güiro*, a *tres*, hips shaking, heads thrown back, an atmosphere—*gaiety*, that was the word. "We spent two weeks in a fancy hotel—maybe a Hilton pre-revolution?"

Yes: the Habana Libre, formerly the Habana Hilton. It opened in 1958, with five days of celebrity-studded festivities, as the tallest hotel in Latin America. Then the revolution hit and, in 1959, Castro made it his headquarters. By 1964, it was a place to accommodate official visitors, sympathizers, Harvey and Del.

As Del tried to make contact with Fidel, Phillip and Rob

cannonballed into the pool and ate that coconut pudding whose taste Phillip was to recall his entire life. The family toured Havana and, eventually, the island, courtesy of the Cuban government, which provided them with a car, driver and translator. "We were taken around in an old Cadillac. They took us to a refrigeration plant, a sugar cane mill, industry places—the government was apparently seriously considering hiring Harvey.

"At one point, we were in a ballroom all lit by chandeliers—an old Mafia hotel—and our driver asked for the lights to be turned down. He asked again, pointing his finger like it was a gun, but they didn't do it, so he took out a real gun and pointed with that. That's when it clicked for me: This guy's a little more than a driver. Anyway, they turned down the lights."

Within a month, they learned they wouldn't be staying after all. Del told Phillip that Harvey was "rejected because the authorities read him as racist. They said he treated the black people differently from the light-skinned people, with disrespect. *Uppity white person? No, we don't want you here to help.* They told Del that they didn't like his kind of communism."

Back in Canada, Harvey could only find a job way up north, in Kitamat, so that's where they ended up.

"We didn't have a lot of money and we'd sold everything, so Del got all our furniture from the dump. And she had a gambling den, poker. She was good—real good. The mayor would be over and the chief of police and everybody, and everybody would compliment her on the place and she'd brag, 'It's all from the dump! Every piece!'"

A few months later, Harvey got a job that let them move back to the Fraser Valley, a place locals called Strawberry Mountain, adjacent to the Peters Reserve, where they acquired forty-four acres for $8,000, the proceeds from Del's poker game.

They terraced and planted and started building a beautiful A-frame house from timber they harvested from nearby public lands (everyone did it, apparently). Harvey really did have practical skills and know-how.

"Harvey harnessed the creek that ran down through the property and ran irrigation hoses off it. He also jerry-rigged a pipe that ran into the house and through the stove, to heat it, so we had lukewarm running water." His skills also came in useful for other less legitimate enterprises, such as rustling a cow that wandered over one too many times from the neighbours' farm, or distilling moonshine from cider the kids made by running apples through an oak press. They made do, got along to get along.

In Cuba, Del had been conveniently out of reach of the RCMP. Now, on Canadian soil, the whole family was implicated in her secret. Phillip picked up tidbits of her former life. Her late husband, Lew Lloyd, had been a longshoreman—a crooked, opportunistic profession, as she sketched it, but victimless. Or almost: a few months after they committed the robbery for which Del served time, Lew had turned up dead of a bullet in Edmonton, courtesy of some former associates.

They had two daughters, both under five when Lew was killed and Del convicted, who were sent to Lew's sister to be raised. Del was letting them stay there. She said the elder one, Lorraine, was exactly Phillip's age.

Del's recollections also came with lessons in vocabulary. Kites passed bad cheques; boosters were shoplifters; skinners were rapists;

The Edmonton Journal

One Of Canada's Great Newspapers

Bullet-Pierced Body Found At Outskirts

29 Are Killed In Airline Crash

British Plane Burns After Hitting Tree At Takeoff

Victim's Wife, Man And Gun Sought By Police Investigators

Friend Tells Of Night Call

Fatality Presents Puzzles

Queen To Open Seaway?

New Jets Dominate Moscow Air Display

diddlers were pedophiles. Rounders: "a solid type of crook, only robs people who can afford it—businesses, banks, corporations. Has a real clear sense of morals and ethics."

Del and Harvey married a year or so after the Cuba trip, but they were perhaps not suited to a life of simple industry and domestic harmony. The sense of lightness and adventure faded. They started to fight.

"There was a lot of physical abuse by Harvey. We would be walking on eggshells. Numerous times we would go and see the police because Del was beaten up by Harvey, and the police would put us up in a motel. There weren't any battered women's shelters. Welfare couldn't do anything." The *negative pressure* had returned; its weight was blackmail.

"Harvey would say, *You get back to the farm or I'm turning you in.* Going into town because she's got a couple of black eyes, going back home the next day because there was no choice."

One time, out working in the fields, Del fainted. "I'm pretty sure she'd aborted herself," Phillip guessed. "She never talked to me about it, but I overheard a fight later, where she said, 'I never wanted your fucking baby.'"

Eventually, I would see a photo of Phillip as a shy, chubby thirteen-year-old, his arm around Del, who wore a slinky, strappy number. It was New Year's. "She finished sewing up the dress that night, because it had to be skin-tight, and when they got home, they were fighting. He was accusing her of flirting with people at the party. Whether she did or not, I have no idea, but she was looking pretty spiffy."

The fight lasted twenty-four hours. The next day, "Del ran into the kitchen, stark naked, picked up a glass coffee pot and took his lunch out of the fridge. She threw the lunch on the floor, threw the coffee pot onto it, and ground it up in the lunch. She would take it for a while, then not take it."

One Saturday morning, they clashed terminally.

"Come into town with me," Harvey told her. "I'm going for groceries."

"No," Del said.

"Get in the car."

"Phillip," she said. "You want to come?"

He sure didn't. You got in the car with Harvey, he would cuff you, backhand you, who knows what. There was no room in their little VW Beetle to get away.

Anyway, Harvey didn't want him along. "He's not coming."

"Then I'm not," she said.

"I'll see you out there," Harvey said on his way out the door.

"I'll see you in hell."

In a couple of minutes, Harvey stormed back in. "Where are you?" he roared from the door. She went straight to the knife drawer and grabbed a meat cleaver.

"Come here, you motherfucker," she roared back. Harvey turned and ran.

He didn't return for two weeks. They had no money, because Harvey held the purse strings. Maybe they should have gone shopping after all. They made out all right for food—they were essentially self-sustaining—but Del ran out of coffee and cigarettes, which couldn't have helped her mood. Plus they were terrified, wondering what Harvey was planning.

Two weeks later, he walked in and ordered the kids out of the house. When he couldn't stand it anymore, Phillip went back inside. "Where's Del?" he asked when he didn't see her.

"I'm leaving," he heard her say, and he ran toward the bedroom, but she was already walking out with a bag.

He put his hand on her sleeve. "I'm going with you."

"No," Harvey yelled from the kitchen, "you are not."

Del went to stay with a family friend, a prison guard who knew her true identity, unlike the rest of their circle.

After she left, Phillip said, "Del and I would talk on the phone, because Harvey wouldn't be home when I got home from school. I'd phone her and say, 'I'm not staying here, I'm going to run away.'"

He wore her down. They made a plan.

"It was midnight. I opened my bedroom door, and I heard Harvey get up. I froze while he went to the can and back to bed, and then the grandfather clock starting chiming midnight, which gave me twelve steps to get to the door. Then I ran like hell." He made for the neighbours' house, where Del fetched him the next day.

They were a unit now, for better or for worse: "fugitives on the run, trying to hide in plain sight, a deep camaraderie."

I have imagined these events so many times—the poker nights in Kitamat, the midnight escape—that they are as real in my memory as events from my own life. Maybe even more so, since I accept that my own memory is fragmentary and elusive, whereas I have grasped hard on every substantiating detail of Phillip's, trying to bring them to life on the page.

And while I only recall wanting to write about Del, back there in Genoa Bay, my journal records my fascination with Phillip as well. He was not only a conduit to a story I wanted to write but a character in it, glowing in that magic-hour sun, ringed by the survivor's ennobling halo.

I hit pay dirt, I wrote in my diary that week, about the denizens of Genoa Bay. *What an ugly term. I feel a reluctance to pin them down, especially Phillip. But I must—kill the butterfly to preserve it.*

TAKING NOTES

Can a writer and subject be friends?

Walter Kirn, in *Blood Will Out*, his strange account of his relationship with the serial con artist and murderer Christian Gerhartsreiter, berates himself in retrospect for letting his man-crush on Gerhartsreiter blind him to the killer's true nature: *I was degrading my vocation. My grant of literary immunity to the strangest creature I'd ever met violated my storyteller's oath. Writers exist to exploit such figures, not to save them. Our duty is to the page, not the person.*

But page and person are usually commingled in the writer's psyche, or at least they are in mine. Also, when Kirn says "person," he means the subject, but what about the writer, who is also, typically, a person?

What kind of a person, though? Recently, I was discussing the Alice Munro story "To Reach Japan" with my book club. On a train, an actor, Greg, draws all the children into a game: *He managed things so that he turned the attention first drawn to himself into the children's awareness of each other and then into games that were lively or even wild, but not bad-tempered. . . . It was a miracle, how much ease with wildness was managed in such a small space.*

The protagonist, Greta, is both impressed and gratefully relieved of her own child, as she admits to Greg's girlfriend, Laurie.

"He's mostly just there," Laurie said. "He doesn't save himself up. You know? A lot of actors do. Actors in particular."

Most of my book-club fellows are theatre people—talented, accomplished—who have tempered their artistic ambitions for the sake of life and loved ones. One, also an actor named Greg, commented, "That's what I like about us. We don't save ourselves up."

Munro's protagonist is a writer. She responds to Laurie's comment the same way I did to real-life actor Greg's: *Greta thought, That's what I do. I save myself up, most of the time.*

I didn't tell my friends my reaction. I saved it up.

Greta admires Greg's way of being, but it doesn't change hers: watching, writing, thinking, *fussing and probing, secretly tough as nails . . .*

Secretly tough as nails. Saving myself up. Pinning the butterfly. Maybe the writer isn't, can't be, much of a person after all.

There is a cryptic entry in my sketchy, badly organized journals, suggesting that I had doubts about the truth of Phillip's outlandish story or about his role in it. Even if it was true, what were the chances that it all happened to him?

He told me that Neil Fleishman, a flamboyant Vancouver lawyer who eventually helped Del clear her parole violation charges and get a divorce from Harvey, had written a memoir featuring her. On returning home to Edmonton from Genoa Bay, I found the book, *Counsel for the Damned*, in the University of Alberta library. It's a mishmash of braggadocio and pulp, studded with sketches of Fleishman's most infamous cases. His clients are pseudonymized, but Phillip told me to look for "Ruth Pasjack," one of Del's underworld aliases.

"When Fleishman's book came out," Phillip said, "the story was—true or false, I don't know—that he got calls from Toronto and Montreal looking for her, people from the underworld. She didn't want anything to do with them."

I mailed Phillip photocopies of the relevant Fleishman pages as well as a sequence of *Vancouver Sun* articles I found about the trial that had sent Mary Lloyd to jail. Fleishman's account lined up with the newspaper report; neither contradicted what Phillip had told me.

In spring 1956, Mary drove the getaway car when her husband, Lew, and another associate robbed a bank of $5,100. The articles I found, from January 1957, said the jury returned a guilty verdict after deliberating for only ten minutes. Mary and the associate were the ones who stood trial; Lew was already dead. The justice, A. M. Manson, imposed sentences of twenty-five years each, with the associate additionally sentenced to fifteen strokes of the paddle.

It was a ridiculously outsized sentence for a single, small-potatoes robbery; observers thought it was the judge's way of making Mary pay for Lew's murder, a crime for which she was suspected, but never brought to trial. Funny detail: the prosecutor appealed the sentences as too harsh. Mary would have to go to Kingston Penitentiary. The only federal facility for women in the country, it was thousands of miles from her young daughters and her aged parents.

She ended up serving seven of fifteen years, the second-longest term served by a woman in Canadian history to that point. (The record holder had killed her husband and baby; the baby was found encased in concrete.)

The final *Vancouver Sun* article, January 15, 1957, included pictures of the convicts. Mary Lloyd has a long face with strong cheekbones, thin lips and large, clear eyes. Her hair is arranged in soft waves around her face. Her surviving co-conspirator, a fellow by the name of James Kempster, has thick dark hair combed back from a high forehead and close-set eyes under heavy brows. While

STANLEY KEMPSTER
... 25 years, paddle

MARY LLOYD
... stiff sentence

Holdup Pair Get 25 Years Each

NEW WESTMINSTER — Stanley James Kempster and Mary Eleanor Lloyd were each sentenced Monday to

he seems to glower at the camera, his mouth pursed in a slight frown, Mary's straight-on look is more ambiguous: frank or appealing or even slightly amused—one eyebrow slightly higher than the other, mouth tilting up a tiny bit on that same side.

She's a looker, as Phillip said, groomed and in control, even in her mug shot. I spent a lot of time imagining what it would be like to encounter her on her own terms, then more time imagining what those terms would be.

Can a writer and a subject be friends? Depends what you think of as friendship.

In Helen Simpson's short story "Opera," a couple is getting ready for a night out: their wedding anniversary. The wife loves opera; they're going to Berlioz's *Orpheus and Eurydice*. But the husband is doubling up on the occasion, using it to entertain some clients, which dampens his wife's pleasure in ways she can't get him to understand.

"Clients aren't friends," she said.

"They can be," he said. "You're so narrow-minded. They can become very good friends."

"No," she mumbled. "Clients are about money."

"Oh, wicked Mammon," he hooted. " Everything's about money if you're talking in that ignorant way. Music certainly is."

"Clients are business," she persisted. "Not pleasure."

"Client entertainment is all about pleasure," he snarled. "Good tickets, champagne, the works."

"You can't get drunk with clients," she said.

"You certainly can," said Christopher. "I do."

"True," she conceded. "But you couldn't ever be really rude or insulting to them."

"You won't keep many friends that way either."

"You don't make friends for their usefulness," she said. "There can't be strings attached."

"Why not?" he said. "Mutually beneficial relationships, that's the

way the world works. Special relationships; hadn't you heard? Symbiotic's the word. Hadn't you noticed?"

I doubt I'm the only reader of "Opera" who feels the wife is being gaslighted. She's making a legitimate case poorly. People have been trying crudely to distinguish categories of friendship at least since Aristotle. He had three—friendships formed for mutual benefit; friendships formed for mutual pleasure; and friendships formed by people drawn to each other's aretē, or virtue. Broad theoretical types, useful up to a point, but not terribly accurate to the nature of friendships as they are lived.

Aristotle said his last category was the best, truest, even maybe the only true type of friendship, and perhaps that had some aspirational truth in 350 BC, but I put my most-valued friendships in the second category, even when they have valences of the first or third.

William Hazlitt took my side, a hundred and fifty years ago: *In estimating the value of an acquaintance or even a friend, we give a preference to intellectual or convivial over moral qualities. The truth is that in our habitual intercourse with others, we much oftener require to be amused than assisted.* Phillip would have helped me, if I'd ever needed it, but friendships are more about fun than function. *We consider less, therefore, what a person with whom we are intimate is ready to do for us in critical emergencies, than what he has to say on ordinary occasions.* We might even forgive lapses, unavailability or insensitivity, *if only*, per Hazlitt, *he saves us from ennui.*

Phillip amused me, and I admired him. Our friendship had been occasioned by proximity, though, and after I went home, there was little to bind us. Still, we began phoning each other, every month or couple of months.

He would tell me about his work as a nurse's aide, his daily life in Victoria, his prolific sexual escapades. He was unapologetically promiscuous but what he really wanted was to find a love, someone to cherish and dedicate himself to.

He described the patients he tended, their families. I'd had several surgeries myself and felt in my body how reassuring it would be to be cared for by someone so solicitous and attentive, so committed to the spirit of his profession. In his time off, he volunteered at a community centre, giving pedicures to seniors and the homeless. He radiated love: *eros, philia, agape*.

What did I talk to him about? Maybe my work, my daily life, but not in depth. He was a good reader but not a close observer of culture and we shared few reference points. I informed him when my marriage ended, but he didn't particularly inquire into the reasons. We had no friends in common outside of Genoa Bay, and I hadn't kept in touch with anyone else from there, anyway. Our conversations were limited in a way I recognized: I glossed my life for him the way I do for relatives, people I love who don't share my interests the way my friends do.

And indeed, after a few years, he started to refer to me as his little sister, his signal that we were now chosen family. Our dynamic, owing to my voluminous, non-chosen, extended family, was perhaps more familiar to me than he might have realized.

A couple of years after we met, I returned to the west coast for a visit. He planned a lovely day out: canoeing Victoria's inner harbour, visiting a historic tall ship temporarily docked there, eating thick sandwiches in a café-terrasse. I returned a couple of years after that, and stayed with him, and then it became a thing I did: having a visit with him whenever I went west.

Through his twenties, Phillip had struggled with addictions, alcohol and hard drugs; now, as if to prove all that instability was behind him, he bought a condo and worked extra shifts to pay it off in less than seven years. Now he quit pot; now he took up long-distance cycling. It appeared from the outside as though he was channelling the energies formerly taken up by substances into an obsessive pursuit of stability and health.

The first time I stayed in his condo, the bathroom smelled like a Players Light doused in Lysol: he used to smoke in there with the fan on, until he quit cigarettes and took up antiques.

Fifteen years into his occupancy, the condo was filled with objets d'art and items of use, nothing fussy or flowery, but rather a collection dominated by earthy tones and robust textures. He appeared to concentrate on the era of Canada's settlement: whale-oil lamps, a human yoke, a wood plane, harmoniously arranged and curated, perfectly dusted and ordered, alongside more rarefied items. Victorian creamers stood in groups like gossiping villagers, copper kettles more aloof. Vancouver Island was, throughout the twentieth century, a retirement destination for former colonials, who washed up here with their bric-a-brac, *life being, as Ortega y Gasset once remarked, in itself and forever shipwreck.*

Whenever I visited, Phillip pointed out items I might otherwise miss. Once, he hoisted what he called a "Chinese vase"—blue-painted porcelain, a covered pot with a handle and a spout. I cautiously admired it—I'm not a collector and struggle to grasp the governing principles. As I pretended to mull, he started giggling: the "vase" was a urinal.

His bed, where I slept, was covered with a Dresden Plate quilt in pinks and greens. At its head, a series of eight prints showed Inuit figures bent to tasks. Against the wall leaned a folding luggage rack, "what the Via Rail cars used to have to put your luggage on in the olden days," Phillip told me. As far as I knew, it never served that use in his home for anyone but me.

We might not have had much in common to start with, but once the relationship took hold, we accumulated shared experiences, running jokes, the sense of keeping track of each other across time and distance.

Years passed. I divorced, remarried, moved to the US, had a baby, went to graduate school, bought a house, brought my parents to live with us, had another baby, published a novel, became a professor, published another novel. During our phone calls, I would dust, fold laundry, pass notes to my kids or husband—*milk on grocery list?* or *screentime over clean yr room!*—to keep the household wheels turning.

Sometimes, he went on about matters that didn't much interest me, such as his study of the psychic arts and communication with those "on the other side." He would refer to colleagues or friends by name without context or reminder—the way I referred to my parents or husband or, eventually, kids. (I had so many family members in my daily life that I never even tried to tell him anything about my friends.) I felt ashamed to interrupt and ask for a reminder of who the people were that he was referring to. Fact was, I couldn't remember who they were because I wasn't that interested in them. I just let him talk.

Consumed as I was with life, family, career and community, and considering how far he was from any of those, it was sometimes difficult to find the time to call him, occasionally tough even to pick up the phone when he called me, which he inevitably did when I took too long to get in touch.

So what allowed our friendship to take such deep root? What was the extra glue in those early years that held us together long enough that I came to love him as I did?

It was the book, the book I wanted to write, the book that didn't exist yet, and that never would, unless I had the whole story.

When we talked, Phillip would drop references to Del, to the precarity and excitement of their pre-and post-Harvey life.

Anytime he did, I would open my computer, holding my phone to my ear with my shoulder through those first years, then, later, putting in earbuds.

I would take notes.

Fleeing Harvey brought Phillip and Del even closer together. They were a unit now, for better or for worse. Del looked out for him and he would do anything for her, and she knew it. It was during this time that Phillip recognized glimmers of the telepathic connection between them: "You'd just have to think, *I wouldn't mind a cup of tea about now*, and the other would get up to make it. I always thought, if I married someone, it would have to be like that." The gold standard of love.

Del found them an apartment under a new alias, the second floor of a house. Phillip kept going to the same school as before, but he was always on the lookout for Harvey.

This peace was short-lived. Maybe three or four weeks into their time there, Phillip had come home from school and was gabbing to her, drinking his glass of milk. "BANG-BANG-BANG on the door. Open the door, there's Harvey." He'd followed Phillip home. "I'd been keeping an eye out for his VW, but he was driving a brand-new Mazda. He came in and kicked me out."

Phillip waited in the yard. April—cherry trees in bloom. After a while, Harvey descended the stairs and drove off in his new car. Phillip watched him go, filled with fear, despair, claustrophobia—Del's feelings flowing through him—and knew what Harvey had said: *I'm turning you in, bitch. You stole my kid, I'm turning you in.*

The worst had happened and now they had to figure out what to do.

Del stashed Phillip at a boarding house and went to ground, but she was arrested within a month at her mother's house in Vancouver and incarcerated in Matsqui, a women's prison on the lower mainland. Phillip would hitchhike out to Vancouver every Friday evening, stay with Del's mother, hitchhike to visit Del in Matsqui on Saturday, come home Sunday.

Del instructed him to contact Simma Holt, a *Vancouver Sun* reporter who had advocated for her parole back in '64. Lew Lloyd's sister brought Del's elder daughter, Lorraine, to visit. The two teens went together to talk to Holt.

Holt recruited Neil Fleishman, the lawyer, who directed Phillip to collect testimonials from their old neighbours as to what a good mother Del had been, how responsible and caring, what an upstanding member of their community. It worked. The only parole condition she'd reportedly violated was skipping out on her supervision. In all other ways, she appeared to have fulfilled its intention, living a respectable, law-abiding life.

Free from parole and, soon, free from Harvey: Fleishman, arguing physical and mental cruelty, got her a divorce and half of their shared property.

The final question the judge asked in the divorce proceeding: "And as to the disposition of the children?"

Harvey, quivering with suppressed rage, stood, pointed to Phillip's older brother Rob, and declared his intention to take custody of him, just that one boy.

A long silence ensued, the stenographer's fingers poised above her machine, the judge looking expectantly from one adult to another. The silence lengthened a little more, lengthened toward its breaking point as Phillip felt an old emotion creeping toward his core: abandonment. Was that Del's emotion? Or was Phillip recalling his own trauma, his actual mother's departure when he was only six?

She'd come out that spring, Lucille, his biological mother, a month or two after Del was reincarcerated. Phillip was still living at the boarding house and assumed his school or social services had called her—*this kid, he has no one to look after him.* She'd asked Phillip if he wanted to come back east with her, but he turned her down. He'd hitched his wagon to Del. He waited now, in the courtroom, his heart unnaturally still, sweat coming out on his palms.

Finally, Del stood. "I take custody of Phillip Dennis Totten."

The judge nodded. "So granted."

Phillip and Del hugged, flooded with her relief and his pride. He had won her freedom and won her for himself.

They withdrew to a nearby café, together with Fleishman and his whip-smart legal secretary, the one who kept all the details straight. They toasted with their coffee cups. As Fleishman glanced at his watch, the secretary said, "Del, you've just made legal history again. You're the first criminal in Canadian history to get legal custody of a child who's not your blood relative."

They all looked at Del and shook their heads. She smiled, raising one eyebrow, mouth tilting a tiny bit higher on that same side. She was something else.

Twelve or more years into our friendship, I confessed to Phillip my longstanding desire: "I want to write your story. That is, Del's."

"I'm not surprised," he said.

"It's a great story," I said. "Your story, too," I added, uncertain of how or whether to let him know that it wasn't just Del—crooks and Cuba and cow rustling—but also his role (and his way of speaking and all he'd endured) that attracted me to the idea.

"You should talk to Del," he said.

"I'd love to," I said, a little breathless at the thought.

"Would you have any idea how to find her?"

"Nah. I could try to find her, but"—his voice was lightly serrated—"when you talk to her, don't mention me."

They had parted ways long ago in circumstances still unclear to me, but he said he was willing to try to find her. He offered to help in any way he could, to introduce me to his brothers. He hadn't spoken to Harvey since his twenties, but heard that he had moved to Nicaragua, married a widow there and adopted her daughters, and, when he died, had been buried down there. Maybe I'd be able to find out more.

We agreed, also, that I would interview Phillip more formally, record him and try more systematically to chronicle his journey from that patchwork of a childhood into the integrated person he was now.

Mostly, we lived our friendship as a twosome. Occasionally, though, others would be inserted, deliberately or accidentally, into our closed system. He came to see me in Edmonton when I brought my husband and new baby to spend the summer with my parents. He met me in Vancouver on my first book tour, when my father accompanied me as nanny to our second child, a daughter.

In Vancouver, Phillip took us for dim sum. He knew Chinatown intimately—he'd ended up living on the street there for a time in his twenties. He guided us past the medicinal herb stores, past grocery stores with bins full of creatures I couldn't identify but that smelled of the sea—I pointed to one bin and asked a woman slurping jade-green soup what was in it; "Food!" she barked—to a nondescript door in a block of two-storey walk-ups, tailors and accountants, up a set of stairs carpeted in ratty red and into—surprise!—a restaurant the size of a ballroom, packed with families brunching loudly. The waiters pushed their dim sum carts between tables like Pac-Man and ghosts. Phillip would lean back, raise a finger and ask to look under a silver dome or inside a bamboo basket, order with authority, theatrically savour every taste.

Afterwards, he took us to the Dr. Sun Yat-Sen Classical Chinese Garden. It was one of those drizzly Vancouver afternoons. My dad took pictures of us standing by tall, pocked grey rocks, in front of bamboo, under a magnolia. In one photo, Phillip laughs at the baby as she grasps our fingers as though pulling herself up out of the stroller into the light.

Vancouver's Chinatown has been, for some years, the epicentre of Canadian homelessness and, at some point that day, we narrowly avoided a threat. I don't remember it: Phillip protected us, he said, heading off the attacker almost without us noticing. Maybe I didn't realize how significant it was; I have no memory of it. But Phillip would refer to it from time to time, how we didn't register the risk, how his street smarts let him come to our rescue.

A few times when I visited, he introduced me to friends of his. Mostly, they were lovely, as he promised. A couple of friends, though, whom he'd described as "delightful" and "brilliant," struck me as pretentious. One made subtle digs to Phillip's face about his spiritual pursuits and his weight (he'd gained a few pounds after he quit smoking) and, when Phillip went to the loo, asked me, "How did *you* get to be friends with *him*?"

Phillip's eldest brother, when I interviewed him, asked the same question, his curiosity perhaps tinged with jealousy that Phillip had an intellectual for a friend, especially one who thought him interesting enough to write about. A Cuban biologist we met in the Havana airport would ask it, too, with a snobby sneer, in Spanish—literally speaking a language my friend couldn't understand.

I didn't care how people saw us, but I saw in those moments how they saw him: as unlettered, unfiltered, unsophisticated. I would feel insulted and defensive, protective of him and proud that I could see what they failed to: his genuineness, his gentleness, his resilience and genius for life—how he was *the single maker of the song he sang, the single artificer of the world in which he sang.*

I get it. I recall friends who wanted my taste in men to be the same as theirs: *Isn't he so cute?* they would ask. *Um, no,* I would think. Ditto others' babies, others' outfits.

Vive la différence. As Michel de Montaigne said of his dear friend La Boétie, in "Of Friendship": *If you press me to tell you why I loved him, I feel that this cannot be expressed except by answering: Because it was he, because it was I.*

The philosopher Alexander Nehamas, in an extended argument comparing friendship to art, resolves this by resorting to Kant's "antinomy of taste"—the dilemma of aesthetic judgment: Can a book or painting be judged objectively or are all aesthetic judgments reducible to personal taste? *For Kant,* says Nehamas, *our sense that something is beautiful is produced not by that object's features but by a particular feeling of pleasure that object occasions in us.*

Perhaps the most common experience affirming the truth of this is parenthood: I adore my children abjectly; I fawn over them. Yet I'd never expect anyone else to find them so gorgeous and astonishing, the lyric of their little bodies on push-scooters, the sound of them calling *Mommy* as they bumbled into a room.

Nor, even when I feel consuming admiration for a person or a work of art, do I abandon my critical sensibilities, which, according to some people, are overdeveloped. "You're the most critical person I know," my daughter told me when she was about ten.

What are we, after all, asks psychoanalyst Adam Phillips, *but our powers of discrimination, our taste, the violence of our preferences?*

"Well, at least you know you can trust me when I praise you," I told her, probably small compensation for having a mother who is a writer.

I'm a writer. This means I'm cleft. Part of me lives and loves; the other part is watching and weighing, turning people into phrases, not only saving myself up but saving *them* up, all my observations, all their stories.

Hans Christian Andersen quite literally embodied this cleft self in his creepy tale "The Shadow." In it, a scholar's own shadow leaves him to go spy in the house of poetry, then moves on, not returning until he's gotten rich off of invisibility, slinking through streets, peering through windows, learning evil secrets. *If I had written a newspaper, everyone would have read it, but instead I wrote directly to the persons themselves,* he slyly confesses to the scholar, who is writing about *the true and the beautiful and the good,* not a route to material success.

"The Shadow," says Andersen biographer Jackie Wullschlager, *is about how we accommodate, or fail to accommodate, the darker side of our souls.* She, like many people who read the story, thinks about Jung, about the shadow everyone carries, *the selfishness and thwarted desires* and the dangers of failing to acknowledge these. *The scholar refuses to face his dark side, so it defeats him*—his shadow has him put to death.

But of course, Wullschlager goes on, *Andersen is not only the scholar but the shadow as well, a shifty dark figure watching behind the scenes—he artist as a man without identity of his own but finely tuned to all experiences.* She quotes an 1855 letter from Andersen to a friend: *"I am like water, everything moves me, everything is reflected in me, I suppose this is part of my nature as a poet and often I enjoy this and receive blessings from it, but often it also torments me."*

This double nature is inevitable, taken for granted in the writer. We can't do our work without it. *The look that one directs at things, both outward and inward, as an artist,* says Joseph Campbell, is not the gaze of your human self. *As a man, you might be well-disposed, patient, loving, positive, and have a wholly uncritical inclination, but as an artist your demon constrains you to observe, to take note of every detail that in the literary sense would be characteristic, distinctive, significant, opening insights, recording all as mercilessly as though you had no human relationship to the observed object whatever.*

Again, if only it were so simple. It's not.

I found the Joseph Campbell quote in Janet Malcolm's book-length essay *The Journalist and the Murderer,* about writer Joe McGinniss, who pretended to befriend an accused murderer in order to get access to his story. At least, McGinniss said he was pretending: during the years of research and writing, when he stayed close to the subject, it was pretty hard for any external observer, including the accused himself, to tell the difference.

You would think, according to what so many writers, including Campbell, say about their art, that the necessity of cleaving self from self would ensure McGinniss his success, just as you would think it might ensure my failure. I observed Phillip, but not mercilessly. I listened and took careful notes because of an instinctual chemical attraction that deepened over time: I loved him.

But Malcolm says love is the secret sauce. Contrasting Joe McGinniss with Joseph Mitchell and Truman Capote, she says, *a crucial element of the transformation from life to literature that the masters of the nonfiction genre achieve is the writer's identification with and affection for the subject, without which the transformation from human being to literary character cannot take place. The Joe Goulds and the Perry Smiths of life tend to be windy bores and pathetic nutcases; only in literature, after they have got under the skin of a writer, do they achieve the ambition of fantastic interestingness that in actuality they only grotesquely gesture toward.*

Did others see Phillip as a windy bore? I didn't trust them. I looked on Phillip with love; I saw his *fantastic interestingness.*

Alexander Nehamas's main argument is that we seek rewards in friendship much the way we do in a painting or a poem we love. I think that fails to take account of friendship's open-endedness and reciprocity, but it's true that Phillip held my interest in the way of a book I might return to, again and again, seeking pleasure and meaning.

All of these writers, though—philosophers, journalists, mythographers—are silent on what happens if you actually confuse a friend you love with a book you want to write.

OF DUCKLINGS AND SWANS

"WOULD YOU RATHER GO to bed with Elvis Presley or Diana Ross?" Del asked Phillip with that not-really-playful smile she had. He was twelve.

"Diana!" he said, indignantly, because he didn't want her to think he was weird. He loved Diana Ross, her voice, her hair, her clothes. But what did Del mean, go to bed?

"I didn't have a clue, not till the hormones jolted in. But I always took that as an indication that Del knew," he told me. She knew more about him than he knew about himself: that's how tight they were. "She purposely put a man first and a lady second."

Del saved Phillip, that was clear, but from what or whom? From the chill and loneliness of being unseen.

"*Coincidence,*" says Rebecca Solnit in *The Faraway Nearby, is often used to mean accident but literally means to fall together. The patterns of our lives come from those things that do not drift apart but move together for a little while, like dancers.*

We call a good coincidence serendipity, *the faculty of making happy and unexpected discoveries by accident.* Horace Walpole coined the term: on making a happy, unexpected discovery about a sixteenth-century Venetian painting, he referred to it by way of a sixteenth-century Venetian tale set on the isle of Serendib, as Sri Lanka was called once upon a time.

That story tells of three princes who indeed make unexpected discoveries, not by accident, but by rational deduction—guesses based on acute observation. The only thing accident has to do with serendipity is the accidental misuse that birthed it into English. Still, it's a beautiful word and a useful one.

Serendipity brought Del into Phillip's life; his persistence ensured they didn't *drift apart but moved together for a little while, like dancers.*

In childhood, Phillip stuck to the margins, not because he was an outcast, according to him, but because it gave him the best view. Now, Del's pointedly serendipitous question let him see a pattern in his own life.

"When did you realize you were gay?" I asked.

He said he always knew, just didn't have a way to express his longings, nor even, really, a name for them.

"Was it hard for you, growing up?" He shrugged, and mentioned a boy from high school, an athlete. "He talked a girl into going for a walk with me." An act of charity. "She and I held hands, but I didn't know what else to do. I wanted to get into his pants."

Phillip insisted that he never experienced homophobia at school, but I couldn't quite believe him. Homophobia back then was like lead or asbestos; it was a flavour you recalled when you drank the water in some other town; it was the smell of your own house.

There was one incident he mentioned, however: he'd been ogling a boy who, passing him in the hall later, shoved him into the lockers, no eye contact, nothing said. Leaning there, the breath knocked out of him, he thought, *Oh: you gotta hide this.*

Back in grade one, his eyes were always drawn to one particular boy who played baseball at lunch. "I remember looking at him," Phillip told me, twinkling in his soft way, "and thinking that if I could just go and stand beside him, everything in the world would be okay."

Was it significant, I wonder now, that this recollection dated from about the time Phillip's biological mother, Lucille, left their family, when nothing in his world was okay?

If I put this to Phillip, he might narrow his eyes, frown, make resistant sounds—"Mm. No, no, no." Or he might open his eyes wide and cock his head—wryly impressed—as he did when I suggested to him interpretations of his own life that had not occurred to him but that struck him as possibly true.

I no longer have a way to ask him and maybe, at this point, I trust my telling of his life as much as I trust his. After twenty-five years of thinking about his story, I see some patterns, too.

If I consider Hans Christian Andersen's "The Shadow" to be the fairy tale of my life—and I do—I might consider his tale "The Ugly Duckling" to be Phillip's.

It opens on a mother duck, feeling a little sorry for herself because brooding her eggs *was taking so long and hardly anyone came to visit her.* To her relief, they finally hatch, except for the biggest. An older duck comes by and sows a seed of doubt: *"I am sure that it's a turkey egg! I was fooled that way once."* Against this elder's advice to abandon it, though, the mother duck keeps the big egg warm and protected until it hatches and her misfit tumbles out.

At first, as he is chased away and nipped at by other ducks and turkeys, she defends him. *"Leave him alone!" shouted the mother. "He's not hurting anyone!"*

Before long, though, she's tired of the situation. *The poor creature was mocked and laughed at by the whole farmyard. Even his mother said, "I wish you were far away."*

The duckling runs away. He meets some wild ducks who tell him he better not try to marry into their family, but he's far yet from any such fantasy, still paddling around at the bottom of

Maslow's hierarchy. *All he wanted was to be allowed to swim among the reeds and drink a little water when he was thirsty.*

He tags along with a couple of wild geese who end up getting themselves shot out of the air. He gets taken into other houses, other farms, whose admission price is that he recognize the superiority of their values. He leaves all of them, suffering a winter of privation *en plein air* rather than conform. A choice? Depends how you look at it.

Andersen considered "The Ugly Duckling" to be the most autobiographical of his stories. As a youth, towering over other children, he was mocked for his social awkwardness, but he felt always that his tribe awaited him somewhere and that eventually they would be united. In the magical, metaphorical transference of this beloved tale, says Jackie Wullschlager, Andersen *fused a record of his own suffering with a wish-fulfillment ending which promised hope and consolation.*

On an evening at the start of that lonely winter, *just as the sun was setting gloriously, a flock of beautiful birds came out from among the rushes. Their feathers were so white that they glistened; and they had long, graceful necks. They were swans. They made a wondrous loud cry, then spread their powerful wings, flying south to a warmer climate, where lakes were not frozen in the winter. Higher and higher they circled. The ugly duckling turned round and round in the water like a wheel and stretched his neck up toward the sky, filled with a strange longing. He screeched so piercingly that he frightened himself.*

Oh, he would never forget those beautiful birds, those happy birds. When they were out of sight, the duckling dove down under the water to the bottom of the lake. When he came up again, he was beside himself. He did not know the name of those birds or where they were going, and yet he felt that he loved them as he had never loved anyone else.

All he is thinking is that he desires them, those powerful silhouettes soaring against the dusk. It will be some time yet before he understands that he is one of them, that the desire whose expression so frightens him is that of plunging among his own.

But why refer to fairy tales at all?

If I asked Phillip, he would say, "Girl, because I want my story *packed* with fairies!" And I would snort and hit his arm. Haha.

Really, though: I keep coming back to Andersen's tales.

Partly because of the *tough core of most of the stories,* as Rebecca Solnit puts it, *the struggle to survive against adversaries, to find your place in your world, and to come into your own. Fairy tales are children's stories not in who they were made for but in their focus on the early stages of life, when others have power over you and you have power over no one.*

Fairy tales are equated with childhood, but what happens to us in childhood happens to us our whole lives.

Objectively speaking, Phillip was terribly, terribly vulnerable.

"When I was fourteen or so, I worked at berry picking."

The first time he told me this story was on a trip we made back to where he grew up, in the low green valley of the Fraser River.

"There was a man who used to prey on the kids of the poor families who lived in the picking shacks: He'd lure a boy back to his place, feed him booze, and molest him, *wham, bam, thank you ma'am.* That was the first guy to molest me. He plied me with booze and raped me, but I liked it. I went back to try to find him, but he knew I would come on Sundays, and so he would disappear. He was worried he'd get caught."

Most sexual violations occur unwitnessed and are absorbed into a sexual trajectory. In Alice Munro's story "Wild Swans," an adolescent girl, brimming with her mother's warnings about strangers who could victimize her on the train, gets on the train and is duly victimized. Maggie Nelson talks about the story in *The Argonauts*, talks about Munro's character being *jerked off by a male stranger on a train.* It happens *without her consent or protest but also without being forced to do anything to his body.*

There is perhaps a spectrum of violation. But what Nelson says next, about what the story meant to her, seems also meant for Phillip, *how the force of one's adolescent curiosity and incipient lust often must war with the need to protect oneself from disgusting and wicked violators, how pleasure can coexist with awful degradation without meaning the degradation was justified or a species of wish fulfillment; how it feels to be both accomplice and victim; and how such ambivalences can live on in an adult sexual life.*

One day, when Phillip and Del were living on their own, he hitchhiked into Hope to get some medication for her. "I was hitchhiking back, and this old guy picks me up in his car, Edwin Mingham, an old pedophile. He lived in Vancouver and used to drive the highway picking up hitchhikers with the glove box open and full of pictures of guys' cocks." A dangerous game, but it must have worked often enough. Phillip was interested. It wasn't that this man was any more appealing than the itinerant berry picker: make no mistake, neither of them was appealing. But he saw no other route to what he wanted.

Trucker hat, stubbled chin, ice-blue eyes sliding over, an energy emanating from man and boy, bouncing back out of the glove box so that the dirty pictures were lit and obscured at the same time.

I'm going to Vancouver, Mingham said. *You coming?*

I've got to take my mum her medicine. Phillip held up the white paper pharmacy bag, the top now moulded by his damp, clenched fist.

I've got things to do not far from you. Mingham leaned over the wheel, his eyes focused straight ahead on some distant unseen point. *I'll be passing right by in, oh, half an hour, maybe, if you need a ride.*

Phillip walked up to their trailer. Del was under a crocheted afghan, watching TV. He couldn't get close to her because she was sick and maybe that's why he headed back out that night, but he was heading that way some night or other, no matter what. *I'm going to Vancouver,* he told her. *I'll be back.*

She looked up at him then. He knew she knew—telepathy, right?—but she just said, *Okay,* and he went to Vancouver with that pedophile and met up with another pedophile and made out with them and, after a few more such trips, told Del, *I'm sleeping with guys.*

In spring of 2021, almost twenty-five years after meeting Phillip, I went on a writing retreat to start my third attempt at writing this book. I had written two failed drafts and, after each, weighed whether I should abandon it, but I hadn't managed to. This would be my last try: I needed to find a way either to tell this story or to move on.

In the evenings, during my retreat, I planned to watch a brand-new TV series, *It's a Sin*, whose dramatic arc is powered by AIDS. The show opens on three eighteen-year-old Brits in 1981: boys, gay, leaving home in pursuit of their own lives, who, while very different one from another, end up rooming together in London.

One morning, all three have big appointments—a meeting, an audition, gates that might swing open into their future if pushed at the correct angle. Each steps into the bathroom for his turn as the previous boy emerges fresh and groomed and ready. At breakfast, they give and receive good luck wishes and head optimistically out the door. Watching the third go, I burst into tears. *Oh, such faces.*

Yes, the pressures of the retreat—alone, immersed in this book I feared I would never materialize—had broken me down a little and, yes, I'm a sap, but also, over these years, my own life had caught up to the story I was trying to write. I was now mother to a teenage boy, sweet, obnoxious, ignorant, curious, vulnerable, lithe, as full of life, and hunger for life, as these boys onscreen in 1980s London, as teenage Phillip, back in 1960s Fraser Valley, was, seeking fun and beauty, the glory of sex and gorgeous guys, seeking camaraderie, revelry, *their real lives.*

Del was watching him keenly, serendipitously, Phillip's shepherd. Her gift to him on his sixteenth birthday, for example, was an object lesson in the dangers of heroin.

"Del took me to the skids in Vancouver, the Pacific 66 Café. Right in the first booth were a woman and her lesbian girlfriend." Del had done time with them both. "The older, butcher one? Her son Roger was dealing junk in the back of the café. The mother was watching the entrance, and when junkies would come in, she would give them a nod of the head. I remember his name was Roger because there was a junkie there who was desperate but didn't have money, who kept moaning—*Roger, I need a fix! Roger, I need a fix!*—over and over."

When they got home, Del delivered a lecture: "If you ever come around here shooting up, I'm going to throw you over the top of that mountain."

Phillip recalled one night a year or so earlier, when they'd heard a knock. "Aunty Mary?" Another knock. "Aunty!"

Del frowned and went to the door: it was her sister's kid, a skinny boy of about nineteen. Del offered to fix him a plate. He slunk into the kitchen, a dim-looking fellow, no one for Phillip to care about, except he was Del's blood, her kin. She boiled water for instant mashed potatoes—this was how they ate, now that they no longer had the garden—and set the plate down in front of the kid, meat loaf and canned green beans. She rolled and lit a smoke as he started shovelling in the food. Picking a shred of tobacco off her tongue, she said, "You're still using."

He looked up, at her, at Phillip, who was standing, not sitting. "Yeah," he said.

"Where's your rig?" she asked.

"Um." He forked up some more meat loaf, but she wasn't going to let it drop. "In my sock."

She looked at Phillip, so quickly it wasn't even a look. "Get the fuck out of here," she said, taking her nephew's plate and putting it in the sink.

"But Aunty . . ." He raised his fork in his fist, sunken eyes indignant.

"I said get out."

He did, slamming the door. Del stepped out onto the landing to watch him go, flicking her embers into the darkness.

She knew just by looking at him.

Phillip, on his sexual forays out to Vancouver, was starting to use drugs as well. His first time on acid: "Holy fuck, it was mind-blowing. Colours and strobes. These two guys were fighting over who was going to take me to bed, so I turned my head to the wall so all I could hear was the music." When he eventually slept with one of them, "it was this yucky thing. It's almost like the acid made a person so at-one you didn't need to do the sexual act. The love of it all was right there." He shrugged earnestly. "It was all right there."

Ever the dutiful son, he told Del all about the acid. I guess he needed someone to tell. Del herself—with a younger boyfriend, of which there were many—was the one who introduced him to pot. She told him she had tried cocaine, maybe down south somewhere. But he never forgot her warning about the needles.

The summer after high school, he got a job as a waiter in Harrison Hot Springs, a resort town. Many of the workers lived in a compound in the shadow of the Harrison Hotel, in little white cottages with green-painted eaves, smoking dope and having sex with each other and with passers-through, in the way of young labourers in every seasonal industry, at ski destinations and in tree-planting camps from Smithers to Banff to points east.

In Vancouver for a weekend, Phillip met his first real boyfriend, Michael. Gorgeous, blond, Michael twirled on a barstool, enchanting everyone there with invisible fairy dust.

And he had money: he dealt speed and MDA to the gay crowd, though he himself was clean at the time.

"Don't ever let anyone put a needle in your arm," he said sanctimoniously to Phillip that first night, lying in the unmade bed in his apartment—playing the older man, though he was probably no more than twenty-two. Phillip tongued the veins in Michael's wrist, the tracks up his arms, the porcelain blue softness of his inner elbow. A few weeks later, Michael fell off the wagon.

"He shot me up with speed for my eighteenth birthday," Phillip told me with a cold, clinical interest, his customary tone when retelling the worst things he had done to himself. "The first person to ever put a needle in my arm."

Del came to Harrison once in a while, attracted to the party scene. It was the height of flower power, and she was still at the height of her powers, too—white patent leather boots, mini-skirts, wide collars, wide belts—though she was forty-five. Her boyfriends were in their twenties.

"Forty-five?" Phillip was flabbergasted when I told him.

"No, she was thirty-five," he insisted, but I had done the math.

Inevitably, a boyfriend, Andrew, moved on to the land she owned on Strawberry Mountain. He and Del scavenged wood to build a two-room cottage on the property. They did meditation. They sold art from a roadside stand. Phillip, visiting every month or two, saw the changes. When Del used to come out to Harrison and flirt and go home with someone, he had felt proud: she was gorgeous, everyone said so. The two of them would compare conquests and trade stories, like that was really the point. But now her energy was caught up in Andrew's. When Phillip went to visit, he couldn't tell anymore what she was thinking.

Why had he ever left? It had seemed the responsible thing to do—he needed to earn and didn't have a car—apart from which he was also getting laid regularly. But now he saw that he had abandoned Del, and that the channel between them had been polluted and weakened.

He decided to quit and move back. He was family, after all. Andrew didn't look happy at this development, but that was to be expected. He and Phillip built a little guest shack on the far side of the property. Andrew spent exactly a day on it—no windows, no electricity, no running water—then went back to live with Del in their skookum little cottage outfitted with all rustic amenities. Phillip slept alone in his shack. With each passing day, it smelled more and more of him and him alone, until he realized it wasn't only Andrew who wanted him to move on.

He stuck out his thumb and landed at the Gemini Steam Club, a Vancouver bathhouse, where he paid thirty-five bucks a week for a bed and the privilege of turning tricks.

Though Phillip often refers to any given gay bathhouse as *the whorehouse* (as in, "One time in the Quebec City whorehouse, I heard this story about the last time Pierre Elliott Trudeau had come through . . ."), prostitution is not officially part of the culture of the tubs (his other moniker for them). Still, the owners allowed the hooking as a sort of service. "It kept the kids off the street and added to business. There were five or six of us in there."

Phillip would make out with "older guys of thirty or forty," an activity he was already accustomed to engaging in for free. Now he earned thirty dollars a trick. "In a couple days you'd have enough to pay for your food and lodging for the whole week. You always had a roof over your head."

He was only nineteen, but he could tell that this life had an expiration date, and that it would be better to get out while it was still his choice. He'd acquired another burden, though—a heroin habit—which made it even harder to go home to Del, not that he thought that was really an option anymore.

I eventually interviewed him formally in his immaculate, antiques-lined condo. It had been a long day of story upon story of drinking and parties and chaos and misadventures, and I wondered aloud whether Phillip missed all that.

He shook his head. No.

I pressed him: "I know you ended up in a very bad place at the end, but you make it sound like there was a lot of fun and camaraderie."

"Oh, yes," he conceded. "I'll say it: that's something that straight people don't understand, that camaraderie of living on the streets and shooting up and drinking and living hard." He elaborated. "You have your friends in Fayetteville, you call them your friends, they're your neighbours and all that, but in all honesty, I doubt that the core soul feeling of friendship that you have with any of those people would ever reach the feeling of friendship you get when you sit down and crank up with somebody."

I was offended: I'd hardly ever spoken to Phillip about my other friends, so who was he to generalize?

"You come together as one," he continued, oblivious to my unspoken reaction. "That intensity . . . that's why it's sometimes hard for people to quit. The closeness."

I stiffly clarified what he meant by "straight"—not sexually straight but people who hadn't been around the block the way he had.

"That's right. The learning that I did through that makes it all worthwhile, though it was so brutal. That deep soul learning is what I give today in my job."

We took a break. I was quiet, filling the kettle. He occupied the silence with a recollection: "I'd been sober maybe seven years or something like that. I was back in Vancouver. And I thought, I'm going to go back to the old haunts, where I was shooting heroin and all that. So I went down to Hastings Street, brutal, third-world, deserted. The Sunrise, the old library, the Chinaman's store." Places he shot up, places people died, in the alleys, on the steps. "Anyway, this squaw is coming toward me and she puts the bead on me because we're the only people on the street."

I made a mental genuflection and prayed, *Don't say squaw.*

"I'm sober and clean," he recounted, "and she's watching me and I'm watching her, eh. And she says, *Get the fuck out of here. You don't live here anymore.*" I was still silent. I couldn't tell any longer what I was offended about.

"It was neat," Phillip said, hopeful and wary, "very cool."

I took a breath and addressed the point I knew how to address. "I am actually slightly upset by your comment about . . ."

"Friends," he finished my sentence.

Clearly, Phillip had been aware of my reaction and barrelled through because he wanted to clarify. He hadn't really been talking about me; he was trying to draw a distinction between the obscure intimacy of heroin friendships and the blinding arena of respectability. Instead of listening, I took it personally and took him to task.

"Yeah," I said, chastised by his essential kindness.

"I'll qualify my statement there, little sister. The moment you put a needle in your arm, you have lost a virginity of a type that you will never get back again. You go into a land of ecstasy that, as one guy put it, *it's God's kiss to us here.* When you do it with a friend, the energy kind of comes together. You leave this realm, and you go where it's just pure love, you don't question a guy's politics"—this was shortly after Donald Trump's election and he was getting earfuls of my frustrated activism and rage—"you don't give a sweet flying fuck about any earthly matters. You just float together in euphoria.

"So that's why I said that, not to be degrading. It may have come out wrong, but if there was a junkie sitting here, he would say, *I think he's right.*" A silence fell again between us. Again, he broke it: "Does that—do you get it after that explanation?"

"Well . . ." I said. "I get your point of view. But you don't know anything about my other friends."

What was all this defensiveness? A dark river of worry: What did I really know of Phillip and his world and what right did I have to tell the story *and and and.* But instead of saying all that, I monologued on the gap between how people see me—a writer and professor, happily ensconced in heterosexual marriage—and who I really am.

"Yeah," Phillip attempted to interject. "I apologize if I offended you."

"I think you love a lot of sides of me, but I feel uncomfortable that you see the shiny side more than anything else."

On the recording, Phillip's voice changes. He takes a tender, authoritative tone. "Kiddo," he says, "I know nobody's perfect.

But permit me the indulgence, this fantasy that in our friendship we will see the finest sides of each other. We only have limited contact. I know the magnitude of you wouldn't fit through that fucking door. But please: I'm not judging you."

"I sat here thinking, should I say something, should I not . . .?"

"Oh, absolutely!"

"You've been . . ."

"Honest with you."

"Baring yourself, so I didn't want to upset you but . . ."

"No, no, no. Spit it out. Yes."

"That's how I was feeling."

"I was using you as an example of a straight person. You don't like it, but there's a very big difference. That's why I told you that story about that squaw."

Don't say squaw.

"She knew. She knew I was the same as her. I'd been there. *Get out of here. You don't live here no more.* You and I could pass each other on the street and you would never say a word if we didn't know each other. So," his voice on the recording turns tentative again, "do you kind of get that a bit?"

"I need to absorb it," I hedged. "Now I'm thinking, *Is Phillip the same as an Indigenous woman on the street? Phillip's going to get out of there. Is that Indigenous woman going to get out of there?*"

"You never know." Phillip shook his head. "You never know."

Lovers are normally face to face, absorbed in each other; Friends, side by side, absorbed in some common interest, says C. S. Lewis, a line repeated by philosophers, and often, it seems to me, taken as a given.

Lewis is defending the underrated and under-elaborated pleasures of friendship. Unliinke eros or familial affection, friendship is neither born in a hot burst nor essential to raising the next generation. It has not generated reams of immortal poetry (though we do have a small canon of novels and films). It eludes norms. It's considered optional among many adults who otherwise lead full lives.

Lewis's take strikes me as gendered: most of my female friendships (which is to say, most of my friendships) are based on intimate conversation. By contrast, my husband's male friendships more often stem from shared interests: he lives friendship side by side on bicycles, or, if face to face, over a Scrabble board or pool table.

This is too general to be wholly accurate. I also have dance friends, bonded not through the baring of our souls but the synchronizing of our bodies. And my husband's cycling friends often end up talking confessionally over a beer at the end of a ride.

Still, in rough terms, such categories exist and my cross-gender, cross-generational (cross-class, cross-race) friendship with Phillip confounded them, not least because we were side by side absorbed in *him:* his adventures and misadventures, his outsize parents and the historical currents in which they swam or sank.

When I think of the two of us gazing together into his life, his story, I think of Narcissus and Echo: the youth entranced by his own reflection; the nymph entranced by him but unable to express this other than by repeating his own words. *I am like water,* after all: *everything moves me, everything is reflected in me.*

In a less-quoted bit of that same essay, Lewis distinguishes one-on-one Friendship, in which a pair of friends *stand together in an immense solitude,* from "the Companionship," in which groups of friends magnify one another's qualities for everyone's mutual delight. His refinement breaks down the divisions between forms of love and, in doing so, creates a new category, closer than any other I have found to what Phillip and I had:

The Companionship was between people who were doing something together—hunting, studying, painting or what you will. The Friends will still be doing something together, but something more inward, less widely shared and less easily defined; still hunters but of some immaterial quarry; still collaborating, but in some work the world does not, or not yet, take account of; still travelling companions, but on a different kind of journey.

By his early twenties, Phillip was working oil rigs, hydro dams, sawmills—jobs that gave him a bunk, regular meals and lots of drinking money.

He'd gotten off heroin by getting out of Vancouver, camping out on a friend's property on Lasqueti, a tiny off-the-grid island in the Georgia Strait, until he was through withdrawal. The friend turned out to be scamming the government for prescription pills, so he had a well-stocked pharmacopeia, plus Lasqueti's forest floor was thickly carpeted with magic mushrooms. Phillip got over heroin by wandering around the island stoned on other substances. At least he got off the heroin.

Now, out at the bar, he'd toss back liquid courage. He was muscular and competent, like the men he loved to fuck, but if the wrong person figured out he was gay, he'd pack up in an instant and move on, chasing sex and running away from it all at once, pillar to post, pillar to post.

On the road, hippie houses would take him in: he'd come across them in clearings on the outskirts of mining towns, the hippies dancing out front or some shit. He looked like them, too: long hair and patches, bangles and beads. They'd feed him rice drizzled with sesame oil—it's all any of them could afford—and tell him he could stay as long as he wanted.

He retained it all in Technicolor detail: A chick in a middle-of-nowhere bar who carried her little dog—as alcoholic as she was—in a little purse. A horrifically bungled attempt, with a fellow traveller, to rustle a cow. A car accident, driving in an alcoholic blackout, waking up in hospital. Okay, maybe he didn't remember that quite so clearly.

It sounds, in retrospect, like a grand if involuntary adventure, a picaresque: a callow youth, cast out to make his way, nothing but still-nascent wit and survival instinct keeping him intact as he ricochets toward a destination he can't suss but that readers know is his own becoming. Battered he will be, but the only way out is through.

I have a particular fondness for picaresques in which the protagonists are animals bearing hidden identities, such as Andersen's "The Ugly Duckling" or Apuleius's The Golden Ass. The duckling, trying only to find peace and shelter, is clueless as to who he really is. By contrast, Apuleius's Lucius, turned into a donkey through his own reckless overreaching, thinks he knows exactly: a privileged youth on a gap year, now trapped inside the body of an ass.

Both these stories culminate in recognition. The ugly duckling, at the end of his long solitary winter, sees again the tribe of swans. *They floated so lightly on the water. The ugly duckling felt again that strange sadness come over him.*

"I'll fly over to them, those royal birds! And they can hack me to death, someone so ugly daring to approach them! What difference does it make?"

And he lighted on the water and swam toward the magnificent swans. When they saw him, they ruffled their feathers and came gliding toward him.

"Kill me," whispered the poor creature, and bent his head humbly, waiting for death. But what was that he saw in the water? It was his own reflection, and he was no longer an awkward, clumsy grey bird, so ungainly and so ugly. He was a swan!

It's the Narcissus story inverted, a late arrival at self-love, the reflection giving life instead of death.

Lucius, by contrast, started out perhaps a little too fond of himself. Even though he caused his asinine transformation, he's furious about it. The antidote? A rose. He needs to eat a rose. Such a simple magic and yet it eludes him, almost fatefully, for a full year. Finally, in a procession, a *komos*, the goddess Isis conveys to him a rose garland, which he gratefully devours.

This is a story of metamorphosis, though, and, like a caterpillar, Lucius, inside his carapace, has been altered at his very centre.

(I can't honestly speak to whether caterpillars feel their essential identities to be changed in the cocoon, but the Greek word for soul is cognate to butterfly.)

Formerly a selfish, arrogant, lusty youth, Lucius emerges chastened and chaste, destined to become a priest for the goddess who descried him in his abjection.

And Phillip? Well, one big difference between him and the ugly duckling was that he knew who he was. He learned young, *Oh: you gotta hide this.* But what happens when your truest self is not a regal swan or temple priest but a persecuted sexual identity? You drink, that's what—not a plot point you see much in canonical tales.

One feature of the picaresque is a certain kind of dramatic irony in which the reader is enlisted. Unlike our hero, we can flip ahead and check how the story turns out; we are also capable of a clarity brought by distance. Occasionally I wondered if part of my role was to bring that reader's eye (a writer is a reader first) to Phillip's life, to make it more legible to him, collapsing the ironic distance between events and meaning.

On a break one day during our interviews, for example, I was fretting about Trump's approaching inauguration. Phillip considered politics a waste of time and mental energy—this, too, will pass. I could see his point, but I had hopes that the activism I was participating in would yield results sooner than later.

"The thing you're not talking about," Phillip burst out with a sudden energy, "the thing that no one talks about, is that for Trump to win, he would have had to have the nod from Israel and be backed by the Jewish money that runs the world."

What the fuck, I thought, except nonverbally, more like the equivalent neural cramp. "Do you have any idea what you're saying?" I asked him. "That's, like, straight out of *The Protocols of the Elders of Zion.*"

He looked at me like, *Listen.* "I was called up one day when I was staying at the hostel in Winnipeg: this older couple in a nice house needed their garden turned over for the winter. Well, this farm boy knew how to do that. When it was time for lunch, they called me in and fed me at the table. That was unusual: usually, people fed you on the back step. After lunch, I was all fired up. I turned the beds and got it all squared and nice. And when I finished, normally the wife pays you at the back door and sends you on your way. But this time, they brought me into the house and sat me down. The husband was sitting in a big chair, and he told me, *We're Jewish. Did you know?* I said, *No, I can't tell if someone's Jewish.* Well, it turns out that Jewish people are required to take care of their kids first, set them up in business or whatever, but then when they die, they're supposed to leave their money to the church. And you can go to the bank three times, if you have a business proposition or whatever, but only three times. Well, they didn't want to leave their money to the church, so they wanted to buy a ranch. And the idea was that I would look after it, convert to Judaism, work with their son for a few years, to make sure I was doing a good job, and then when they went, it would go to me.

"Well, I talked to some people and decided I didn't want to do that, convert to Judaism, all of it, and so I said no." I was incredulous, not even at what he was saying—at him. "And you believed them? They needed a tax dodge or something."

"I met the son," Phillip insisted uncertainly. "He had a business, a car wash."

"So what?" I shrugged. "He had a business. Doesn't prove there's a worldwide Jewish bank running the world."

We dropped it. A few minutes later, though, he started shaking his head. "That just never occurred to me: tax dodge or whatever. I'm so gullible." Chuckles foamed over into giggles. "I knew you and I might get to the point where we would have a . . ." He made a noise, a revving, growling sound meant to represent conflict. Apparently, when he mentioned Jewish banks running the world, I held up a hand like Diana Ross: Stop. His imitation of me made me start laughing, too.

I was his negative capability, a receptacle he filled with stories I would parse later, alone.

Susan Sontag, writing in "Against Interpretation" about literature, says *interpretation is the revenge of the intellectual upon art*, since the interpreter inevitably reduces the text while claiming to do no more than make it intelligible, *disclosing its true meaning.*

But what happens when a friend you love is also a book you want to write?

One cannot think without metaphors, Sontag admitted in her essays against the metaphorization of illness. *As, of course, all thinking is interpretation. But that does not mean it isn't sometimes correct to be "against" interpretation.*

Sontag had cancer; I can understand wanting to push back against abstractions of the phenomena that most literally, physically affect us.

Phillip is not a metaphor, an aggregation of allusions, an ugly duckling or a graceful swan. He's an actual person. Was I, am I, wrong to interpret him, to metaphorize him?

Psychoanalyst Adam Phillips, in *Unforbidden Pleasures*, advocates for what he calls overinterpretation—multiple, flexible views on ourselves and our stories—since *tragic heroes always underinterpret, are always emperors of one idea.* I think of this when I tell my mother or my husband something puzzling or upsetting that happened at work or tell a friend something upsetting that happened with my mother or husband. Sometimes I can't understand the story I'm telling; some times I'm in tragic thrall to a single idea about it. My family and friends interpret for me when I can't. I trust them to do that, to know me better, at times, than I know myself.

What we don't know, what we haven't understood, can be the realest thing about us.

What made me think I could understand the events of Phillip's life better than he could?

I didn't think that to start with. In my first draft of this book, I tried to present the events of his life simply as he had told them to me, in his words, unmediated. It didn't work.

There is such a thing as robbing a story of its reality by trying to make it too true, as Oscar Wilde warns in "The Decay of Lying."

My agent's assistant set up a call so my agent could tell me, "We don't like this."

He didn't answer my email when I asked for more details, but his assistant volunteered, "Maybe it could be of interest to the family?" Kinder, but no more helpful.

My mother listened sympathetically when I told her what the agent and his assistant had said. I had given her the manuscript, too. *They're right,* she said. She'd been afraid to tell me. The book droned, I gathered, in the way of self-published autobiographies: too many details, not enough thrust. With no centre to hold, it couldn't transcend its particulars.

My husband, Geoff, a writer and reader par excellence, was the one to explain what my underinterpretation had done to my friend. He knew very well how I saw Phillip, but he said that my perception of him, his *fantastic interestingness* (which Geoff never quite got), wasn't coming through on the page.

"It's like reading the lyrics," he said, "without knowing the tune."

People tell journalists their stories as characters in dreams deliver their elliptical messages, says Janet Malcolm, *without warning, without context, without concern for how odd they will sound when the dreamer awakens and repeats them.* My mistake was thinking that anyone else could walk into my shared dream with Phillip, could hear his song without my singing it.

Literary characters are drawn with much broader and blunter strokes, are much simpler, more generic (or, as they used to say, mythic) creatures than real people. Real people seem relatively uninteresting in comparison because they are so much more complex, ambiguous, unpredictable.

I know the magnitude of Phillip wouldn't fit through the fucking door, but merely thrusting his infinite varicoloured facets forward into the light caused him to fall apart on the page, not cohere.

My enjoyment of him, the ongoing surprise of him, his complexity and ambiguity, could intrinsically mean nothing beyond the friendship itself. *Art itself is really a form of exaggeration,* as Oscar Wilde explains, *and selection, which is the very spirit of art, is nothing more than an intensified mode of over-emphasis.*

The only way to convey the mythic profundity of Phillip's story—to *write it*—was to overinterpret those few aspects salient to the story I wanted to tell.

I loved Phillip as a friend. My self-serving daemon constrained me to write him as a writer would. But didn't the second depend somewhat on the first? Malcolm said it was *my identification with and affection for* him that would allow me to transmute the human being I loved into a literary character others might also love.

Interpretation amounts to the philistine refusal to leave the work of art alone, says Sontag, but if I replace "work of art" with "friend" or "person," since that's what, let's be honest, I was doing, her essay says this: *Real friends have the capacity to make us nervous. By reducing the person to their content and then interpreting that, one tames them. Interpretation makes them manageable, conformable.*

Who was I fooling? We never know our loved ones the way we think we do. We deduce their characters, serendipitously, based on what little we can see; we love them based on the ways they fulfill our needs.

After he got off the junk, Phillip went back to visit Del. He hadn't seen her in months, maybe close to a year. He found her sitting with Roberta Peters, a matriarch from the reserve, in the A-frame, a strong energy between them. Del was living there now, while the little cottage she'd shared with Andrew rotted on the hill above. Roberta got up. She didn't say anything, but she laid her hand briefly on Phillip's head as she left.

Del looked him over, but not thoroughly. Not maternally. "What're you doing for money?" she asked.

"Lumber," he said. He'd been up north for a few months; he'd been a few places. "Where's what's-his-face, Andrew?"

"Ah, he split. Ages ago."

He'd already known about Del's "magic relationship" with Roberta, since he'd met someone from the reserve working up north and caught up a little. He didn't bother telling Del he knew they were involved.

She stubbed out her cigarette. Something was coming—what? She seemed . . . closed, somehow.

"You still doing your art?" he asked.

She was. Could he see it, whatever she was working on?

No, look, here was the thing, the talk she hadn't had with him before: *he was coming to look too much like Harvey, and his face and his voice,* Phillip's voice, which may as well have been Harvey's, brought back the trauma of that abusive relationship, even when he smiled.

She didn't want to see him anymore. She couldn't.

"And after that, I never did go back," Phillip said.

We were on a trip together when he told me this, touring the sites of his youth. It was dusk, his face in shadow, but his voice was that voice I had become so attached to over years of nurturing our friendship by phone.

"You know, I understood, I got it. Didn't want to offend her. We parted on good terms."

Good terms or Del's terms? It would be a while before we both learned how either of those were defined.

TONAL RESONANCE

AFTER DEL BANISHED HIM, Phillip found a job that stuck for a bit, on the oil rigs in Alberta. The stints were two weeks long; the job included isolation pay and breaks back in Edmonton. He got his first apartment, boyfriends: a gay rig pig was good pickings. It was a different class of life. He spent generously, sometimes $5,000 a week in booze and drugs and food. When he quit the rigs to stay home with a long-term, live-in boyfriend, Victor, he lost some friends he could no longer pay for. And then he and Victor broke up.

By then, he was working at Russell Steel, taking home about what he'd paid in taxes when he worked the rigs. Still, it was enough to rent an apartment in Edmonton's River Valley, a dream of a building, an old walk-up with big bay windows, pocket doors, hardwood, an oak cistern and toilet seat. Maybe this was his real life, finally beginning.

The building manager lived downstairs. She'd kicked her husband out and was struggling with her teenage kids, especially her son, Carl.

Carl got friendly with Phillip, so much so that he asked if he could bring his girlfriend to Phillip's place to have sex with her. Phillip said yes; no judgment. He'd go out and leave the place to the kids. He knew Carl was drinking and smoking dope, but it wasn't like Phillip was on any moral high ground there.

So Carl was hanging out at Phillip's place and his mother was talking to Phillip about Carl. "I'm having a really tough time," she'd say. "These kids are not listening to me. They're not going to school." She'd invite Phillip for dinner, to have a man around when the kids got home. Finally, she said, "You're down here all the time anyway. Why don't you move in?" She never suggested she wanted anything other than company and a masculine influence. She might have wanted more, but the arrangement was that Phillip would share Carl's room, not hers. (Where was Carl supposed to have sex with his girlfriend now? That detail was left dangling.)

Phillip called the school and got the kids re-enrolled. Carl's drinking subsided. One night, Phillip told him to do the dishes.

When he said no, Phillip brought him in line the way he'd been taught by Harvey: "I threw him against the wall: *You're doing the dishes, prick.*" And Carl did.

Phillip didn't just share Carl's room. He shared his bed. And *one thing leads to another*, as Phillip put it. *Boys will be boys.* "You wake up and you have a morning hard-on and I'd do him and that was about it. There was never any real affectionate sex-making. We were buddies."

One evening, Phillip got home after work, unlocked the door and called, "Hello! Can I speak to the man of the house?" Their little joke. He shucked his steel-toed boots outside the door, hung up his hard hat, went into the kitchen, and was pulled up short by seeing a man sitting at the kitchen table with Carl, his mother and his sister, the man giving off hostility like an odour.

The husband. He watched Phillip come in. No one spoke. Phillip got a glass of water, drank half of it, and opened the paper bag he was carrying to take out the bottle of rum he'd bought on the way home.

Carl's dad raised his chin, drew a line with it from Carl to Phillip. "So how long you two been sleeping together?"

Phillip froze.

Carl glanced at Phillip, nonchalant. "Oh, a little while." Phillip threw his hands in the air and backed away. "This has got fuck all to do with me. I'm outta here." He went to the room and started throwing his things in his pack.

"No!" Carl yelled. "If he goes, I go with him. Let me stay with him." He was crying. "Mom, please. He's my only chance."

Carl would eventually end up on the street. Phillip could see it coming as well as he could. "I dreaded what was going to happen to him. I knew and he knew." He felt terrible.

But Carl's mother wouldn't let him go.

"Carl made a big scene," Phillip told me. "But there was nothing I could do. He was underage. I was twenty-seven. I could have been arrested."

After Phillip left, got a new place and a phone, Carl found him and called: "I want to come over and have sex with you. My dad and I have sex."

Yep, that's right.

Phillip refused him. "I mean, I'm not saying I could have raised him. But if we had hung out together maybe we both would have taken a different path. Especially after I found out that the father was fucking the boy! Like, *hello?*"

Did Carl's father ask his question because he detected a sexual charge between them or because of his own inclinations? There's no way to know. Anyway, what interested me more was that, in Phillip's telling, both he and Carl saw this relationship, which most people would see as predatory and certainly harmful to the child, as something that could save them both.

Phillip had told me earlier that his boyfriend Victor would "fuck around" with his favourite nephew, "literally—Victor had no qualms about doing straight guys or relatives or whatever."

In an era when gay couples marry and raise families in the suburbs, it's easy to forget how long queerness was associated with defiance of all kinds of socio-sexual norms, and how the queer movement has made visible and acceptable what was previously unseen and stigmatized.

In Jan Morris's 1989 autobiography, *Pleasures of a Tangled Life*, she muses on convention, pleasure and taboo. On incest, for example, Morris says she is *unreliable*, though she also suggests that it's the Welsh in her. Telling of an elderly widower in her neighbourhood, hauled to jail for sexual relations with his unmarried adult daughter, she says, *I was not alone in thinking it a mean-spirited response to a primitive expression of affection which, far from being the cruel abuse of one by the other, undoubtedly brought comfort to them both.*

That *undoubtedly* now sounds unreconstructed, and yet: I appreciate, as in the case of Carl and Phillip, the possibility that people without many resources might give and receive something good in a proscribed relationship.

Phillip insisted that he wasn't defined by his sexuality. "The fact that I'm gay doesn't say what kind of a person I am," he told me in another conversation. "That's what I do in bed, that's not who I am."

It reminded me of an interview I once heard on the radio, Terry Gross talking to James Baldwin about gay liberation. Was it important for him to join a movement?

No, no, no, Baldwin says. *I had been afflicted with so many labels that I'd become invisible to myself. No, I had to go away someplace and get rid of all these labels to find out not what I was but who.*

But the relationship between what we do and who we are is complicated. As Phillip also said, "Being gay and in the minority, I'm very tolerant of everybody. I don't care what colour you are, if you dress up, if you eat shit, if you do any of that. It's your business. Toe fetish. No judgment."

Queer sex is creative rather than procreative, though Phillip was in every sense a pro. (One bathhouse story: neither he nor his partner recognized each other, but when he was running his tongue along the man's ass-crack, the guy said, "Whoa, Phillip, right? I forget a face, but I'd never forget that tongue.")

I have another dear friend, a straight woman, who is sexu-ally prolific. Like Phillip, she is discriminating; like Phillip, she has been physically intimate with an extraordinary number of men. Both talk about their encounters with an unapologetic, literary wonder, in the way of travellers who know how to get to the heart of a place. My woman friend describes herself as monogamous: for as long as she is with a partner, there is no one else for her.

"Have you heard of tonal resonance?" Phillip asked me once. I nodded yes, though I had no idea—I was just keeping the conversation going.

"When I go to bed with guys," he said, "the energy that flows through me? Sometimes, I put them to sleep." He described it in more detail: with long-term and short-term lovers and also a gay friend he always refused to have sex with, he would hold them and a sort of energy would flow from him, surround the bed and transport them into perfect sleep.

Tonal resonance, tonal resonance. I loved how Phillip pronounced *resonance*—emphasis on the second syllable, the o not a schwa but a short vowel, giving the phrase a melodious ring: trochee + iamb + trailing syllable. I have done west African dance for most of my life, and now this phrase sometimes goes through my head when I hear the drums' aftertones mingling into a single suspended sound—*tonal resonance, tonal resonance*—a harmonic energy layer, a silk scarf in wind.

Eventually, Google revealed to me that "tonal resonance" is in fact a theory of reincarnation. Your Resonant Tone *is as eternal as your soul, and for all intents and purposes is your soul, which is propelled once again into this physical life-school to expand,* one website says.

Um, I thought.

After a rest in the astral (energetic) realm, the densities of your Resonant Tone *eventually pull you back into the physical Earth realm, so you may once again evolve.*

Phillip's version made more sense to me than this mumbo-jumbo. I know for a fact that Phillip gave the men in his life the gifts of his intuitive energy. He gave them good rest, which is to say: health, sanity, reassurance. *Tonal resonance* is a metaphor and metonym for the physical effects generated by the generosity of his gestalt.

As with my woman friend, the way Phillip talked about his sex life—and he talked about it a lot—seemed a corrective to received narratives of pathological promiscuity. I couldn't read Phillip's libertinism as emanating from power hunger or emptiness or insecurity. Rather, he saw sex as an expression of love, a synonym for emotional intimacy, perhaps even a version of what he experienced with Del.

It's a mirror of what he said about trying acid as a teenager—*The love of it all was right there*—and about heroin friendship. Andrew Sullivan recalls that the drug ecstasy, a key part of gay male gatherings early in the club scene, *instantly simulated an intimacy so many men found almost impossible to achieve, and an exhilaration they could not otherwise allow themselves to feel.* Phillip wasn't after a simulated intimacy, though, but a real one, "just pure love." Drugs were, in a way, another route to that.

Jan Morris was married to her wife for more than fifty years, through *a greater permutation of sexual relationship than a Grecian fabulist could conceive.* (Adam Phillips: *The object of life is not to simplify it.*)

And out of it all, Morris says, *I have drawn the conclusion that the ultimate object of sex is spiritual, the sealing of profounder unions, and its ultimate delight is nothing less than a glimpse of that final unity, the infinite.*

If my story is "The Shadow" and Phillip's is "The Ugly Duckling," the fairy-tale analogue of our adventure together is Hans Christian Andersen's "The Snow Queen."

The preface to this multi-part story shows a demon inventing a magical mirror. It has *the power of making everything good or beautiful reflected in it shrink to almost nothing, while everything worthless and bad looked bigger and worse than ever. The loveliest landscapes appeared like boiled spinach and the best people became beastly.*

The demon thinks this is hilarious, while his acolytes say that it showed, for the first time, *what the world and human beings were really like.* There is a bifurcation in nature, opposites—good vs. evil, lovely vs. hideous—that must do battle.

The devils' disciples have the idea to take the mirror up to heaven, whether to relieve the angels' boredom or to expose their hypocrisies (while perhaps sowing a little discord into the bargain) but *the higher they flew, the more slippery the glass became.* The mirror falls and shatters into *a hundred million billion pieces, which flew around the wide world. When one landed in a person's eye, it stuck there, and from that moment he could see only the worst side of what he looked at. A few people even got a fragment of the mirror in their hearts.*

The story proper commences with two children, Kai and Gerda, bosom friends, who live in adjacent garrets. Each has a window box of roses, which climb and mingle into a bower, under which they meet and play.

One winter night, watching huge snowflakes swarm like bees, Kai wonders aloud whether they have a queen. "*To be sure they have,*" his grandmother replies. "*She is flying there where the swarm is thickest.*" Later, alone, Kai peers out through a little hole he has made in the thick windowpane frost, and sees one snowflake ontogenize into *a beautiful, elegant woman, made of ice—dazzling, glittering ice—and yet she was alive. Her eyes sparkled and stared, like bright stars, but there was no calm or peace in them.*

The demon and the Snow Queen are unrelated, just a couple of restless forces out in the world, but, whether because of Kai's curiosity or his vulnerability, both will act on him. A fragment of the mirror lands in his eye; another pierces his heart.

In spring, he sees the roses' wormholes and asymmetries, and tears the flowers down and stomps on them, to Gerda's dismay.

When Grandmother told any stories, he would interrupt her with "but" or get behind her and imitate her to make people laugh. His impressions earn him a reputation: *All that was peculiar or disagreeable in a person he would imitate, and people said, "That boy's very clever!"*

Kai is no longer affectionate with Gerda, teasing her instead. Come the first snowfall, though, he has one sincere moment, when he uses a magnifying glass to show her a snowflake's crystalline symmetry: *"Ingenious, isn't it? Much more interesting than real flowers. Not a single fault. Snowflakes are quite perfect, until they begin to melt."*

The Snow Queen comes for him. On a winter afternoon, when *all the most daring boys* are hitching their sleds to country carts, Kai snags a ride on a great white sleigh circling the square. Anytime he thinks of freeing himself, *the driver, wrapped in white fur and wearing a white cap, turns and nods pleasantly at him as if they were acquainted.* When he finally succeeds in unhooking his sled, it makes no difference—it's towed along all the same.

The obvious reading here is Phillip as Kai: Phillip's father, Harvey, cast as the demon, gave him a distorted self-image, making him vulnerable to the enchantments of a glamorous, maternal-yet-unattainable ice queen who leads him far away from everything familiar. Even when he unhitches from her, he can't go back. Also, as will become clear, Phillip was prey to the dichotomous, all-or-nothing thinking undergirding this tale. Plus, he's the boy.

But I, too, identify more with hypercritical, performative Kai than with sweet, stalwart Gerda, the one charged with locating and restoring Kai, the one who still sees *his finest side.*

There is a splinter of ice in the heart of a writer, said Graham Greene, describing a time when he was proximate to a tragedy. While everyone else tried to avoid it or were traumatized by it, his demon constrained him instead to watch, listen, take notes.

The Snow Queen seated him beside her on the sleigh. "Are you still cold?" she asked, and kissed him on the forehead. The kiss went through his heart, which was already half-frozen; he felt as if he were going to die, but only for a moment. Then he felt fine again and didn't notice the cold.

Kai could not imagine a wiser or lovelier face. She no longer seemed made of ice, as when he'd seen her through his window. In his eyes, she was perfect. He told her he could do mental arithmetic, as far as fractions, and that he knew the square mileage and population of many countries.

She kept smiling, until he thought he didn't know nearly enough. He looked out into the vast night sky as she flew higher and higher, into a black cloud. Far below, wolves howled and snow crackled, while, all around them, a storm blew and keened as if singing old songs.

Phillip had withdrawn from his social scene while playing house with his building manager and her son. Now that he was on his own, it started to accumulate around him once more. One buddy, Brian Barito, was a central feature. A biker from Toronto, he and Phillip would drink and fight—he never beat Phillip up, but he loved to fight and Phillip was game, so they'd go looking for trouble.

And, every once in a while, they had sex. As soon as it was over, though, Barito had to leave. No cuddling, no spooning, no talking about it afterward. Fuck and run.

But he and Phillip really liked each other, loved hanging out. *Trouble*—that's what they were, and everyone knew it.

One time, Phillip got his paycheque from Russell Steel and they went on a bender. They bought forty-four cases of beer direct from the Molson brewery to drink at home, blacking out and coming to in bars, drinking nonstop for a week. Friends who saw them at the Boots and Saddle, Edmonton's gay bar, told Phillip later, *We were watching you two talking and having a great old time but there wasn't a fucking word that the rest of us could understand.*

And somewhere toward the end of the week, they made wild, passionate love—not like buddies, like men in love. They kissed, which they had never done; they gazed at each other, breathed each other in.

When it was over, Brian said to Phillip, in tones hushed and tender, *You know I have to go now.*

Yeah, I know, Phillip replied in a tone that matched his friend's. *It's okay. Goodbye.*

Always before, his boss had covered for him when he was on

a spree, because Phillip only got paid for the time he punched in and was a good worker when he showed up. But he'd rarely ever missed more than a day or two, apart from which, this time, his boss was on holiday.

He lost his job.

He used his last money to get a case of beer, drank it all, and didn't even feel drunk.

He lost his apartment, no money for rent.

The bottom fell out.

"It was wintertime. I think I was doing day jobs. It's a bit hazy." In Edmonton, if you said you were destitute and tried to get welfare, they'd send you to the hostel, but if you were drunk, you couldn't stay.

"I remember sleeping over heating vents in car parks. Or there was a guy used to leave the back door open in his apartment building, so when it was bitterly cold I'd go in there and sleep on the cement floor. My friends didn't want fuck all to do with me. Eating out of soup kitchens. Nasty, hard living."

He left for Vancouver, where you could get a welfare cheque with no questions asked. When he made it to the coast, he called a wealthy gay couple he used to know when he first worked the bathhouse. "They'd been together twenty-nine years, which, back in that day, was a phenomenal fucking feat. The effeminate one was a set designer for CBC and the butch one, him and his dad owned a construction company."

They told him to come over, met him at the door in happy anticipation: Phillip had been a hot little number, back in the day. Seeing him now, they were stunned.

"*What happened to you?* It hadn't dawned on me how bad I looked. I was only twenty-eight and I looked eighty."

He stayed with them a night or two, until he got his welfare cheque. Then he drank it up. He went to stay in the bathhouse, but he got thrown out for drinking.

"I thought, *If you don't do something, you're going to be pushing your stuff around in a shopping cart. I had a damn good talk to myself: Listen, man. Get your head out of your ass or that is going to be your life.*

"That's when I remembered seeing a notice on the hostel wall." He searched it out. *If your life is unmanageable,* it said, *come give us a call.* The Salvation Army's detox program. As he stood there, considering it, a narrow escape of a few years earlier came back to him.

One night at the Winnipeg hostel, Phillip had spied a new guy, in government-issue prison-release clothes, giving off a vibe: in trouble, scared. Phillip edged closer. "It's okay," he said. Fuck, he was hot: cute, rough. "It's cool. I got you."

The guy, Richard Belanger, had been paroled to Winnipeg, where his brother lived, after five years in Kingston Pen, but right when he got to town, he told Phillip, he somehow hooked up with a couple of lesbians and got drunk and stoned and ran out of money and went out to get some more money and ended up killing a cabbie. As you do.

Phillip reassured Belanger that he wouldn't give him away. A couple of evenings later, though, they got back from mowing lawns or whatever and the police were in the hostel lobby. Belanger freaked out: Could Phillip help him get to the train yards so he could escape to the States?

Phillip obliged, enlisting a hostel resident with a station wagon. They dropped Belanger off. Phillip was in touch now and again with his mother's sister, Blanche, who lived in Winnipeg. They headed to her house now for a bite to eat.

Blanche came to the door with an apron over her dress and a scarf over her curlers, the smell of a roast wafting past her, extra-long cigarette ash dangling over her tumbler of gin.

Phillip kissed her, took hold of her shoulders and looked her in the eye: "Aunty Blanche, you can't repeat a fucking word you hear here tonight."

"All right," she said, because what else could she say?

Phillip and his buddy dissected the evening's events as Blanche served them, knocking back the gin, ears popping, eyes starting out of her head. The minute the men left, she called Lucille back east.

From Ontario, Lucille called the Vancouver police and asked, "Are there any arrests or warrants for my son?" Nope. She phoned the Edmonton police. "Are there any arrests or warrants for my son?" No. Winnipeg police. No.

Then she got a call from the RCMP in Ottawa: "We have reports that you're phoning everywhere, asking about your son. What's going on?"

She spilled the beans.

Phillip was blacked out in his local when the bulls barged in, cuffed him, threw him in the back of the car, took him back to the train yards. He came to in the back seat, a cop whaling on him, and talked.

They charged him with accessory after the fact to murder and stuck him in the Winnipeg city jail to await trial.

"The elevator at the jail is stainless steel with a drain hole for water. I grabbed the metal handrail and felt where the metal had been chewed up." Phillip knew how to read those details: "They stop the elevator, cuff you to the handrail, and beat the living fuck out of you. Then they can hose it down. Stainless steel: fuckin' right.

"That was back in the day when, in the prairies, if there was a drunken Indian that was too much trouble, little town, big town, didn't matter: throw him in the back of a police car, drive him forty miles out, kick him out in a blizzard and drive off. You got a dead Indian in the morning. There were a lot of cases of that."

Scary shit. Scary shit. The cops escorted Phillip through grey hallways toward a holding cell, pushing a button on the wall to unlock the doors, one, and then another. They shoved him in. His cellmates' hungry, calculating gazes held him like lines hooked into his body. The door clanged shut behind him—BOOM. His asshole slammed up into the bottom of his throat.

Criminals. Real criminals. As the cops departed, his cellmates ambled over.

"The fuck you in here for?"

"Looks like a diddler. Don't he look like a diddler?"

"No fuckin' way, man," Phillip said, sounding shrill.

"Good thing," one guy said, shrugging. A deep scar started under one of his eyes and disappeared under his chin. "You know what diddlers get in here." He pulled another guy forward. "Tell him."

"For the first six months, we kick the shit out of them every day," the other guy recited. "Beat the fuck out of them. Every day. And after that, nobody will talk to them. You are a dead entity."

"That's right," said Scarface, encouragingly. "And at any time if anyone has a cranky day," he looked around at the others, "you can just start whaling on this fucker at any time."

"I'm not a diddler," Phillip squeaked.

"Hey, remember that skinner that came in when we were in together that last time?" another guy said to another guy, as though Phillip wasn't even there.

"They kicked the shit out of him," said the other guy, "right here in the holding cell."

"Then when the guard came to deliver meals," the first guy explained, "he was made to kneel at the bars and ask, 'May I suck you off, sir?'"

"That one time he said he didn't want to . . ." the second guy shook his head. The other men snickered to recall what happened then.

One hardened-looking old guy frowned, and the crowd receded as though trying to save him the trouble of stepping forward. "What *are* you in here for?" he asked.

"Accessory after the fact," Phillip responded, eager to please.

The mood of the crowd shifted. "What'd he say?" one dim-looking fellow asked.

The guy beside him hit him lightly in the chest. "Rat."

Rat: that's what his charge meant. Phillip was being held in case they needed him as a witness. It turned out that Belanger had turned himself in; Phillip had been detained as insurance in case Belanger decided to plead not guilty.

He held his breath, waiting for someone to tell him what they did to rats in there, or, worse, to show him. But the old guy had given some signal, and everyone let him be. Phillip had been given protection: why? Maybe in expectation of future favours, but he never found out. When he got to court for his bail hearing, another miracle occurred.

His aunt Blanche had, by this point, told everyone she knew what was happening, including her next-door neighbour, Louella Winterton.

"Once, I'd been in Louella's house when her grown son came home," Phillip recalled. Louella's son told her to kick Phillip out. "She said, *No. There's something good going to come of this guy.* That's what she said."

And now, "in the courtroom, unbeknownst to me, is Louella Winterton. They read out the charge, legal talk. I didn't have a lawyer. I'd been in the middle of a piss-up, then was two days in jail, scared shitless and hungover. Louella stands up in the middle of the courtroom. *Your Honour,* she said. She was a homecare nurse and presented as very professional. *Your Honour, I will vouch for this gentleman. I will make sure he abides by all bail and release requirements. I will make sure that he comes back to court on any appointed date, if you will release him into my custody.* And the judge did, thank God."

Phillip's prison drama brings to mind Michel Foucault's distinction between the offender and the delinquent: roughly speaking, the offender *does* criminal activities, the delinquent *is* a criminal. But the relationship between what we do and who we are is complicated. As Louella Winterton recognized.

Now, as Phillip hit bottom in Vancouver, standing in front of that notice at the hostel, he heard again Louella Winterton's voice: *There's something good going to come of this guy.*

"That's when I decided: I'm going to prove her right."

Italo Calvino, in the introduction to his book on Italian folk and fairytales, says that these *repeated yet varying stories of human events, brought down to us from ancient times, are a general explanation of life, a catalogue of destinies. The division of humans, despite their essential equality, into kings and peasants; the persecution, then vindication, of the innocent; love unrecognized at first blush and then lost in the instant when it matures; subjection to spells, which is to say, having one's existence determined by complex, unknown forces; the duty to free oneself, to struggle toward self-determination, and free others as well in the process; fidelity to a goal and purity of heart as basic values; beauty as a sign of grace; and, that which unites everything on earth, the ongoing possibility of metamorphosis.*

Phillip went to the Salvation Army and was granted an entry interview with a counsellor whose kind face encouraged him to lay himself bare: "I'm gay. I'm a drunk. I'm unemployed and homeless My life is Fucked. Right. Up."

The counsellor listened, nodded, slid a form across his desk.

It was a three-month detox program. Residents were accommodated in a separate, better-appointed dorm from those in the nightly hostel. They worked half days for the Sally Ann, in the donation sorting room and so on. The other half of their days were spent in AA meetings, counselling, whatever else would help them along this new path.

"After two months, I went in the bathroom one morning to have a shave. I looked at myself in the mirror: the haggard look had gone. They say it takes two months for the fog to lift.

"*Oh!* I thought. *Oh! Well, maybe you're not that bad ugly mean person everybody was talking about.* Because when I was drinking, I was this mean motherfucker. Loud, obnoxious. I was a prick."

I must have smiled.

"Mm-hm." He smiled back. "I will admit it. So that was when the real sobriety kicked in."

Sober, maybe, but not straight, in any sense: he hadn't given up his other substances. Post-detox, he boarded with Aunt Pitty-Pat, an older gentleman who had taken an interest in his welfare. They got along marvellously, Phillip helping with the cats and garden, until Aunt Pitty-Pat discovered him shooting up and threw him out.

Phillip believed wholeheartedly that Aunt Pitty-Pat had been right to do it. "Fuck holding addicts' hands," he said, with a burst of conviction that startled me a little as I took notes. "If they're gonna croak, let 'em croak. You're not going to end up standing on your own two feet if there's someone behind you holding you up. The only way I ended up where I am is by falling flat on my face." Then he pointed to my phone, on his dining table between us, recording our interview, and said something even more shocking: "I hope you're going to put that in verbatim."

I felt my face flatten out in disbelief. Phillip had never told me before what I should write.

"Why do you say that?" I asked cautiously.

"Because if an addict reads it, that might get through to them." He poked the table in front of the phone for emphasis.

I told him I couldn't promise to put anything in verbatim. "If I literally put in every time you said fuck, this book would be unreadable." We laughed and he apologized.

"You're going to make what I say elegant," he paraphrased.

"No," I cavilled. "I hope to give a true sense of how you talk without putting your statements in 'verbatim.' But this won't be a self-help book. There might be a copy in a hostel that someone might incidentally pick up," but it was a different kind of hostel I had in mind: for backpackers, with a rotating foyer library of beach-wrinkled paperbacks, Colm Tóibín and Louise Erdrich and José Saramago. *Need a book? Take a book. Got a book? Leave a book.*

It was my first glimpse of Phillip's motivations in talking to me. My research into other aspects of this book had, by this time, brought him some difficult revelations. He had talked about them with another friend, who asked him, "If it's all so painful to you, why do you want it put in a book?" Phillip didn't tell me what he answered, though I pressed him. Now I thought I knew:

He was reliving the wounding shame of his worst days in hopes of helping others. To him, his was a cautionary tale. The book wasn't about him, but about something bigger.

He was thankful that he had known so much want, and gone through so much suffering, thinks the ugly duckling in the end, when he's happily ensconced among the swans, *for it made him appreciate his present happiness and the loveliness of everything about him all the more.* The *deep soul learning* Phillip said he gives today in his job was what he also hoped to give in this book.

Phillip was fond of saying that all the terrible things that happened to him *happened for a reason.* It's a platitude I instinctually resist, but, for him, perhaps the book was proof he was right. Perhaps, for him, this book *was* that reason. Or it would be, if I'd only put his words in verbatim.

Whose story was this?

Phillip's? For many years, I treated it like that, listening hard, full of respect, trying to see his stories as he did, not because I always agreed with him but because I thought I was supposed to represent him as he saw himself.

Did I have a right to tell his story? An obligation? Or was he obliged to me, for listening to him in a way no one else ever had?

What Art really reveals to us is Nature's lack of design, her curious crudities, her extraordinary monotony, her absolutely unfinished condition, says Oscar Wilde in *Intentions.*

Nature has good intentions, of course, but, as Aristotle once said, she cannot carry them out.

I had found this out the hard way: left unmediated, Phillip was unintelligible on the page.

When I played spies as a kid, we used lemon juice for invisible ink. The contents of our communiqués were revealed by holding them over a flame.

If this was Phillip's story, delivered to me through friendship's codes, it would remain invisible without my transforming filter. Me: I was the flame.

Seeking a proving ground for his sobriety, Phillip moved back to Edmonton, scene of his final descent, and got a job in a bar. All around him, people he knew were careering toward their destruction. One old friend died by suicide. Brian Barito overdosed, fatally. Young Carl descended into addiction. But the real onslaught of deaths was yet to come.

It was the early eighties. Phillip ran into a guy he knew, maybe five years younger, who looked awful: he'd lost weight and his glands were swollen. His body looked tiny and fragile, his eyes huge and scared.

They were just shooting the shit, until he asked Phillip, out of the blue, "What do you know about it?"

"I know it's killing people," Phillip responded. "You better go see a doctor."

Phillip never saw him again.

The second person in Edmonton to die of AIDS was a doctor. He owned the bathhouse. His lover was the seventh to die of the disease. Phillip, back in his drinking days, had had a fling with the doctor's lover. "I understood that it was a disease passed sexually, with guys," he told me.

Death was counting off or counting down. But for Phillip, all these years later, it was still counting.

I had wondered, ever since I first learned the outlines of his story, how a gay former junkie of his generation in Vancouver had managed to stay alive. Phillip would test positive for HIV shortly after meeting that old friend. Though he waited, it never developed into AIDS.

There was just one brief strange episode: "I got sick. And I mean really, really sick. My whole scalp was moving like there was a whole whack of leeches or bugs in there. Hallucinations. I'd never been that sick ever, never ever. Four or five days, it was brutal. And then it was all gone."

Phillip would eventually see a documentary about a genetic mutation called Delta 32, found in less than 0.1 percent of the world's population, which prevents HIV from developing into AIDS, and surmise that he had that kind of luck. The documentary's subject was a New Yorker called Steve Crohn, whose lover had been among HIV/AIDS's earliest casualties. Some seventy or eighty of Crohn's friends succumbed while he stayed healthy. Mystified and almost ashamed, he badgered the medical community to investigate and eventually learned of an AIDS research centre looking to test "nonprogressors." It was then that the mutation was discovered.

When Phillip told me about his brief and unusually violent illness, he speculated that it was his immune system "kicking into this genetic thing that's supposed to keep you from getting it."

In *Love Undetectable*, Andrew Sullivan talks about how AIDS both exposed and created what we now know as the gay community. Previously, there had merely been gay men, isolated from each other. At best, they were integrated into—masked within—the community at large. *AIDS as a homosexual experience created bonds and loyalties and solidarities that homosexuals had never experienced before. As it forced gay men out into the world, it also paradoxically intensified the bonds among them. The old question of assimilation-versus-separatism became strangely moot. Now, both were happening at once.*

I'm not sure why, when we talked about it in 2018, Phillip didn't seem to know what Sullivan calls the telltale signs of seroconversion, the moment when, several weeks after infection with HIV, the body starts manufacturing antibodies to try to fight the virus's invasion.

Sullivan said he himself felt like *an animal thrashed around by the neck by a predator desperately trying to break its spine. It went on for two days: a relentless, hostile, virulent thrashing, a deep, spiking fever that I had never experienced before and had no idea how to confront.*

Ruth Coker Burks, in *All the Young Men*, a book about her work with gay male AIDS patients in Arkansas, asked a doctor early on, "What do they think is causing it?"

"I guess they're saying it's a virus and when you get it at first you have the worst flu of your life, and then it passes. But it starts to destroy their immune system. They're sitting ducks for anything that comes along."

Although it seems likely that what Phillip experienced was the flu-like seroconversion, it also appears that, in his case, his genetics did take him down a very different path. Antibodies are supposed to keep you safe; maybe his did, so that he wasn't a sitting duck for opportunistic infections. Hard to know.

Steve Crohn died by suicide in 2013, a death mostly attributed, in the news, to survivor's guilt. But Crohn had been gregarious, and his community was decimated; the love of his life had been taken from him. A perceptive feature about him in *New York* magazine put it differently: *Survivor guilt he could work on . . . surviving was a harder problem. It meant facing mortality, in essence, alone.*

Phillip never mentioned such difficulties to me; rather, he seemed to think it a moral duty and an accomplishment to have survived, not just HIV but also addiction, abandonment, his mother's departure, his father's abuse, Del's blockade. His friends died (or were heroin friends and, so, temporary); he never found the great love he always wanted and so richly deserved. But while Steve Crohn struggled to find connection, meaning, and the means to go on after his loved ones disappeared, Phillip was an artist of survival.

It wasn't just the people who died of AIDS, says Ruth Coker Burks, who buried so many young men. *Even many who did not have the virus ended up committing suicide. They lived through the depths of the epidemic only to take their own lives. But I knew the memories they were living with, and why it might be too much to bear.*

There were other memories, as well, though:

In the TV series *It's a Sin*, many boys go home to die amid virulent homophobia. One, Ritchie, whose mother has sequestered him from his friends—his chosen family—reflects on his deathbed. *"Boys die in London, and they say it's cancer or pneumonia, and they don't say what it really is."*

"Look, maybe we should think about tea," his mother interjects, Britishly, but Ritchie won't be stopped.

"They just lie and I don't want that. Do you know why? I had so much fun." He laughs. *"I had all those boys. I had hundreds of them."*

"Oh, Ritchie, don't talk like that."

But he's on a roll now, overriding his poor mum's decorum.

"And do you know what?" he goes on. *"I can remember every single one of them. Some boy's hair or his lips, the way he laughed at a joke, his bedroom, the stairs, his photographs, his face as he cums. Seeing him across the club six years later and thinking, oh, that's him, and he's with someone and he looks happy. And I think, oh that's nice, 'cause they were great. Some of them are bastards, but they were all great. That's what people will forget, that it was so much fun."*

Andrew Sullivan, who has now lived HIV-positive for many years, says, *I promised a friend of mine that we would never allow ourselves to forget just how truly frightening it was. But of course we did forget.* Which was sort of the goal—to live normally—but Sullivan found himself unable to do that either, unable to engage, he said, with a world oblivious to what he had witnessed. *Some call this survivor guilt, though it didn't feel like guilt. I was glad beyond measure to be alive, to be well, to be here; but the sadness still surrounded me like a blanket, muffling everything. Post-plague, post-death, post-mortality, post-career, post-fear. It was not a memory or a regret. It was a puzzlement. A numbing, deadening, saddening puzzlement.*

Sullivan lands on the spiritual:

Maybe that puzzlement is something we should always feel but cannot bring ourselves to . . . a gift of a heightened sense of what is actually real, and what I cannot understand. . . . I sensed that the key to living was not a concentration on fighting the mechanics of the disease or fighting the mechanics of life, but an indifference to both their imponderables . . . the safety of knowing and the relief of not knowing. But in that of course it resembled merely what we all go through every day. Living, I discovered, is about the place where plague can't get you.

Hans Christian Andersen may have considered "The Ugly Duckling" to be his most autobiographical tale, but he was a writer, both scholar and shadow, both duckling and swan. *I am like water,* he said, but he was beside himself at all times, both Narcissus and his own reflection.

Andersen's actual autobiography was a book he titled *The Fairy Tale of My Life*: a romanticized, sanitized, idealized account of dignified privation in a provincial town, presided over by a devoted, unimpeachably pious mother, giving way to glittering success—literary accolades, hobnobbing with European cultural and actual royalty, the patronage of Copenhagen's best-known families.

In real life, there were some skeletons in the Andersen family closet; in real life, young Hans Christian suffered at school and in town. He was neurotically insecure through out adulthood and not without reason: the families that supported him never treated him as though he was their equal but always as a misfit—a genius, perhaps, but awkward, not one of them. This was at least in part because of his sexuality: he proposed to several women, but never married; he was often simultaneously in love with a man, but this love dared not speak its name.

"The Ugly Duckling" ends as fairy tales are supposed to, with a happy, uncomplicated resolution, the swan fully fledged and nestled securely in the bosom of his fellows, the terror and shame of his past nothing but a distant memory.

But what happens to us in childhood happens to us, in some form, our whole lives. Andersen was a proud survivor of bullying and exclusion, executing his artistic vision with confidence and drive, but was also maniacally obsessed with social status and longed for an intimacy that eluded him.

Phillip's childhood suffering, too, both scarred and strengthened him.

The ugly duckling's story begins before he hatches, before memory, before conscious experience. He is born into a world made by others and his life's work is not to shape it but to find his bespoke place in its multiform design.

Somewhere, we dream, the universe has a hole in it cut to our shape; we are the peg custom-crafted to fill it.

Phillip would gradually wean himself from his other addictions. He would qualify as a nurse's aide. And then there he was: a homeowner; a professional; a fine, upstanding member of society. My friend, and a friend to others. Louella Winterton had been right.

He was pretty much out of the closet at work, where he occasionally faced homophobia—more informal than institutional. His actual closet at home was filled with whips, chains, some kind of elephant harness, or so he told me—he wouldn't let me look.

He got a computer, then got rid of it because it was pulling him into the internet ugliness that most of us engage with routinely. He was relieved to see it go, though he missed looking at pictures of puppies and kittens before bed. He'd started sending me short emails, in addition to our phone calls, but now he did that from the hospital on his lunch break.

There are many other stories I could tell from his life: funny ones, shocking ones, sad ones. I had to kill a lot of darlings, as they say, to keep this story moving. But I think now that if you're inclined to love Phillip at all, I have given you plenty of reason to do so. If not, it's fine. *If you press me to tell you why I loved him, I feel that this cannot be expressed except by answering: Because it was he, because it was I.*

Regardless, that wasn't what lured you or me into this story. What about the woman bank robber travelling under an alias? you might be asking now.

What about Del?

THE SNOW QUEEN

It was summer 2007, as I recall. My husband and I were in Edmonton, staying with my parents, who were looking after our toddler to let us work. I was heavily pregnant with our second child. My first book had sold to a Canadian publisher, a two-book deal that included a second novel, already nascent, and was getting international offers. I was feeling confident—my only two goals in life had ever been to be a writer and a mother, and look: I was both.

Now, back in western Canada, not yet working on this book actively but always keeping it at the back of my mind, I thought I'd do a little research on Del.

I'd had no luck finding her online, but I easily tracked down Simma Holt, the feminist journalist Del had asked Phillip to contact when she got thrown back in the slammer. I phoned Holt at home. She was eighty-five and remembered Mary Lloyd clear as day, forty years after they had met.

"She was a victim of all those bastards, was with someone who was blackmailing her and needed a divorce from him. I got Neil Fleishman involved, took him to the prison to talk to Mary. He was a mean-spirited divorce lawyer, a wild man, mustached, reddish hair. His language was terrible. If you ever want anything on Neil Fleishman, I've got lots for you. You would have fun writing his character and he's dead so you can say whatever you

Sun's Simma Holt Canada's Top Woman News Reporter

Vancouver Sun reporter Simma Holt took top honors in the field of news reporting by women in Canada for 1955.

Mrs. Holt was presented with the Canadian Women's Press Club memorial award Tuesday night at the club's biennial convention dinner in Hotel Macdonald, Edmonton.

The award for best news story is worth $100.

Winning story was Mrs. Holt's scoop headlined "Blackmail Made Me Quit." It told why lawyer T. G. Norris, QC, resigned as former police chief Walter Mulligan's counsel during the Tupper police probe.

DECISION EXPLAINED

The story appeared in a Vancouver Sun "extra" last September.

News story judge J. B. McGeachy, former editorial writer for the Globe and Mail, now associate editor of the Financial Post, explained why he had chosen Mrs. Holt's story as the top news story in the nation-wide contest.

"Many of the entries in this category were, in my judgment, features rather than 'news stories,' as I have always understood the term.

"The distinction is sometimes hard to draw but I judged on the assumption that a news story must refer, at least in its main point, to some current event, incident or disclosure; and that the criteria for deciding whether or not it is a good news story are:

"1. public interest.

"2. competence and liveliness in the writing.

"3. early and speedy reporting.

"A scoop, of course," Mr. McGeachy said, "scores top marks under the last of these headings."

PRAIRIE-BORN

Born in Vegreville, Alta., Mrs. Holt joined the editorial staff of The Vancouver Sun in 1944 after graduating from University of Manitoba.

She received honorable mention for a news story in the press club awards of 1953.

That year she was honored by the Vancouver Fire department, and became Canada's honorary woman fire chief.

Honorable mention for good news reporting went to Phyllis Griffiths of Toronto and Jo Carson of Cobourg, Ont.

Other awards were given for best magazine articles, columns and features, radio scripts and fashion articles.

want about him. I wrote that book for him." Apparently, Fleishman made his own revisions to her manuscript and gave her no credit. Simma seemed gratified that it hardly sold any copies.

I appreciated the encouragement, even if it was partly revenge. I couldn't imagine why she would have wanted credit for Fleishman's memoir—*In Cold Blood* it wasn't. But she was also no Harper Lee, and once I read more of her work, I understood better. She didn't write to make literature, she did it to tell stories that needed telling. She was a crusader: a woman journalist and, eventually, a member of Parliament, part of a very small female minority in that era. She wanted credit for Fleishman's book because she had done the work.

"Mary was lovely, elegant," she recalled. "She would have been a grand lady if her life hadn't turned out as it did. I think she was a lookout in those crimes. She was used by the men in her life."

Simma asked me if I had talked to her. I hadn't. Did Simma know how to find her?

No, but she told me to pass on her address and phone number when I did. "I'm sure she's still alive because she's younger than me."

She also directed me to the University of Manitoba archives, where her papers had been housed, telling me she had a file there marked "Mary Lloyd."

I was busy, as I've said—baby and book in their respective pipelines, not to mention a toddler and other projects. One way or another, it was 2011 before I got around to ordering copies of the file, one for me and one for Phillip.

My copy hadn't yet reached me at home in the US when he received and opened his. When we spoke by phone, his voice was different.

"It was a real Pandora's box," he said. What was it I was hearing? He wouldn't elaborate; he wanted me to read it for myself. We had plans to meet shortly, in the Fraser Valley, where we would spend a few days going through the file's contents together and visiting the places where he had lived with Del.

But he was right. When we opened that file, dark things flew out that couldn't be put away again.

When Phillip, coming east from Victoria, alighted at the ferry terminal in Vancouver, I was waiting for him, leaning on a rental car. I always take the smallest and cheapest car available, but the smallest and cheapest that day was a white convertible.

Phillip didn't disappoint: "Oh, my goodness, would you look at that? We are travelling in style."

The sky started spitting as we barrelled east along Highway 1, the Trans-Canada, but we refused to raise the top. The highway runs roughly parallel to the Fraser River, which carved this valley, though the road is straighter. Phillip had chosen a cozy B&B for us at a crossroads with little else around it but fields and mountains and forest. When the owner came out to greet us, Phillip expressed admiration for the hulks of farm equipment she had rusting in the yard. They compared notes on similar displays of agrarian antiquities we had passed en route, a fashion in these parts for which I perhaps failed to show sufficient enthusiasm. In the foyer, I stooped for a closer look at a decorative mouse hole in the baseboard, complete with a natty mouse family just coming or going. The father wore a hat and carried a briefcase; the mother held a mouse baby's paw.

Phillip and I had adjoining rooms. He had brought matching printed cotton kimonos for us—a hilarious, elegant gesture. We would wear them in the mornings during prolonged continental breakfasts on the patio, as we went through the Holt documents at our leisure. (From then on, whenever I visited him, I would pack my kimono to reprise the ritual. Now, it hangs in my closet and gives me a pang each time I push it aside.)

The rooms were smallish, but he gave me the one with French doors giving onto the backyard, where each day I would see a rabbit bounding slowly through the early-morning mist.

It was a place whose charms might salve the abrasions of the Holt file, a little green space in which to recover.

Topmost was a stapled sheaf of articles. The first headline read, *2 Sisters South of City Describe Finding Man's Body Beside Ditch*. The story was an account of how, one June afternoon in 1956, a couple of kids came upon Lew Lloyd's body lying face up just south of the Edmonton city limits. It had been raining heavily the night before; his truck lay half-buried in mud in a ditch nearby. A bullet had entered his right side and exited below his heart.

Edmund Gendron, a roommate and an associate in a landscaping business, told police Lloyd received a phone call about 1 a.m. Sunday, became excited and suddenly left the apartment they shared in a quiet street, close to downtown. The call, it seemed, was from Del. *He returned a little later, borrowed $20 from Gendron, took the truck keys and left, saying he was going to a motel to see his wife.* He never came home.

Del had told Phillip that Lew's murder was a mob hit. He'd believed her and I believed him, but when he read this, he told me,

"It was like, *bing!* There was something wrong with the story I believed all these years."

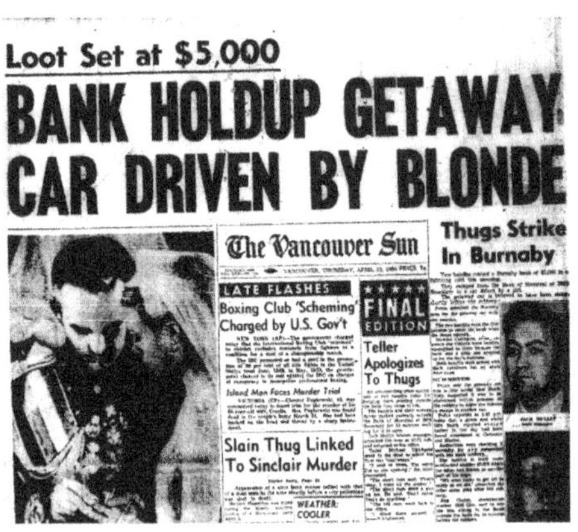

Loot Set at $5,000

BANK HOLDUP GETAWAY CAR DRIVEN BY BLONDE

The Vancouver Sun

Thugs Strike In Burnaby

LATE FLASHES

Boxing Club 'Scheming' Charged by U.S. Gov't

Island Man Faces Murder Trial

FINAL EDITION

Teller Apologizes To Thugs

Slain Thug Linked To Sinclair Murder

WEATHER: COOLER

So many unforeseen details—the file was a magnifying glass, showing us what we'd missed, burning holes in what we thought we knew.

Five weeks after the robbery, James Kempster, Mary and Lew's alleged partner in the crime, had reportedly gone on a *$2,200 spending spree* with Mary, buying furniture and appliances for the house in Vancouver where they were eventually arrested. Mary was masquerading as Kempster's wife, the newspapers reported. "I knew her as Mrs. Kempster," said the man who sold them the house. Their down payment combined a five-hundred-dollar cheque with a thousand in cash, made of hundreds, fifties and twenties, plus about twenty-five dollars in quarters. *"We asked if he'd been robbing a piggy bank and Mrs. Lloyd said he had won it playing poker."*

The bank loot had included quite a sum in quarters.

All this was given as evidence at the robbery trial and duly reported by the *Vancouver Sun*, whose attempts to sensationalize the story are quaint and malicious. *All through the three hours of Thursday's hearing, Mary Lloyd and Kempster held hands,* one article tittered. *Her right arm was pressed against his through the sleeve of her transparent blouse as they frequently smiled and muttered to each other.*

There's also the parallel drama of Mary's gun charges: a friend of the Lloyds, Kenneth Bird, testified that, in early April, after the robbery and before Lew's murder, Mary came to his house in Vancouver *and demanded to know the whereabouts of her husband.* Bird wouldn't tell her, so she pulled a nickel-plated revolver out of her handbag. *She pointed it right between my eyes,* he said, demanding,

"You either tell me or I'll blow your head off." The article doesn't say whether he caved.

Nineteen days before the murder, Mary and Kempster paid the last two premiums on life insurance policies held by Lew Lloyd. After his death, they came together to claim the payout.

It was the lead investigator on the murder, RCMP Sergeant Norman Lee, of Edmonton, who linked Lew Lloyd's death to the still-unsolved bank robbery. A 2003 memoir by Wallace Craig, the lawyer who represented Mary and Kempster, suggests Sgt. Lee had help connecting those dots: *The police had acted upon information received from the murdered man's father. He said that shortly after the robbery, his son had visited him and told him that he and his wife and Kempster were the persons who had held up the bank, that afterwards Lewis Lloyd had found himself the odd man out in a love affair between Mary Lloyd and Kempster and that, fearing for his life, he was moving to Alberta.*

When the police raided Kempster and Mary's Vancouver home, they found, sketched on the back of a pay stub, a floor plan very much like that of the bank.

Phillip had known that Kempster and Del lived together; he hadn't known they *lived together.* She told him they had bought a big fancy house with the proceeds of their crime.

He recalled a story Del's daughter Lorraine had told him.

A policeman somehow cut himself while searching the house, and Lorraine, then four, screamed at him for "getting blood on mommy's new floor."

Phillip was doubly crushed—by Del's deceptions and by the crime's tawdry scale. "I got the story of a real top-notch criminal with underground ties, someone of importance, but what I read is just a lowdown criminal. They paid for the house with quarters?

"And did she have something to do with her husband's death? I would say yes, without a doubt."

He wasn't alone in thinking that. James Kempster stood trial in Edmonton for Lew Lloyd's murder, and Holt's file included an article on the acquittal, where the judge made his own reading of the evidence very clear: *"Don't ever kid your self that this jury, or I, feel that you were not implicated in this death. The only problem all the way through has been whether or not the case against you has been proved. You are a young man. You have time to mend your ways. I personally feel that you embarked on this course of action at the insistence of Mary Lloyd. If you are going to be governed by Mary Lloyd from now on, you are going to end up in trouble."*

I don't know how Phillip missed that Kempster and Del had been lovers. Holt had shown him and Lorraine the newspaper coverage when he was a teenager. The ignorance seemed almost wilful.

And what about Del's political beliefs, which had been so inspiring to Phillip and informed his ethical development?

In the case of the only robbery she was convicted for, the proceeds had gone not toward the revolution but a house in the burbs.

But who was she before she was caught? Who was she now?

"Did you know that when I was in my late twenties, I was a red-hot Marxist Socialist?" Del asked Neil Fleishman the first time they met. *"That's French for a Communist!"*

Fleishman's book lets her tell her own backstory:

In 1953, I lived in Mexico City for about a year, and I still speak pretty good Spanish. When I was there, you'll never guess who I was chumming around with—two of my very best friends were Fidel Castro and Che Guevara! Sure. Che was a doctor then doing medical work in a Mexico City hospital. Fidel was planning how he was going to take over Cuba. How do I know? Because we were all planning together. Seems hard to believe, doesn't it? A curvy little prairie broad sitting in on planning sessions with men who changed the destiny of the Western World? But it's all true. Every word. I loved them both very dearly, Fidel and Che.

"Have I ever spoken to the External Affairs Department about this?

Hell, no. Nobody's ever bothered to ask me. I could tell them all about it, what they should know, what to look for, why all these things happened. I'm no Communist anymore, not even a theoretical Marxist. I've made my peace with myself. I've made my peace with the world. I'm not in that old bag anymore. That time in 1965 when we went to Cuba I never met Fidel but all I had to do was let him know we wanted to come and everything was on the house. He remembered me—just as I'll always remember him, in a very special way.

"A great man? Sure he was a great man, he knew what he wanted. You know, it's funny. When I was in Kingston Penitentiary from '57 to '65 somebody put it on my record that I had become intensely Communistic there. Well, they could believe what they liked but you know my history now. I told them I had done it to annoy the staff. I annoyed them, all right. They resented me thinking of myself as having superior intelligence. They used to accuse me of reading impressive books which I didn't understand. Go away! I knew what I was reading and I knew what I understood. Okay, it's all over now, it's all in the past. I really don't care anymore. I'm not going to shake the world, hell, no woman is ever going to shake the world. I thought I was going to once, but no more."

Would Del still sound like this, if I could find her, if she would talk to me? I couldn't square this voice with any way of speaking I know from western Canada: she was mouthing lines better suited to Bogie and Bacall. Were these her words, or was Fleishman playing pulp-fiction ventriloquist?

As it turned out, Del had many different voices, or sounded different depending on what you wanted to hear. Which, in a way, amounted to the same thing.

Holt's file contained an eight-by-ten picture: tall black bookcases, laden with hardcovers, meet in a corner; on top of them, a couple of cats. A woman with her back to the camera plays with them, holding out one end of a cord dangling into the photo from above the frame. In the foreground, Mary Lloyd sits upright in a hard

wooden chair, wearing a crisp white blouse with the same skirt and cardigan as the other woman. A thick book lies open in her hands. Her legs are crossed, her eyes are down; she looks absorbed. Her mouth pulls slightly to the right. Dark bangs curve in a yin-yang upon her pale brow.

Where is this? Doreen Meyer, in a 1992 master's thesis on the Kingston Prison for Women, *A Prison of Their Own*, says, *The women's "library" consisted of a small bookcase of books which were drawn on request from the library of the men's prison.* The space in the photo looks more capacious than that, and none of the descriptions say anything about cats. What was the picture taken for? Some kind of brochure, maybe on progressive initiatives in prisons? There are no other clues.

Nor can I make out the cover of Mary's book, which drives me nuts, though it would turn out to be just one maddeningly illegible patch among many. In this case, at least, I know what I'm not seeing.

Mary was sentenced at what turned out to be a time of significant change in the Canadian penal system. There was only one place in the nation where women could serve federal time, the women's prison in Kingston, Ontario. This meant that female inmates in Canada were usually hundreds or thousands of miles away from their families.

Until the 1930s, women sent to Kingston Pen were housed in a unit within the men's prison. When they got a dedicated building, it was built with forbiddingly high stone walls topped with barbed wire, a remnant of Victorian philosophies that emphasized punishment and isolation.

Reformers were chagrined. The late-nineteenth-century view that women criminals were degenerates, a breed apart from "normal" women, was giving way to the theory that they could be remade into law-abiding citizens. A prison's intended function, and therefore its design, was shifting along with this view, toward providing a sort of family environment, setting standards and boundaries and providing nurturing that it was supposed criminals must have been deprived of early in life.

There's not a ton written about all this as it pertains to women, but when I visited the site of the old prison, now a museum, an enthusiastic young historian put me on to some academic writing on the Prison for Women, or P4W, as it is known, including Punishment in Disguise, by Kelly Hannah-Moffat.

Hannah-Moffat quotes a couple of 1920s commissions on penal reform, whose efforts reflected this sea change. *So many people seem to forget that human nature in the convict does not differ from that of the person outside the walls, and that most of those within will some day be again without. . . . Offenders are sent to prison as a punishment and not to be punished; the function of those in charge should not be to repress but to stimulate their charges with fresh hope for better things and better days.*

By the 1950s, the P4W had a prison psychiatrist, who offered diagnoses and interventions, as well as vocational training, including a home economics program run by a professional in that field. While male inmates were given work that would increase their chances of becoming responsible breadwinners on release, women were coached to become good little ladies—chaste, continent, knowledgeable in the domestic arts.

The P4W had female matrons and female staff to counteract insalubrious side effects of male staff (sexual temptation, sexual exploitation, etc.). The matron, living on-site, took the role of a surrogate mother. Ironically, while matrons were hired in part to model appropriate feminine behaviour, they were often ambitious career women, scrappy and single, such as Isabel Macneill, who became the P4W's first dedicated superintendent in 1960.

Despite her own unconventional career choices, Macneill *firmly believed that domestic training could provide skills that were important for women who were likely to spend much of their everyday lives in the kitchen or doing household chores.*

The Little House

One emblematic initiative was the fully equipped and functional home she had built within the prison walls. Six women inmates lived together in the little white bungalow, ten weeks at a time, to train in *meal preparation, home care, and personal grooming,* adhering to strict standards set by a domestic science instructor. The meal preparation curriculum included budgeting and menu planning, as well as an occasional lecture on starving people around the world. Home care included doing floors and furniture, silverware and laundry, and learning how to set a table, serve tea and say grace.

Personal grooming was considered as essential an aspect of vocational training as any other, given its intended outcome: a Federal Corrections newsletter article describes the current inmates of the Little Bungalow as *attractive girls in their late teens or early twenties. Most are not married and while the way to a man's heart is through his stomach, the old adage tells us, he must first be lured by a pleasing appearance.* This philosophy was common in correctional facilities across Canada: in 1953, Oakalla prison started offering plastic surgery as one of *the new treatment techniques to correct any disability which might have contributed towards delinquency, such as scars, squints, unsightly or obscene tattoos.*

In the prison system as a whole, conventional feminine attractiveness and social habits were promoted as a critical aspect of the aim of reintegration. Together, both would lead to "healthy" relationships, which in turn would decrease recidivism. (In the 1970s, concerns about lesbian activity in the P4W led not only to the reintroduction of male staff but also a short-lived experiment in Saturday night dances with students from nearby Queen's University, later discontinued in part *because* of concerns that students would develop relationships with inmates.)

ISABEL MACNEILL
... backed parole bid

Macneill's thinking on individual inmates' possibilities in the world, though, may have been slightly more imaginative. In a letter to Simma Holt about Mary Lloyd's employment prospects post-incarceration, Macneill mentions that Mary might make a good receptionist or hospital worker, *a crack steno.* Presumably training for all of these (admittedly pink-collar) jobs was available within the prison.

Phillip told me that when Mary was paroled, she was to have entered training in something "writing-related," but he couldn't tell me what, and of course she skedaddled before it could take hold, leaving her to fall back on those other qualifications cultivated at the P4W.

When Phillip and I drove by on our tour, nothing remained of the Totten family's A-frame at Strawberry Mountain: BC Transportation had bought Del out when the highway was built through there. But we found the rental house where Phillip had lived from age eight to twelve, the one the family gave up when they went to Cuba, a dank, low-slung bungalow with a view of Vedder Mountain from the front, Chilliwack Mountain to one side. The property was limned with a row of cottonwoods, planted by Harvey as a windbreak. When the wind came through, the current occupants told us, the leaves all turned so they looked white, a signal of approaching rain.

They let us walk through the house, which they believed to have been built in 1954: when they'd pulled up the kitchen floor to replace it with hardwood, they'd found a Vancouver Sun from that year.

I had scoured microfilm of the *Sun* 1956–57, the years of Del's arrest and trial. It was a provincial paper, reflective of postwar values. Headlines invariably referred to communists as "Reds." Obituaries of innocuous local folk were used as filler, sometimes on the front page. Hunting for relevant bits, I would scroll quickly through the "Ladies'" section, past recipes for gelatin moulds and advice on the smooth handling of boorish guests, text and photos blurring as I imagined Del thumbing through the paper in that kitchen or other kitchens. What if anything did she think the ideal life of the 1950s housewife had to do with her?

He was a great man, she'd said of Fidel, *he knew what he wanted.* What did Del want? *She would have been a grand lady*, Simma had told me, but I'd only seen the conditions preventing that, not what might have made it possible.

Phillip and I peered into the three bedrooms. "This one was Harvey's, this was mine, and this was Rob's," said Phillip. He and Rob had shared until their elder brother, Ben, took off for good.

"So where was the housekeeper supposed to sleep?" I asked. He paused and frowned as we arrived simultaneously at the answer. "Well, with Harvey, I guess."

In the file, Holt described Del as having answered a "wife wanted" ad. I would later confirm that sex was implicit in the job description, along with housekeeping and childcare. The vocational directors at the P4W knew whereof they spoke.

How did Simma Holt get involved with Del to begin with? The one time we spoke, I hadn't thought to ask.

Likely, it was while researching rehabilitation, parole and the P4W, possibly because Macneill wanted Holt to write about the women's prison. Canada's National Parole Board was established in 1959, a year before Macneill was hired. Its founding dovetailed with Macneill's belief that, for most women at the P4W, long years of incarceration so far from their families were wrong and probably counterproductive.

In a lively exchange of letters during fall 1963, Macneill sent Holt some recidivism statistics, then later berated her for getting them wrong in the press. I never found that article but I did find a 1964 profile Holt wrote of another inmate.

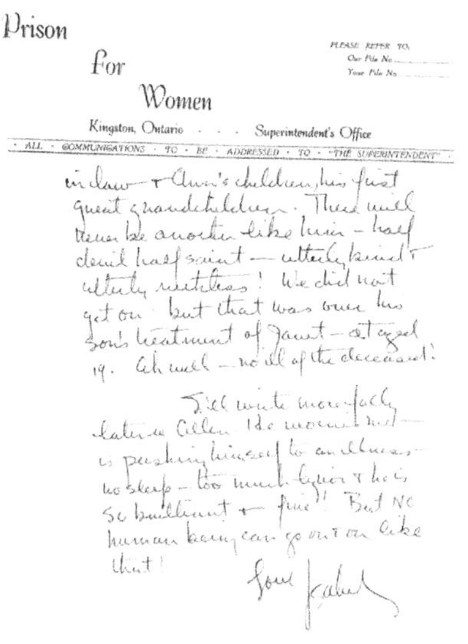

Prison
For
Women

PLEASE REFER TO
Our File No. ....
Your File No. ....

Kingston, Ontario . . . . Superintendent's Office

· ALL · COMMUNICATIONS · TO · BE · ADDRESSED · TO · "THE SUPERINTENDENT" ·

in law + Ann's children, his first great grandchildren. There will never be another like him – half devil half saint — utterly kind + utterly ruthless! We did not get on but that was over his son's treatment of Janet – at aged 19. Oh well – no ill of the deceased!

I'll write more fully later. Allen [illegible] — is pushing himself to an illness – no sleep – too much liquor + he is so brilliant + fine! But NO human being can go on like that!

Love Isabel

Holt, for her part, thanked Macneill for the help and kindness she was given while in Kingston. *I do appreciate your patience with this wandering scribe who was too thick-skulled to get the message of Kingston in the first four or five hours, she wrote. I sit here stalling the writing and wondering if I have it. I keep telling the boss: "Great story" and he asks "What is the story?" And I say: "I don't know, but it is great."*

Not an uncommon sentiment among writers.

By late 1963, Holt was a fully committed recruit to one of Macneill's pet causes: getting Del paroled. Despite legal eligibility and good behaviour, not to mention young children and aged parents three thousand miles away in BC, the Parole Board turned down her first application. Macneill and Holt traded outraged letters about it, and then Holt started writing to others—the head of the Parole Board, her member of Parliament—pleading, cajoling, sometimes flattering, sometimes threatening to take the case public in ways that wouldn't look good.

She even contacted A. M. Manson, the judge who'd presided over Mary's robbery trial, suspecting he was the one who *put the kibosh* into her application (a prepositional reconfiguring I sometimes repeat for my own amusement). *The minute I mentioned her, he said, ". . . she is a very very wicked woman . . . a very evil woman." He went on to explain that he had sentenced her to 25 years for the bank robbery, that she was older than Kempster and was the influence probably in both crimes.*

Holt was not impressed. *Judge Manson's tone when he talked about Mary's "young paramour" indicated his feelings not only about her part in the murder, but even worse her affair with a young man,* she later carped to Macneill. *You know these puritanical types (whose name incidentally was in the records of customers at a big call girl establishment here. . . and you must destroy this letter or I will be haunted by Manson through the courts for the rest of my life).*

She knew how to work the judge, though, and quickly brought him over to their side. Mary was due for release within two years no matter what, she told Manson, but parole would ensure she had resources and support to ease her transition.

The most convincing argument appeared to be Mary having *said that the first person she planned to see when she returned was Manson because she had to thank him, for in the long run he had given her a purpose in this life,* that of helping other fallen women get on the straight and narrow, a bit of flattery that, Holt said, recruited the judge to the cause of Mary's rehabilitation.

Another inmate wrote to Holt in hopes of assisting Mary's case: *I want you to know that when I came here last yr I was a very sick person mentally. And Mary was the person who has got me on my feet. Now I am just a few months away from the front door. And I am quite stable now. And also since I've been associating with Mary I feel now that it is much better to work for a living. And I feel Mary is responsible for my straightening out.*

Macneill believed Mary herself had a similar trajectory: *Mary WAS a borderline psychotic at the time of the crime and subsequently, in our opinion. She is now better, much better! My firm conviction is she should go out on PAROLE not release. If released June 24 1966 she is free as the birds! I think that parole for 5 years is a much safer course for society than release in under 3!*

She and Holt were unified in their purpose—trying to get Mary paroled as a means of extending the prison's influence over and involvement in her life. Holt railed in long, closely argued letters to the powers that be:

It seems phenomenal—and the height of folly—to keep this woman confined until she reaches the period of unconditional release (only two years from now) rather than to let her out on supervision on parole. Her case exemplifies the very reason for the creation of your board in Canada.

In Holt's view, if Mary got out in two years without supervision and reoffended, the board would be to blame. It was derelict, undermining its own purpose.

If more time is wasted she will decide against parole which will keep her "prisoner" outside for eight years. It makes sense that she should be made into the best possible human before she is released.

The more times I read this statement, the more nakedly chilling I find it. Holt and Macneill were progressives and champions of women, but their single-minded efforts toward parole for Mary were not aimed at her autonomy but rather the extended vigilance of the state.

Foucault put his finger on it, in *Discipline and Punish*. Progress in prisoner treatment through the ages is usually described quantitatively—*less cruelty, less suffering, more kindness, more respect, more humanity.* In fact, he says, reduced sentences treat prison as purgatory.

By paroling Del instead of releasing her, the authorities would retain power over her movements, her choices, her future, power that extended beyond the prison, beyond the punishment, into and around her very self.

If we are not locking up or maltreating the prisoner, what is the object of punishment?

Since it's no longer the body, it has to be the soul.

Holt's view of Del, as *a victim, being used by the men in her life,* didn't quite square with Phillip's. He agreed that his father was a bastard, but he saw—he needed to see—Del as a scrapper, a fighter, resourceful and sharp. He recalled her going after Harvey with a butcher knife; he watched her manipulate the joint property assessment after the divorce so that she came out ahead.

"So, a shrinking violet, exploited?" Phillip looked skeptical. "No. That might have been the story she spun for Simma, but I don't buy it."

But Holt, the crusader, wasn't fighting for someone who could fight for herself. Nor did I find her anywhere engaging with the possibility that Del had any involvement in the murder. I can't tell if this is due to fair-mindedness or closed-mindedness—in either case, if Holt condemned Mary for a crime she hadn't been tried for but likely had something to do with, it would make it hard for her to promote Mary's cause.

This is Holt's description of Del's marriage to Harvey, in the chapter she wrote for Fleishman:

She built a home with him and became a respected member of the small community. The marriage was a shambles, though a strong bond of love had grown between the new mother and the stepsons, particularly the youngest of the three, who was thirteen and had already been in trouble with the law. The husband, described by a psychologist as a "sadist with a castration complex" gave her as a Christmas present in 1967 a black eye and a broken nose. Subsequently, he threw her over a chair and damaged her back. After a particularly serious attack on February 1, 1969, and his continuing threat to turn her over to the parole board, she left him.

Fleishman *filed the papers for divorce on the grounds of mental and physical cruelty,* telling Del, *"You deserve matrimonial relief and I damn well will get it for you."*

In any telling by Holt, Del is the heroic victim. Despite spurning the therapeutic resources of parole (or failing to abide by the terms of parole, depending on how you want to tell it), Del became an upstanding (i.e., conventional) mother, wife and community member. She had not only *rehabilitated herself at no expense to society* but also *saved a boy everyone believed was headed into a life of crime.*

Phillip.

Holt reports that Phillip testified, at his own request. *He told of the love and help she gave him and his older brothers, and that it was she who kept him from sinking further into the delinquencies he had entered before his father married.*

The judge, too, became a believer, restoring Del's parole instead of sending her back to jail. *So little of what she did was bad,* Holt reported him saying as he delivered his decision. *What offense she committed against organized society was so overweighed by the aid and comfort she gave to salvage from society's wreckage a boy who already was on the way to becoming a reject. The boy chose to defend his stepmother against his own father before the courts when the battle became public. He loved this woman and knew that she had saved him from a life in institutions.*

Holt's file is thick with layer upon layer of talk *about* Mary. We were deep into it before it yielded a letter *from* Mary herself, in spring 1964, a full page of pretty cursive straight out of a handwriting textbook, except that the lines of her terminal *s*'s and *t*'s slant upward like flying scarves, and, in place of lower loops, her *y*'s finish in insouciant hooks.

Dear Simma,

Received your charming letter and was pleased by every word therein. You are a truly wonderful person Simma and I haven't the words to express my deep appreciation for your thoughtfulness.

The letter reads as though the writer wants badly to please and is tacking in different rhetorical directions to do so: sunny, intimate, sincerely grateful, gratefully sincere. I'm not saying Mary isn't on the level, but it's a bit like a job applicant letter in that its purpose is to appeal. She stresses that she's aware of all the roadblocks and *psychological barriers* to her success on the outside, but vows she is dedicated to making a go of her life. But before seeking a job that will set her on the right path, she writes, she wants to spend time with her parents, supporting her aged mother and ailing father. *I hope and pray that Papa hangs on. . . . If anything further happened to him while I was in here, it would be a dreadful blow.*

Mary was still in prison when, in July, Macneill broke to her the news of her father's death.

She dissolved in tears—really shattered, Macneill wrote to Holt. I took her home—gave her a DRINK—she wouldn't take a sedative—put her in the garden whilst cooked dinner.

Mary slept there. The next day, Macneill received a call from a *minion* informing her that *no decision could be reached in time to get her to funeral. I am livid,* she ranted in a letter, comparing Mary to the most notorious criminals in recent Canadian history: *Dion got a chance—Boyd got a chance—Evelyn Dick got a chance—but no chance for Mary Lloyd! If the mother dies before parole I think I will have to resign.*

The father's death pushed Holt to make good on her threats: she published an article in the *Vancouver Sun* about Mary's plight. It was intended to generate sympathy for Mary and to further her case for parole, but this publicity turned out to have unintended consequences. The next letter in the file is from Maude Stark, Mary's sister, raking Holt over the coals for having humiliated their family.

That article was all past and gone information not to be rehashed publicly. At this time my mother is with me and should be more upset over the loss of my dad but thanks to you she is emotionally upset beyond words over your article. Furthermore none of the family will ever read your paper again.

The last sentence was an afterthought, crammed between the letter's body and signature, but the problem went well beyond the *Sun*'s loss of this (admittedly large) family's readership: Macneill, too, received a letter, co-signed by Mary's mother, saying they didn't want Mary at home.

Holt wrote directly to the mother: *I saw Mary at Kingston and she is still a wonderful and gentle woman. . . . In fact I met a youngster in prison who has been greatly helped by Mary's advice and kingness* [love this typo] *and it seems that this young beautiful woman will for the first time lead a good life because of Mary's influence. This is the fifth girl who Mary has helped.*

In various places, Holt numbered "the girls Mary helped." What did she think Mary, who had been in jail for seven years, could do to rehab young women for life outside prison? Wag a finger at them and say, "Look, you want to end up like me?" What had she actually done to "save" Phillip and his brothers?

In the wake of Mary's father's death, Holt flew out to see her in prison. When Mary wrote to thank her, she projected undimmed resolve: *I want you to know Simma—that no matter what fate has in store for me—my faith in God and in mankind on the whole, will never be lessened. My goal in life is to help others and I know that I am quite capable in this field.*

BULLSHIT ARTIST

"DEL WAS SO PERCEPTIVE in judging people, figuring out what they would like to hear," her daughter Lorraine would tell me. "If she spoke to anyone, she would be very endearing to that person. She had one way of speaking to this person, a different way when she spoke to an ex-con. There were all these different Dels."

It seems a given that we speak differently to different people. If I used the same tone with my children as with my husband, my students, a bus driver, I would seem socially maladjusted. Sociologist Erving Goffman, in *The Presentation of Self in Everyday Life,* proposes that all our interactions involve personas—variations on a self.

But that healthy, rote role-shifting didn't seem to be what Lorraine was talking about. "Sometimes different people ended up in the same place who knew very different Dels," she told me in her quiet, straightforward way. "Then there was a problem."

A few weeks after receiving Maude Stark's tirade, Holt got a short, strangely formal letter from Mary.

Dear Mrs. Holt, it began.

Mary had called her *Simma* in all the previous letters, but perhaps was creating some distance to deliver news Holt was unlikely to take well: Mary had withdrawn her parole application and wished *no further publicity regarding same.* Her new goal, she said, was to walk out, free of her past, and start anew.

For the first time, Mary was not going along with Macneill and Holt, making me ask: Did Mary herself want to receive all the support Macneill and Holt believed she needed, or had she simply wanted to get out of jail sooner?

It was exactly the outcome Holt had said she feared, but now it seems she might have sparked it herself by writing about the case and inflaming the domestic situation Mary would enter were she to be paroled.

In her next letter, though, two months later and once more addressing her by her first name, Mary denies this, sounding intimate and plaintive. *Perhaps I caused you concern over my problem—if so, I am terribly sorry. In your last letter you mentioned that there must be more to it than I stated. No—my dear friend—there wasn't. I found it quite necessary to withdraw my application, due to the fact of enough waiting, worry and anxiety.*

After softening Simma up, Mary slipped in that she was reorienting her efforts toward early release, free from obligations or accountability, and also asking the provincial appeals court to count the seven months she spent in custody toward her sentence, so she might be able to get out even sooner. *It would be wonderful if I were granted this, wouldn't it.*

But Macneill and Holt hadn't wanted her out early if it meant she was off scot-free. Soon, Del changed her strategy back to the one her champions favoured. Early the following year, it worked.

February 25th, 1965

Prince George, BC

Dear Simma,

Here I am at long last "out."

Del wrote that she was excited to make contact with Simma and chagrined that she had not been allowed to go to Vancouver, where her widowed mother lived.

The main thing though, is that I am at long last partially free. Perhaps I am being a fool by wishing to clear my name—but believe me it is what I desire, more than anything else.

She asked Simma to keep in close contact, and to come up on a weekend if she could. As we know, though, Del didn't last long enough in Prince George to get any visitors.

That year's only other item is a letter from a woman named Ruth, whose last name I didn't recognize, but she was friendly and chatty with Holt and connected somehow with the P4W:

Mary Lloyd's disappearance has not surprised me. I have always felt that she was the only real criminal in the Prison for Women. A very selfish and hard woman. I am sorry that you were not better informed, and got involved and embarrassed. What I am afraid of is that she may be found dead somewhere some day . . .

Holt reported having spoken with Del by phone after she violated her parole and she showed no reluctance to get back on board the Del train when she resurfaced, implying she was sympathetic to Del's reasons for fleeing Prince George, and not at all *embarrassed* by her involvement. I suspect she identified with Del's struggles against her limitations, even while wanting to help her figure out how to live legitimately.

Doreen Meyer, in *A Prison of Their Own*, refers to a 1965 Canadian Corrections Association brief on the female offender, which noted that *women who broke the law were subject to a societal double standard—they were judged according to their refusal to play the traditional female role expected of them rather than, like their male counterparts, according to their transgression of the criminal law itself.* It quotes an equivalent American document, which said that *although the female offender is not significantly different from the male inherently, her violational behavior is defined, and she is treated and/or penalized, when she belies the traditional expectation for females. It is recognized that she has behaved in a way that is symbolically characteristic of the traditional male role.*

This proposition doesn't need to be stretched to fit Del's treatment in the Canadian penal system. Little had changed in a hundred years: *When a woman has thrown aside the virtuous restraints of society and is enlisted on the side of evil,* said a Victorian expert, Mary Carter, in 1864, *she is far more dangerous to society than the other sex.*

Dr. George Scott, the prison psychiatrist whom Del claimed to have assisted in his research, published a memoir, *Inmate: The Casebook Revelations of a Canadian Penitentiary Psychiatrist.* It only has a single chapter on the women of Kingston Pen, but that chapter includes a pointed footnote:

An impressive array of criminologists, female and male, consider deceitfulness to be the outstanding characteristic of the female offender. They base their conclusions on woman's lesser physical strength which leads her to rely on indirect aggressive behavior. In my own experience, I cannot accept the theory of woman's deceitfulness as the basis of her criminal acts. I recall the words of a male fraud offender who kept coming back to prison because of his expensive tastes. He remarked, "Doctor, you have to use what's going for you at the moment." Perhaps the female uses what's going for her at the moment. I believe she does.

Scott was eventually stripped of his medical licence after admitting to having had sex with a patient. (Mary had told Harvey about a prison psychiatrist who used to "book her out for a weekend" when she was at P4W.) Reprehensible, but it doesn't mean that Scott was wrong about the female criminal *using what's going for her at the moment.* It's just that her resources were perhaps more constrained than anyone around her wanted to admit.

As we went through these papers together at the B&B, Phillip said he was puzzled by his own repeated characterization as a delinquent. He couldn't think of what he had done to earn it. When I later interviewed his eldest brother, Ben, I heard a few stories: Phillip stealing fifty cents from a little girl; all three boys shoplifting candy.

I asked Phillip about those offences, and he readily admitted them, saying their mother found their booty hidden in the coal pile, "whupped" them, and made them return it to the shop. These were crimes committed before Lucille left, when he was about six. He further volunteered a story about getting drunk on Harvey's wine after school one afternoon. "I didn't know what alcohol was. I'd seen Harvey drink it and he never wobbled or anything. It tasted like grape juice. It wasn't till I stood up that I thought, *Oh, my god.* I went in the bathroom and puked my guts out."

The incidents all seemed quite innocent to me, but Phillip could see how, collectively, they might be viewed. "I can see a little bit where people might say, *heading down the road.* But inside myself, I walked in terror, all the time."

In addition to the transgressions he owned, however, there were others he denied, such as stealing Rob's newspaper money. I'm not sure it matters what he did or didn't *do*, though, since this is not who he remembers—or admits to—having *been.*

I asked if he recalled feeling rebellious.

"No, absolutely not."

His version of his child self from his vantage point as an adult, though, has to be taken alongside what he is reported as saying in court. In addition to the testimony whose stalwart sentiments so impressed the judge, Holt quotes Phillip in what appears to be an unpublished article drafted about ten days after Del was arrested for violating her parole: *Mary married and took two of the three young sons of her husband as her own. They were headed for trouble and the youngest said: "I was already a delinquent, I think, I was 10 when she came to us. She did so much for me."*

Was this all Holt's spin? The unpublished article contains other characterizations and quotes of dubious provenance. She quotes both Phillip and Lorraine calling Del "Mom," for example, which neither of them did. She says Mary *was angry and bitter* at being denied parole, though Mary herself, in her letters and in Macneill's reports about her, repeatedly and consistently emphasized that she was not. It's possible that there is some other source I haven't found, but I also have to allow for the possibility that Holt conjured these flourishes, which were, after all, perfectly logical. More crusader than writer, her aim was to assist Del; perhaps she thought that anything toward that end was fair game.

But did some of this spin originate with Del herself? Phillip's hackles were raised by things Del said in a letter to Holt when she was first thrown back in prison. Shoulder to shoulder at the breakfast table in Chilliwack with the letter between us, he ran his finger down the page, annotating in real time.

Dear Simma,

Thought I'd drop a few lines to let you know that I heard from Phillip. He was in at Mother's over the weekend and at his brother Ben's. It seems that Ben is more shook up over this than anyone else.

Phillip: "I did go to Ben's, but he wasn't more shook up than anyone else."

If you could possibly find a spare moment Simma I wish you would speak with him. Ben always hated his father on account of the way he was treated as a child and needless to say he hates him more now on account of my being here.

Phillip: "True that Ben always hated Dad, but not likely more because of Del."

He depended on me so much for moral support and guidance.

Phillip: "That's a crock of shit."

It's not impossible that Ben had this sort of relationship with Del or that Phillip's reactions stemmed from jealousy or possessiveness, but Ben was already out of the house when Del arrived, and my later conversations with him made it seem that she hadn't made much of a dent in his life. If Del were lying or even exaggerating, though, why would she ask Holt to contact Ben for her? She must have been confident that either Holt was going to find Ben in the state she described or that Holt would see Ben in the light Del shone.

Ben had done a brief, youthful stint in jail for housebreaking but hadn't committed a crime since and eventually got a pardon. Rob's history doesn't appear to include any crime. Phillip eventually had a couple of brushes with the law: Perhaps Holt should have tallied him in Del's stats as a partial success? But the file gives no sense that Holt followed up with those she counted as "redeemed," including Phillip.

Phillip grew out of childhood mischief to become a relatively docile adolescent, receiving from Del the love and attention he craved, even if he went off the rails into substance abuse after they parted ways. It was sad to me that although Del's letters also contained things about him that seem accurate to his own descriptions of the boy he was, he discounted them because they were couched in what he saw as a series of manipulations: *Phillip is taking this really good and is a great help to me,* that same letter concludes, describing him as understanding, lovable, stalwart and expressive.

So whose idea was it for him to characterize himself as a delinquent at Del's parole hearing? If it was his own idea, as the judge said, why? Was he spinning his story to get Del out of jail? It was his story to tell: he could spin it however he wanted. But he had no memory of having done so and yet here it was, on the page, in his voice.

In Andersen's "The Snow Queen," Gerda unmoors a random boat and lets the river carry her away in search of Kai. She bumps up at the property of an old woman, living in a wonderful flower garden, who wants Gerda to stay with her forever. The old woman buries her rose bushes, knowing that if Gerda sees them, she will remember her childhood friend and the hours whiled away beneath their bower.

One of the many improvements to family life that Del had implemented in the first year of her tenure, before the fighting started and her credibility with Harvey declined, was an allowance for each boy, a dollar a week out of the baby bonus. Every Friday, with some of his dollar, Phillip would buy Del a single red rose.

One day, Del took him aside: *"Your dad is pissed that you're always giving me a rose. It's causing me trouble."*

It was a revelation to Phillip. He'd been saving the rest of the money, though, and now he used it to buy Harvey a pocketknife. According to Del, Harvey cried that night in bed. *"It affected him,"* she said. *"That was the first time you ever gave him anything."*

"Were you in love with her?" I asked.

Phillip looked baffled and denied it, but then accepted that it might have been a little bit that way.

Gerda had been lolling, sunstruck, doldrummed in the old woman's bee-loud garden, when she spied some roses the old woman had forgotten. The sight broke the spell and Gerda rushed off to find Kai.

Phillip had been bewitched, as willingly as Kai. He'd hitched himself to Del and was still wrapped in her cloak, like *sinking into a snowdrift.* Now the contents of Simma's folder had broken the spell, and what had been gained? I was watching my friend recalibrate his own origin story, piece by piece.

And who was I in this story? Was I his Gerda, waving the roses of childhood under his nose to wake him? Was I instead one of the devil's minions, sliding shards of dark mirror into his eye, his heart?

Empty, vast and cold were the halls of the Snow Queen. In the midst of its empty, endless hall of snow was a frozen lake, broken on its surface into a thousand forms. Each piece resembled another, from being in itself perfect as a work of art, and in the centre of this lake sat the Snow Queen, when she was at home. She called the lake "The Mirror of Reason," and said that it was the best, and indeed the only one in the world.

Was Del used by the men in her life, as Holt said? Or was she using them? Phillip now thought the latter.

I started looking for one of those men, James Stanley Kempster, whom I found the way we found anyone in the 2010s, if we were going to find them: on Facebook.

Sixty years had passed since the mug shot published in the *Sun*, but it was unmistakably the same fellow, with a high forehead and close-set eyes over a strong nose. While he looked suspicious and cranky in that long-ago mug shot, though I could be reading that in, here he looked peaceful, strong, forthright.

His first entry on Facebook was dated March 14, 1965. I thought at first that he was still figuring out the settings, but then I guessed that might have been the day he found religion. His location was listed as "Citizen of Heaven" and the entry read: *Man has only one purpose in life as determined by our Creator. Dominant question: "What have I done today to glorify God"?*

In the picture, he sits on a leather loveseat with an unsmiling woman *d'un certain âge* in a red sweater over a leopard-print dress. A dachshund on her lap wears a black cape trimmed in leopard print; another, perched on Kempster's pinstriped lap, is in red. Christmas card photo? They're surrounded by angels, floating on wires and sitting on side tables. Behind them, a light glares as if from the dark beyond the picture window. It could be the reflection of a flash or Gabriel himself, about to come through the pane bearing glad tidings.

Kempster's page said he lived in Deroche, just across the river from where Phillip grew up. Phillip was astonished to hear it. I asked if he thought Kempster had been among those who tried to drop in on them when they were living at Strawberry Mountain. In one instance he recalled, a big black car slowed to a stop in front of the house, but Del ran out screaming at it and the car sped up again and drove away.

The internet yielded several possible phone numbers. I'm not a journalist by training and cold-calling racked my nerves. All the first hits were wrong numbers, which was just as well because I went to the bathroom before every time I dialed. By the time Kempster himself answered, I was depleted.

I explained why I had tracked him down. "I hope it's not upsetting for me to bring this up."

"Well, it doesn't matter if it's upsetting," he responded, "because I have a family and I don't care to have people hurt.

That's a long time ago now and I've had no trouble since then." His voice was a little on the high side, perhaps due to nervous tension. "Mary's daughter tried to reach out a couple of times, but I didn't follow up. It was a long time ago and just a very unfortunate relationship. You know, I was very fond of those girls"—I was startled to hear his voice break a tiny bit when he said this—"very attached to them, but what benefit could there be in it? I have kids getting close to fifty and Lorraine must be fifty-five."

"Does your family know anything about your past with Mary Lloyd?" I was trying to figure out who exactly would be hurt, and how.

"They know I was in jail."

I mulled this, then explained that many aspects of the case were on the public record but that I wanted anyone I included in the book to be represented in their own words and to be treated fairly. "Could I come to Deroche and talk to you?"

He asked for my name. When I spelled it out, he said, "Unusual, I guess?"

"Not in India," I said, chuckling, doing my best to radiate charm and reassurance through the phone.

He took my number and said I could call him back in a couple of days. "I'll think about it and talk it over with my wife." The lady with the lapdog, I guessed.

It was early evening, early December, already dark. I leashed up my own dog and left the house, adrenaline ebbing a little. He sniffed along the roadside as I turned the conversation's details over in my head.

Kempster sounded like a man of conviction. How could he have killed those girls' father if he was so attached to them? The logical deduction: if he thought he was protecting them. But from what?

I planned to wait the forty-eight hours before calling back, but the next day, he left a message asking me to call. The phone was slippery in my sweaty hands. When he picked up, he said without preamble, "Well, I'm not going to talk to you or take any questions. I can't see any good coming of it, so that's the end of it for me." He hung up.

Damn wife. I just knew it was her putting the kibosh into it.

Look, though: he could have ghosted me. Instead, he was honourable.

Phillip had thought a book about his life might help someone. I wasn't so high-minded. Driven by curiosity, I wanted to know who Del was and what she had done, and I had a professional justification, however specious, for pursuing that knowledge. Really, though, the pursuit itself was addictive.

I'd tunnelled so many possible veins in hopes of big discoveries. I'd paged through Vancouver and Edmonton newspapers from 1956 to 1957, looking for mentions of the robbery or the murder or either trial. I'd spoken to the RCMP, to Alberta libraries, to BC libraries, to media relations people, to archivists. I'd been misdirected, forgotten on hold, passed off, cut off and turned down. I chased down dead ends in the BC Provincial Archives, in the National Archives in Ottawa, in the courthouses of Chilliwack, New Westminster, and Burnaby. Some places, there was nothing. In others, what there was had mysteriously been lost. And did you know the Recording of Evidence Act dictates that trial transcripts be destroyed after ten years? So many helpful people, so many shaken heads.

But when I hit pay dirt, oh, the rush. The Holt file, the chat with Kempster, and now: the transcript of the preliminary inquiry for Kempster's murder trial, which turned out to be preserved in the Alberta Provincial Archives. The trial itself was never transcribed, because the verdict wasn't appealed—another policy I learned about—but maybe that kept the record of the preliminary inquiry from being destroyed.

In the fall of 2016, I went to Edmonton for my cousin's wedding and tacked on an extra day to visit the archives. Friends and family asked what I was working on. Their reactions were uniform: *Your friend's stepmom, a bank robber? Yes, and maybe a murderer. Oh, my god, so interesting!*

These responses were something else I got high on, even though I knew they were partly an expression of our cultural appetite for true crime, an appetite I don't share and have never properly understood. Most of those books—okay, I admit to having read a few—are shite.

Is that what I was writing—shite? Of course not: as a literary writer, I would make literature, like David Grann's *Killers of the Flower Moon*, like Casey Cep's *Furious Hours*. It would take unexpected angles, use plummy language, be resigned to what cannot be solved or resolved.

Journalists justify their treachery in various ways, says Janet Malcolm, in *The Journalist and The Murderer. The more pompous talk about freedom of speech and "the public's right to know"; the least talented talk about Art.*

I wasn't so self-deluding as to put this story in the first category, so I guess that put me in the second. Mostly, though, I preferred to believe that if I could hold the attention of a dinner table, I could write a compelling book.

Two holdouts were vocally skeptical of this shallow belief: my husband, Geoff, and my old mentor, DD Kugler, a dramaturg and director.

What is the story? both would ask, visibly doubtful that there was one worth telling, at least about Del, unless I could get closer. I never understood their resistance, and it unnerved me because they knew more about it than anyone else.

"I don't know, but it is great."

In fact, I thought I knew what the story was. At each stage, though it shifted, I thought I knew. I just had to prove it.

In Edmonton, leaning on the curving laminate counter at the Alberta Provincial Archives, I asked for the archivist I had spoken to on the phone. She rose out of a pool of people working in the front area and came toward me with a smile of recognition and three thick files. They had lain, gathering dust, as they say, for sixty years. I was the first person to take them out.

Motherlode and *pay dirt* are common terms from mining, Harvey's profession when Phillip was born, but I had even better ones.

Gold miners call the tunnel a drift; Harvey's specialization—setting explosives to blast the excavation deeper—was called *advancing the drift*, which became my favourite term for work on this book, even though *trying to catch the drift* was more like it.

Also *high-grading:* the miners' practice of smuggling the highest-quality ore out for private sale instead of handing it over to the bosses. *High-grading:* that's what I thought now as the archivist handed over the files she'd excavated from some hidden back shelf.

Lugging the files over to a table, I tremulously opened the first: REGINA vs JAMES STANLEY KEMPSTER, stamped by the Clerk of the Court, Edmonton, Alberta. The inquiry happened just after the robbery trial, nine months after Lew Lloyd's body was found in a muddy ditch. The proceedings were spread over seven seemingly random days from February, when Edmonton is still in a deep freeze, to April, when the twinned smells of melting dog poop and pollinating dogwood might have drifted into the courtroom or to Kempster's cell, where he'd sat cooling his heels for months, wondering if he'd go to trial for murder, one stop on a path to the gallows.

Each of those seven days—a span whose Biblical significance he might have appreciated—Kempster sat in the courtroom as witness after witness came forward to testify to what they'd seen and heard, or what they thought they had, starting with Sergeant Norman F. Lee, the Edmonton RCMP officer whose detective work led to their bank robbery conviction. Del was still in BC and would not testify, though I don't know exactly why.

Kempster's lawyer, Gifford Main (hardboiled name, tailor-made for true crime), asked Sgt. Lee, "Is it not true that you have been responsible to a great degree for the charge before the court?"

"That is correct, sir," Lee affirmed. He'd found most of the witnesses; he'd directed most of the other investigators; he could take credit for pretty much any evidence presented in these months.

Lee's son eventually would tell me, "This was a case he spoke about. I think he felt she was, and this is from my perspective, going way back, he felt she was a bad woman. But he was a cop, an investigating detective, so his perspective was that if crimes are being done, he has to find out who's doing them."

After an initial round of questioning, Lee ceded the stand to a CN Railway employee who gave a ride to a man early the morning of the murder. On hearing about the murder on the news, the CN worker had called the police. He fingered Kempster on a contact sheet of suspects, but Gifford Main hammered him on his poor eyesight, the rain, the early-morning dark, and his eagerness to take part in convicting a killer.

Lee then presented physical evidence: a truck registration, the contents of Lew Lloyd's wallet, a Trans-Canada Airlines ticket to Calgary issued to a Mr. J. Butler, who gave his address as 731 Schoolhouse Road, Burquitlam, the house where Kempster and Mary lived.

Subsequent witnesses were grilled on the minutiae of office locations, flight coupons, a *teletyped circuit copy of a passenger manifest.* Statements of identity, statements of location, a swirl and pump of eternally regressive details. Even the most intriguing—Did Kempster fly to Calgary under a false name on the weekend of Lew Lloyd's murder? Why did he quit his job a few days later? What about Lew's life insurance policies, bought about a month after each daughter was born?—turn out to be nothing but red herrings sandwiched between thick slices of tedium. Even so, reading through page upon page, I understood the exactitude as a kind of ritual, motivated by care that, in the words of a source I can no longer find, *justice should be done.*

Eddy Gendron, Lew's roommate and business partner, told of the phone call that made Lew rush out to meet his wife. Their landlord affirmed that Lew left in a taxi; the taxi driver affirmed taking him to a hotel; a hotel clerk affirmed that Lew arrived and met a man. At some point, Lew came back home for the truck. "That's the last time I see him until the next day," he said, which was when Gendron identified the body.

Kenneth Bird described how Mary came to his house and threatened to shoot him if he didn't reveal Lew's whereabouts. Bird said Kempster stood behind her as she did this. It ended in a standoff. "Finally I told her if she would give me the gun I would phone," Bird said. "She said all right but she wouldn't give me the gun unless I phoned and I wouldn't phone till she give me the gun, so neither one transpired."

The court was shown a letter Mary sent to Lew in Edmonton, though she had insisted she didn't know where he was. Lew wired her $100 in the same period. Kenneth Bird testified that Lew was a good father and a good provider and that there was nothing about Lew he considered "unusual or strange." What the hell did that mean, I wondered.

As I read through the files, I started to see a pattern: a dragnet orchestrated by Norman Lee, targeting Mary Lloyd. Lee spent more time on that stand than anyone else, regaling the court with stories of how he misled and cajoled young Kempster over months of interviews and investigation. He told Kempster that he believed Lew was murdered by an associate from his stevedoring days, which he didn't, and that they had found the gun, also false, and that Kempster's *great affection for Mary and his great love and the things he did for her were misdirected.* He told Kempster that, when he went to interview her one morning, he met a young man leaving their house, someone Mary had picked up at a beer parlour the night before.

Did Kempster believe that Mary betrayed him? He did not.

How do we know? Ironically, our source is the wily Sgt.

Lee himself, who now unveiled to the court a new *eavesdropping technology, the latest equipment obtainable*, that he had used to listen in on Mary and Kempster when they believed themselves to be alone.

Lee had directed an officer to hide inside the basement of Kempster and Mary's house in order to spy on them before they were arrested. After, when they were being held for the robbery in Oakalla prison farm, outside Vancouver, Lee arranged for them to be driven out to a quiet spot on the pretense that they were getting some time alone together. The car had *the latest type of hearing-aid* cemented to its roof. A constable lay concealed in the trunk with a notepad, privy to *the lowest whispers*.

Only Lee's own transcript, however, was admissible in the inquiry. He'd bugged two adjacent cells in the New Westminster court building. Kempster and Mary, awaiting trial there for robbery, were put in the cells, while Lee hid in a cupboard above, recording the conversations in shorthand.

Kempster and Mary, in the cells, had a wall between them, like Pyramus and Thisbe, except, instead of speaking through a crack in that wall, they spoke through the bars at the front.

Lee transcribed his own notes and read the transcript aloud at the hearing. Did Kempster's ears burn as he listened, did he blush as a whole room of people listened to him speak—privately, he'd thought—with his love?

"It hurts me when I think what has happened," he lamented to Mary. "It's all my fault. It is because of me that we are in this awful mess."

"Actually, it isn't your fault at all," Mary said. "I'm just as much to blame." (A very Mary moment: telling the truth but probably just to make him feel better.)

"I got a letter from Noreen," she told him—Lew's sister, now raising her girls. "Lorraine is doing her hair up herself now."

"Would she remember me?" Kempster asked. He's been fretting about the kids forgetting him.

"Of course," Mary soothed. "Lorraine would never forget you." But then she became dismissive, or jealous. "I never think about the kids. I just think about you and me."

"I think about them all the time," Kempster replied.

"Makes your time go harder," Mary said. "I never let anyone out there know I have children. The pictures of the kids I had—I tore them up and threw them away. You were real good to the kids and I'll never forget it."

He seemed to be seeking reassurance: about that beer parlour pickup Sgt. Lee mentioned on the stand, about a woman Mary was hanging with in jail.

"You don't mind me being friendly with Darlene, do you?" she asked.

"I don't mind," he said, "so long as you're just friends."

"Wouldn't you rather me live with her than on the outside with a guy?" He didn't answer, and she stops teasing. "If you are scared of me ever getting a crush on a woman, I can't. I'm just passing the time."

Kempster understood loneliness, and he summoned a good thought for Darlene. "I have never met a person in my life that I couldn't find something good about them."

The conversation meandered, punctuated with plaint and longing. "All you have to tell me is that you love me, Mary," Kempster blurted at one point. "That is good for at least twenty years."

And Mary responded, "I love you very much. I love you so much, Jim."

Kempster recalled feeling her pain in his own body after what he called her *operation*. "I said I didn't want you to have any babies because I thought that was the way you wanted it, and you said you didn't want any babies because you thought that was the way I wanted it, when all the time we both wanted you to have babies."

Mary responded pragmatically to his "Gift of the Magi" regrets: "That's the way it goes. We can't have it back now."

She told him that the matron had stopped in to ask her if she was ashamed of herself. *"That young lad there, he is only 21.* I said, *For goodness sake, is that what he is?"*

Kempster didn't think the exchange was quite so hilarious. "There is a lot of nosey people that stick their noses into other people's business."

Mary wasn't ready to give up on the joke. "I will mother you, dear."

"I won't need a mother," he told her gruffly, or suggestively, or who knows how, really.

"I can always get my face lifted if it falls," she said.

"You won't need to get your face lifted," Kempster responded, and maybe that's what she was fishing for. "I think you're beautiful, Mary."

I tried to hear all this in Norman Lee's voice, because that in fact is what it as: he heard it, he wrote it down, he read it aloud. But I couldn't. I heard Mary and Kempster, because that's who I wanted to hear.

I am committed by trade to urging people to attend carefully to the verbal surfaces of what they read, says Stephen Greenblatt in *The Swerve. But it is nonetheless possible to have a powerful experience of a work of art even in a modest translation.*

Lee's modest translation gives us an urgent dialogue between star-crossed lovers, not criminals hoisted with their own petards, though there are tantalizing hints. He might have made the pair sound the way he heard them, but I don't believe he falsified deliberately. If he had, he might have got a conviction.

The couple toggled, throughout their conversation, between sentiment and their legal situation. They'd hired a crack defence lawyer, Angelo Branca, to represent them at their robbery trial in Vancouver. Though they could agree he was a vast improvement over Wallace Craig, they seemed afraid that Kempster himself might be the weak link. He'd already blabbed something to someone in jail. They had great plans for his defence, Mary told him, but she wouldn't give him details because she didn't trust him.

"I won't crack, Mary," he told her.

"Branca tried you out," she said, "and boom, right off the bat you failed. That question that was put to you, look at the way you answered that."

"I had some ideas of my own," Kempster said. "I just wanted to see what his reaction would be. He asked if I had been there and I said yes. Anything else doesn't make sense."

"All you had to say was that you didn't go there. That would have been all there was to it. You should be ashamed."

Kempster said he was. "He talked so darn fast. Your darn thinker just don't work that fast."

"Shows what kind of a guy you are."

"But how was I supposed to know what answer to give? I had no chance to talk to you about it."

"Never trust anyone except me. Unless you keep quiet they are going to hang you."

Kempster, ardent as Pyramus, was less concerned over his own possible death than with retaining Mary's love. She had said that she should have disappeared when she had the chance, and that he should do the same if he could. It hurt him. He apologized now, abjectly, for talking too much.

Mary mentioned having been in jail before, a bit of her history I could never confirm but have no reason to disbelieve. Sometimes, she seemed to speak in code, referring to people by fake names, suspecting the place of being bugged. Kempster had a hard time following. She alternately berated and reassured him, the young man entirely in her thrall.

They wanted to get their revenge on Kenneth Bird. "Bird sure had a big grin on his face today," Kempster said. "I guess it was because he found out I was charged on that other beef." Lew's murder, I presume. "He was scared that I would get back on the street and put a cork into him."

"I would say we are not finished with him yet," Mary said.

"I can still look after him," Kempster suggested, though it seemed a more strategic revenge was available:

"I wouldn't mind implicating myself just to see him behind bars," said Mary. "While they were digging around our house that time, I wish they had done a little digging around his place."

And did they ever hate Norman Lee. "Don't you think for a minute I don't have plans for him," Kempster threatened, as Lee himself took notes.

They saw through Lee's subterfuge or assured each other that they did. "Lee came and told me how evil I was," said Mary, "and the next day he came out and told me how attractive a woman I was."

"The way Lee talks about Lew Lloyd, you'd think he was an angel," Kempster grumbled. "Lee thinks he's got all the brains."

"He doesn't know the danger he is in," Mary said.

Apparently, that's pillow talk in this relationship. "You get me all hot and bothered," Kempster breathed now. "I wish the lattice work was separating us instead of being in the front of the cells."

His passionate tone awakened Mary's tenderness and regret. "If it hadn't been for me, you wouldn't have got mixed up in this."

"I don't care, Mary," Kempster declared. "You have given me something that happens to very few people. I am proud of you, Mary."

"It doesn't matter what they do—how things turn out. We will never change."

"No, Mary, we will never change."

"They won't crack me, doesn't matter what they do. They have tried everything."

"They have tried some dandies on me. I have got the best woman in the world. You will never crack, I know, Mary."

United in their trials, determined to go down together, they were entirely unhelpful to Norman Lee as he crouched in his hidey-hole, hoping for something, anything, incriminating. There were bits that seem to imply knowledge or involvement in Lew's murder, but nothing to hang a case on.

Kempster said that some guy in prison kept telling him he's not like a guy that killed anybody because he "sure keeps his mouth shut."

Mary pushed him on this. "You know that picture that Lee showed you in here? The one of the truck."

"Yeah?" Kempster asked, warily, or so I imagine.

"All right, why didn't he show you that picture before?" she asked. "I'll bet there's something different there, isn't there?"

"No, Mary, honest to God that was taken the same day, that was taken right off the bat. That's just the way it was." This implied Kempster was there, but maybe he was just repeating what he believed?

I am struck yet again by his earnestness. Yes, he was hot-headed, but he also appeared upright, honourable, almost self-destructively sincere.

At the end of the inquiry, Kempster himself will repeat what he told police: that he was home the entire weekend Lew was killed.

He and Mary continue talking ambiguously—nothing firm, nothing to grasp, always a step ahead of Lee, intentionally or otherwise. Mary is Valjean to Lee's Javert, Road Runner to his Coyote. I can almost feel his frustration, because I share it.

I was playing detective after the fact, trying to suss what Norman Lee and his phalanx of investigators couldn't.

Lee not only gathered information from Mary and Jim without their knowledge, he also took statements from them, at their home. Now, at the preliminary inquiry, he told the court that Lew and Mary met in 1945, when she was still with her first husband; that they lived together, then married in 1953, just before their first child was born; that they moved around, picking fruit and doing other itinerant labour; and that Lew was first jailed for forging cheques.

"He wanted to kill me all the time," Mary had told Sgt. Lee. "He would beat me and I would have to get the kids and run out of the house or go into another room and hide. He never left me any money and Jim was always staying with me and buying the groceries."

Lee explained further. "Mary started mentioning that Lewis Lloyd and Eddy Gendron were *going together.* And then the accused, with a great display of emotion and hatred"—Kempster was, inexplicably, in the room while Lee and Mary talked—"said, *What Mary wants to tell you is that Lew and Eddy Gendron are perverts. Lew even tried to fool around with his own daughter.*"

Homosexual equals pervert equals pedophile: so 1950s. I don't know what Lew Lloyd's truth was, but I'm pretty sure that wasn't it. What's pertinent, though, is what Kempster believed.

"This matter was discussed," Lee went on, "and Mary admitted or stated that Lew was a pervert and that she had caught him in the bedroom with the daughter. Mary then said that Lew preferred the intimacies of men rather than her, and she gave me some details of some horrible perversion on the part of the deceased."

Gifford Main objected to this vagueness and the judge agreed. Lee demurred—he didn't want to get explicit—but the judge insisted, and finally Lee came clean. "Mrs. Lloyd stated that for some time past her husband, the deceased Lewis Lloyd, desired men and that in having intercourse with her wanted to go down on a man at the same time. Those are the words she used."

Kempster and Lee were cut from the same cloth. Honourable men, twinned in revulsion, though Lee was determined to use the law to protect society from Mary—monstrous woman, user of men—while Kempster was determined to violate the law to protect Mary from Lew—monstrous man, abuser of children.

This was it, the motherlode, the explanation for how Kempster could have such affection for Del's daughters and yet kill their father. He believed he was protecting them—my suspicions, for once, confirmed.

Where was Del now?

The only evidence of Mary Eleanor Beatty aka Mary Lloyd aka Delia Totten aka Ruth Pasjack George I'd been able to find online was a legal case summary, in the 2007 BC College of Physicians and Surgeons annual report, saying that Del, now going by her maiden name, had failed in bringing lawsuits against her doctors and against the college. It made me wonder if she was trying her hand at spurious medical claims, a venture that didn't seem out of character.

Maybe I'm just not very good at this kind of search, though, because one day when I complained to Geoff about not being able to find her, he got online and, within minutes, sent me a link to a genealogy website maintained by someone else with the last name Lloyd.

Del had died, in December 2011.

I had always known this was a possibility, but until this moment, she was Schrödinger's cat. Simma Holt had told me that she was likely alive, and back then she was, but I hadn't looked, or not hard enough.

The obituary said her ashes had been scattered in North Vancouver and in Harrison Hot Springs, where Phillip once worked, where she used to drink and dance and pick up younger men, perhaps a place where all these different Dels came to gether, her and her shadow and the glimmering dark shades of her past and the blinding bright silhouettes of her future *falling together, not drifting apart but moving together like dancers.*

THE RIDDLE OF THE SPHINX

THE FINAL SURPRISE IN Simma Holt's file was the most painful and decisive: two letters to Holt from Phillip's biological mother, Lucille, in a large, ornate hand.

The first claimed that Phillip had committed perjury at the divorce case and also said that Phillip had threatened to kill Harvey's current wife, Joan, along with her kids and the child they'd had together.

Phillip confirmed that he had threatened them. "Harvey used to harass us," he reminded me. After the divorce, he and Del were living on Strawberry Mountain, which was still in Harvey's name. Harvey had the power cut off, prevented propane deliveries, and otherwise made life difficult. One time, Phillip lost it. He not only threatened Harvey and his new family, he actually grabbed a hunting gun to make good on that threat, but he didn't get very far before he cooled off and came home. Harvey and Del had both called the cops, but all they did was confiscate the gun.

"After that, Harvey quit the hassling. Maybe the cops told him to cut it out."

Lucille believed that Del turned Phillip against his family. She told Holt that she had secured all the papers on the Lewis Lloyd murder case. She wrote an occasional column for her local paper in Ontario, and had, it seems, an investigative spirit. *I believe she has not changed one bit—She is using Phillip for her own gains, & since the Lloyd case is still open until it is ever solved, my son is in the middle of the whole mess.*

She lamented that when she came out to see him, she had offered Phillip a place with her in Ontario, and seemed to have convinced him to visit her, at least, but that after he went to see Del in prison, he changed his mind.

How that woman must be laughing at all of us, but as the saying goes there's one born every minute.

Lucille's letters were written in 1971, almost two years after the events she described. Why so late? Perhaps a call from Harvey ratcheted up the emotional volume she had muted. Or perhaps she'd had the sort of realization or emotional surge that can happen long after a painful or puzzling event, whether as the outcome of an obscure course of mental metabolism or in response to some other change in one's life.

She wrote that Harvey should have left Mary when he found out she had violated her parole, but *he was a do gooder.* In other words, not the violent man of Mary's stories. In their fourteen years of marriage, she said, Harvey had never laid a hand on her, and *I know his present wife has not beaten him or driven him to a psychiatric the way Mary Lloyd did.*

Whoa. I looked at Phillip, who had told me detailed stories of Harvey abusing Lucille.

Yet no one will lift a finger to get that boy away from her. There are so many why's to all this. I believe Mary Lloyd is using Phillip to get what she wants, money and property by her letter to me.

Del wrote to Lucille? When? And what did she say?

Holt began her response with a "why" of her own. She had interviewed Lucille when she had come to Vancouver and now was checking her notes in disbelief. *Your letter is a total contradiction of what you said, and I wonder: Why?*

Previously, Lucille had told Holt she was grateful to Del for taking responsibility for Phillip, but now she seemed to have joined forces with Harvey. Holt wrote, *I cannot see what you have to gain by it; only you and Mr. Totten seem to know.*

Holt said that Phillip's *evidence of assault by Mr. Totten was corroborated by the RCMP*, and that Lucille herself had said Phillip could have used psychiatric help for delinquency long before Del entered the picture.

As for the property, the court awarded her what was her right, not only as one who shared in the building but also in the life of this man. . . .

This woman, like yourself, has had more than her share of suffering and it seems sad to me that someone like yourself, who is also very hurt, would add to the pain of another.

Lucille's response didn't address Holt's questions about her sources or motivations. Rather, she said she had come late to information that, if it had come to light, would have worked against Del at her parole hearing: the passport scam that got them to Cuba.

I can see now why my son Phillip can say she is his mother—because she was legally masquerading as Lucille, who had now alerted Immigration Canada, the Parole Board, and the RCMP to the impersonation.

She fretted that Del might even have sold Lucille's identity and speculated on what would happen if whoever had it got into trouble: the law would come looking for Lucille, not Del.

She uses people the way I use water. . . .

Mary Lloyd has Phillip so thoroughly brainwashed into thinking he owes her something, for the yrs, she was there. . . . He will have to learn the hard way, & be educated in so many things. I just hope it is not too late.

Holt didn't save her response to this, nor could I find any evidence that federal authorities took any interest. Presumably, Harvey didn't raise this matter with the police because he was complicit. Lucille had every right to be angry, but ultimately didn't come off as too reliable herself.

Phillip didn't see it this way, however. "When the wash is all hung out at the end of the day, she was right. My mother. She called it for what it really was."

We never talked about Lucille and Holt's multiple references to psychiatric treatment. Phillip had told me an amusing story of Harvey having sent him to a shrink to correct his tendency to make friends with Indigenous kids, an attraction Phillip himself attributed in part to his Métis heritage on his mother's side. Phillip had responded by finding Indigenous symbols in all the Rorschach test images—canoe, eagle. If there was more to it, he either didn't know or *had substituted a story of his own*, just like he'd substituted a mother of his own.

Little does my boy realize how easily we can be replaced, Lucille had written to Simma, talking about how Del used people and discarded them.

"Del lied," Phillip pointed out. "A lot. I'm not being mean when I say this, but looking at things now, as a fifty-five-plus guy, she manipulated an awful lot to get what she wanted." He wondered if, once she had what she wanted from her association with him, she came up with an excuse to get him out of her life.

"I'm a good person," he said, breaking my heart a little. "I know I am, and it made me think I was used and abused by a lot of different parties."

What had I started? I was watching my friend's ideas of his own history, its composition and value, shift as he remade his past.

Concerned, I kept asking him whether he was all right.

"It's all good," he kept saying to me, but surely it wasn't *all* good. Finally, he got fed up. "I'm a big boy. Stop worrying about me, stop asking if I'm okay. It's good for me to know these things. I want to know them."

That had been the idea, from the first, the reason I'd had a copy of the files send to Phillip: I was not only writing a book about this story but passing my research findings to him as a kind of payment for his contributions and his cooperation.

When Pandora first received her box, it was closed and locked, all its qualities fast within it. It could be carried from one place to another—solid, existent, meaningless.

Listen: the box was meant to be opened. It was never not going to be opened. There is no story unless the contents are freed, but, freed, they vanish—disappearing, not dis-existing; they dissolve like salt in water.

Did Del believe the things she said, at least when she said them, or was she consciously fabricating and manipulating people and situations for her own invisible ends?

The philosopher Harry G. Frankfurt, in his little book *On Bullshit,* gives a definition of his titular term, per Max Black: *"deceptive misrepresentation, short of lying, especially by pretentious word or deed, of somebody's own thoughts, feelings, or attitudes."*

The liar, says Frankfurt, *must think he knows what is true. Producing bullshit requires no such conviction. A person who lies is thereby responding to the truth, and he is to that extent respectful of it. On the other hand, a person who undertakes to bullshit his way through has much more freedom. . . . He does not limit himself to inserting a certain falsehood at a specific point, and thus he is not constrained by the truths surrounding that point or intersecting it. He is prepared to fake the context as well, so far as need requires.*

It may be that Del believed Lew Lloyd to be a bad person; in this case, even if the accusations were technically false, they might have been, in her mind, metonyms to deeper truths.

Even if she didn't ditch Phillip because of his resemblance to his father, he did resemble his father, and maybe that was a reason not to want to have a lot to do with him.

She told Phillip that her daughter Lorraine had come to her in adulthood, asking for criminal contacts that Del didn't want to provide. When I eventually met Lorraine, she said that was false, though she readily admitted to biographical facts Phillip knew independently of Del: that Lorraine had married young into a criminal family and helped them build up their drug-dealing ring.

At that time, on a hunch, I asked her what Del had said about parting ways with Phillip. Lorraine was reluctant to answer but I coaxed it out of her. "Well, what she said, and I'm not sure I believed it, and I would never say it to him, she said he molested a child. But what a thing to say about a person!"

I didn't tell her that it was also what Del had told Kempster about her father, Lew, except the child in question was Lorraine herself.

Del bullshitted a whole ethos of identity: that she was glamorous, well-connected, nationally notorious. She was briefly notorious, but not because of revolutionary or underworld associations. Rather, she made headlines because she was given an outsized sentence for leading a younger man astray, a man conspicuously absent from the stories of her life that she told Phillip.

Was Del used by the men in her life, or was she using them? It depended who you asked.

Norman Lee's son said that Lorraine had called his father and asked to meet. He and his brother had accompanied their father to the meeting, worried. But Lorraine had a different version:

"Norman Lee was obsessed and vindictive," she told me. "He hated Del, hated her, thought she was evil. He was trying to write a book, saying it's hereditary, drawing me in."

Lorraine recommended I talk to other people, such as Del's old boyfriend Andrew, who had eventually become a distinguished scientist. When I called him, he denied even knowing Del. "It's been a long time since I had madness in my life," he said, "and I don't want to let it in now," while also feeding me some cockamamie story about knowing Del's mother and Harvey but never meeting Del herself. Talk about bullshit.

When I asked Lorraine about Del's lawsuits, she surprised me by saying they were legit: "It was a botched hysterectomy or some other surgery. I had to do stacks of paperwork for it, stacks." In Lorraine's recollection, the cases were dismissed because Del refused to follow up on some technicality.

"She could be manipulative," Lorraine admitted in measured tones, but the stories she told to illustrate this were run-of-the-mill stuff. Del had complained to Lorraine that her back went out—she could barely walk, she said—but when Lorraine flew out to see her, she walked everywhere and had a great time. She'd just wanted attention, the company of her daughter in her dotage.

Lorraine came across as philosophical, dispassionate, and uncommonly able to hold all of Del's contradictions. I suppose she'd had a lifetime to practise.

"I hate to speak ill of the dead," she said. "She was a little delusional at the end: hearing messages through music and that sort of thing. Maybe a touch of schizophrenia? But she tried to be good and do good. Like, she was a vegetarian."

The basic insight of psychology, as it has come to us via Freud, is closely connected to the riddle of the Sphinx, says Elif Batuman, speaking of Oedipus Rex: *"What is that which has one voice and yet becomes four-footed and two-footed and three-footed?"*

The answer is *man—who crawls as a baby, walks unassisted as an adult, and uses a cane in old age.* The riddle suggests that our identities are continuous: that children are already whole people, *with emotions and boundaries and dignity that can be violated,* and that our childhood experiences and knowledge carry forward to manifest in the adults we become.

And what if a childhood *contains* riddles, mysteries? What if, when these are solved in adulthood, the solutions don't confer the dignity of recognition but instead cause pain?

Oedipus's story speaks to this question as well. You might know it: on his birth, Oedipus's father, Laius, is told by an oracle that he is fated to die at the hand of his son, who will then marry his own mother, Laius's wife. The horrified father binds his infant's ankles and tells his wife, Jocasta, to kill him, but she can't, and tells a servant to do the dirty deed.

Instead, Oedipus is adopted. On growing up, he hears his fate from another oracle and, to avert it, leaves the only home he's ever known. At a crossroads, he gets into a fight with Laius, whom he naturally doesn't recognize. Killing him, he proceeds to Thebes, where, as a reward for solving the Sphinx's riddle, he wins the hand of Queen Jocasta. These violations to the natural order trigger a plague; Oedipus, now king, is charged with uncovering the truth and setting things right. His investigations bring before him the Theban shepherd who should have killed him as a baby.

Batuman recounts a production of the play. *At a certain point, the shepherd clearly understood everything, but would not or could not admit it. Oedipus, now determined to learn the truth at all costs, resorted to enhanced interrogation. "Bend back his arms until they snap,"* he commands, and the shepherd screams *in highly realistic agony, a personification of psychological resistance: the mechanism a mind develops to protect itself from an unbearable truth.*

Finally, the shepherd surrenders. *"It was Laius's child,"* he says, *"or so people said. Your wife could tell you more."*

Oedipus delivers the next line, *the most devastating in the whole play:*

"Did . . . she . . . give it to you?" Oedipus asks.

How had I never fully realized, Batuman asks, *never felt, how painful it would have been for Oedipus to realize that his parents hadn't loved him?*

The truth can be devastating, and it would be understandable for Oedipus to see lack of love as his parents' motive, but in fact we don't know how they *felt* about their child. All we know was that circumstances made them *act* as they did.

Holt's file was our shepherd. Was Phillip loved by his parents? We don't know how they felt, only how they acted.

Lucille, Phillip told me, had wanted to keep her sons, but Harvey had also blackmailed her—she had committed bigamy when she married him—and so she fled to Ontario without them.

Harvey himself had been violent and mean and didn't even try to claim Phillip in the custody hearing.

And did Del love him? She acted as though she did.

Phillip was *a good person*, but so was Del, in her own eyes, as most people are in their own eyes. Laius, Jocasta, Oedipus: they were all just trying to do the right thing.

Well, maybe not Laius. But even Harvey, as we would shortly learn, was not so easy to vilify as Holt and Del and Phillip himself made it seem.

Next door to the house where Phillip grew up was a prosperous-looking dairy farm, inhabited by the same folks, Kay and Allan Toop, that Phillip knew from fifty years earlier. We dropped in. Kay opened the door, took a moment to recognize Phillip, and then seemed glad to see him. Although they were not expecting visitors, their homey 1922 farmhouse was, as the saying goes, neat as a pin.

Afternoon sun slanted across gleaming hardwood floors. A smell of cinnamon hung in the air from a pie cooling on the scrubbed kitchen countertop. "It was exactly like this when we were kids," Phillip said. I thought of what the place might have seemed like to him as a boy being raised next door, Harvey at the helm, Lucille long gone, and Del not yet arrived.

The Toops' son Richard lived across the road with his wife. Richard helped to run the farm with his own son, who lived next door to him. His sister had bought a house down the road, and they were fixing up another for a granddaughter. Toopville, locals called it. The family went back generations on this same land.

Kay didn't have anything good to say about Harvey. He had written a letter of condolence when Allan's father had died five or six years earlier, but they hadn't heard from him since. "I think he's probably dead," she said, "because he hasn't written asking for money for his causes in some time."

"He would never ever ask for himself," Allan explained, "but he was always asking for money to help the downtrodden. He was a brilliant guy. Very well read. If you were going to argue politics with Harvey, you'd better have your soldiers lined up."

Allan's father had been very fond of him. "I think my dad would have given money if Harvey himself had needed it. But, as he put it, *there goes Harvey again, trying to save the world.* But he was also very helpful, Harvey. If you needed any kind of help at all, he would drop what he was doing and rush over to help you."

"I liked the women he used to bring around," Kay chimed in brusquely, maybe her way of softening her earlier judgments.

Allan agreed that he and Kay had liked Harvey's wives. They had hardly known Del—she lived next door only for a few months—but knew Joan well.

Kay took us upstairs and opened a closet to show us a trunk Harvey had made and given her as a gift. It was beautifully wrought, with a curved lid of bevelled slats, copper detailing, handles and trim. She said she "figured he wanted to give it to Allan and his father but that would be weird, so he gave it to me." I found her unrelenting gruffness refreshing.

I asked Allan if Harvey was kind. "Oh, yes . . ." he said hesitantly, "in his way. I think of him every Friday when I go to put out the recycling, because there was a group of them in the seventies, who got it into their head to promote recycling. We all laughed at them, even the city council. We called them the Save-the-World crew. And now look."

I mentioned that there seemed a great contrast between Harvey's generosity and concern for the world and his treatment of his family.

"Yes," Allan agreed. He had a gentle, fussy manner. "I didn't want to say it, but now that you have brought it up, that was the one thing. We all thought it: Harvey's a good guy, but he's not very good to his sons. I know it disturbed my dad a lot." I asked if any of them ever tried to talk to Harvey about it. "No, no, we never did. It wasn't . . . we couldn't. And I think all three of you boys were estranged, isn't that right?" He peered at Phillip, as a confessant might through a confessional screen, but Phillip didn't confirm or deny.

I asked if Phillip looked like Harvey. "Oh, yes," said Allan. "Especially when you smile."

Did Harvey laugh, I asked. "Oh, oh yes!" Allan said, laughing just to think about it. "Harvey was definitely good for a laugh."

There is a passage toward the end of William Maxwell's *So Long, See You Tomorrow* that I often recall when my kids bang into the house through our kitchen door, thoughtlessly fling down their bags, sniff for hints of supper, listen for the dog's nails as he trots through the house to greet them—moments so unremarkable and poignant as to bring on nostalgia for themselves before they are even over.

Maxwell's novel tells of a friendship between two adolescent boys. One, the narrator, tells the story long after it happened. The other boy's father killed his wife's lover, formerly his neighbour and friend. It's a rural community. Both families leave, their households dissolved.

It's a slim book, almost unbearably moving, about the emotional inadequacies of adults and the guilt of kids unable to give comfort where they know it's owed, about discontentment, grief and deprivation, about pleasure and its cost, about what—if anything—adds up to a life.

Whether they are part of home or home is part of them is not a question children are prepared to answer. Having taken away the dog, take away the kitchen—the smell of something good in the oven for dinner. Also the smell of washday, of wool drying on the wooden rack. Of ashes. Of soup simmering on the stove. Take away the patient old horse waiting by the pasture fence. Take away the chores that kept him busy from the time he got home from school until they sat down to supper. Take away the early morning mist, the sound of crows quarreling in the treetops.

His work clothes are still hanging on a nail beside the door of his room, but nobody puts them on or takes them off. Nobody sleeps in his bed. Or reads the broken-backed copy of Tom Swift and His Flying Machine. *Take that away too, while you are at it.*

Take away the pitcher and bowl, both of them dry and dusty. Take away the cow barn where the cats, sitting all in a row, wait with their mouths wide open for somebody to squirt milk down their throats. Take away the horse barn too—the smell of hay and dust and horse piss and old sweat-stained leather, and the rain beating down on the field beyond the open door. Take all this away and what have you done to him? In the face of a deprivation so great, what is the use of asking him to go on being the boy he was. He might as well start life over as some other boy instead.

On leaving the Toops, Phillip and I went walking in the woods—his childhood haunts, waterfalls, ravines—and he told me that his ideas on Harvey were changing. "I never saw the caring, giving part of him. Doing recycling way ahead of his time. I never knew about that. Like I asked Allan Toop where he lived in Nicaragua, would he have lived in a city, and he said, *no way, he would have lived out in the country and been teaching people how to grow food. He would never deny a neighbour anything.*

"It makes me want to go down to Nicaragua and see where he lived, and where he's buried," Phillip said, and told me a psychic had conveyed to him messages from Harvey's spirit, something about Harvey having learned from what he did.

As with Del and Kempster, I sporadically plugged Harvey into a search engine in case the internet's contents ever brought different results to the fore. In 2012, I came across a progressive petition, for example, signed by a Wilfred Harvey Totten in Managua, some kind of proof that this was, indeed, where he'd ended up.

Then, in December 2013, I ran across the blog of a *Vancouver Sun* reporter, Gordon Clark. A post from the week prior began, *Have you ever been struck by one of those truly bizarre coincidences, episodes so strange and unlikely that you feel compelled to search for a deeper meaning?* Apparently, Clark had recently been chatting rinkside with another hockey dad, recalling how both of them had changed direction during undergrad. Clark had started at UBC in sciences, but a side interest in politics led him to meet some people involved in the student paper, the *Ubyssey*. Shortly after this, Ronald Reagan invaded Grenada.

Two people I knew from activist circles—Sue Mitchell and Harvey Totten—had been working on aid projects in that Caribbean country for 22 months when the US Marines arrived. When Sue and Harvey, dedicated leftists, were expelled a few days later by the US military, they flew home to Vancouver, where I picked them up at the airport with some other friends and headed to a restaurant. I plunked a tape recorder down between us and was able to get the first sit-down interview with the first Canadians to get out of Grenada.

Seeing his interview in print, Clark was hooked, his new professional course charted. *This is where the story gets weird. The day after I told the story at the rink, I got an email. It was from Totten, who I haven't seen in three decades. He'd wondered what became of me and tracked me down on the Internet.*

"Holy shit." I heard myself say it aloud as I stood up and backed away from my desk. "Holy shit. Holy shit. Harvey's alive."

"Perhaps you have forgotten welcoming Sue Mitchell and myself following our expulsion from Grenada following the US 'Invasion of Privacy,'" Harvey wrote him.

Clark wrote back, saying that in fact this event changed the course of his life. Harvey's response confirmed the outlines of what Phillip had told me: he had moved to Nicaragua in the 1980s and eventually married a local widow and helped to raise her three daughters.

I learned all this on Nov. 4, said Clark, *and decided to look up that article about Harvey—my first byline. It was easy to find. Its*

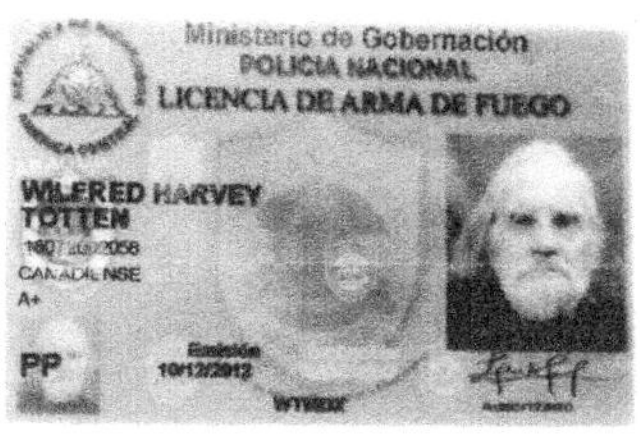

publication date? Nov. 4, 1983—30 years ago to the day.

That was a bit spooky, as perhaps was my stumbling on Clark's blog the same week he posted about that coincidence.

It didn't compel me to *search for a deeper meaning*—that seemed a narcissistic misreading of the universe—but I did send Clark an email saying I wanted to interview Harvey for a book and asking if he might put us in touch.

ADVANCING THE DRIFT

I DREADED BREAKING THE news to Phillip. How had he come to believe his father was dead? Had he relied solely on psychics for his information?

But when I called him, he wasn't really fazed. His reaction was vague, in a way that made me think he suspected—on some level, anyway—that he himself had elicited the supposedly posthumous paternal messages bestowed by the spiritualists.

Phillip's belief in communications from the other side, though, remained undimmed, and he still believed the key aspect of what he'd been told: that Harvey was ready to make amends. When I said that I hoped to go to Nicaragua and interview Harvey, he said that he'd like to come along.

January 7, 2014, I received an email response from Harvey with the subject line "A book you say." *But what is your motivation in writing, he asked, and what would be the slant of your endeavour?*

Dear Mr. Totten, I wrote back, saying that I was a friend of his youngest son's, that my motivations were complex and that the "slant" of the book would emerge from the research and writing. *I am genuinely interested in hearing and retelling your story, from your point of view.* I was vague, and a bit ingratiating.

I recounted how Phillip had learned about Harvey's commitment to progressive causes, and how glad and proud it made him. *He was very young and troubled when he left your home, and I know that you and he had a deep rift. He has turned out to be a person of great strength, character and intelligence, though, and, whatever your differences all those years ago, what he says today is, "I wouldn't be the man I am today if Dad hadn't been the man he was."* He is grateful. I went on to say that he and I both would like to come to Nicaragua.

Padma

Just some random thoughts and a few bits for you to chew upon. I do not like titles including Mr.

He instructed me to call him Harvey or his Nicaraguan name, Javier.

During my life I have been opposed to any form of racism and capitalist oppression, self-aggrandization has not been one of my weaknesses.

He went on to correct what he said were errors of transmission:

#1 Philip is not my youngest son and well he is aware of it.

#2 The recycling project, while I had a secondary part in it, I was not the prime mover. That honour belongs to Sue Mitchell.

I could continue but believe the point has been made. Often of course the greatest task ahead in learning is to unlearn mistaken concepts that we have accepted as true.

He mentioned that he had written some recollections for his stepdaughter, Vivia, and would ask her permission to pass those along to me.

He concluded, *Under no circumstances would Philip be welcome here.*

I responded in the formal register we use with those we don't know well, especially when making requests, agreeing that *having misapprehensions corrected is the surest way to learn,* taking responsibility for errors such as forgetting about the son he'd had with Joan, as well as acknowledging gaps in the versions I had of his story. *It was for these reasons that I wanted to approach you directly,* I said. *I had the sense that you weren't someone who would want such errors to stand uncorrected.*

Honestly, his line about the "greatest task ahead" struck me as sanctimonious in a way I recognized, the customary tone of holier-than-thou leftists. *Get thee to a re-education camp.* It was not hard to detect the person Phillip, Fleishman and Holt had described: defensive, unreflexive, something of a jerk.

But he was not closing the door. Except to Phillip.

It was painful to tell my friend that his father didn't want to see him, although he took it well. "I can understand," he said several times when we talked about it. He would move away from the topic and then come back again as though circling his own pain. "He doesn't want me there, with his family and everything. He's all set up, and I'd be bringing back stuff that's fifty years old. You can't just go and disrupt people's lives like that."

When he said "you," did he mean me or him? Was there a message in there for me, unintentional or otherwise?

He asked to see Harvey's emails and I sent them along. I couldn't sleep that night. Geoff was concerned that my continued involvement might interfere in a possible reconciliation, or that whatever I wrote might destroy a truce if Phillip and Harvey managed to achieve one. My journal shows me deciding not to give myself that much credit:

After all, Phillip and Harvey are not talking to each other now. Each of them is talking to me. And they are adults—how they react to the story will be up to them.

Harvey sent his recollections. They opened with a sort of apologia:

The following account was motivated by Vivia's insistence that I put on paper my experiences in solidarity in the Third World so that she will have something to keep following my death. I have to point out that to take a segment out of a life and to expect it to be understandable is not reasonable. So I have started from my earliest memories up to the present. From this perhaps you will be able to piece together a reasonable image of the person behind the acts performed in his lifetime, that person being the writer of this account.

This effort will necessarily be incomplete (one recalls the good more readily than the bad) so it will be slanted. Anybody expecting to find a "saint" will be disappointed because my feet have always been planted very firmly in the mud.

His account was rambling and dense: his childhood during the Depression in rural Saskatchewan; a one-room school with ink bottles frozen solid; a single pair of coveralls to wear each year; perennial water shortages; a neighbour treating him and his siblings to a handful of peanuts each. He wrote that his eventual conversion to socialism was motivated by seeing families go hungry *in the bread basket of the world*; by witnessing the Canadian government blaming people for having large families when there was no reliable birth control available and *dumping potatoes and beef into the Great Lakes as a price support measure*; that same government later drafting into World War II all those *unwanted children*. He made an early commitment to feminism, taking his mother's side in arguments between his parents about female suffrage; during his brief time at university, during the war, he protested the deportation of interned Japanese Canadians.

How little value are common people to those in positions of power, he wrote to his Nicaraguan stepdaughter, the only one of the nine children he sired or raised with whom he was still on speaking terms. (Which reader, exactly, did he think would be *expecting to find a "saint"?*) *This is a very important point for you to remember, the lack of regard for the poor has a long history.*

At first, I found the recollections almost unreadable, *like sledgehammer strokes in their relentless, repetitive, bombastic self-justification,* as Janet Malcolm said when Joe McGinniss's subject started writing letters directly to her.

Self-aggrandization has not been one of my weaknesses, Harvey had bombastically declared. The fundamental problem was not really his tone, though, not the awkward organization of the manuscript, not even his ungainly prose. It was the knotty question of audience: Vivia would hear his words through a scrim of love and long acquaintance, the way I heard Phillip's. I only had the lyrics, she knew the tune.

But every line of his emails to me hummed with a natural, electric fear, that of falling off a cliff into the oblivion awaiting us all. Most lives are full of unseen events: insights, encounters, slights, transcendences. What are all these moments for? Do they exist if unwitnessed by another?

In one of the last letters in the Holt file, Del wrote, *Something that will really please you is this Simma—I have decided to write my life story—no holds barred. I would need considerable help on this—so hope I can depend on you for some.*

I never saw or heard anything else about this. Holt herself might have wanted to write Del's story—her retention of the file on Del is suggestive—but she didn't.

Holt wrote her own life story, published as *Memoirs of a Loose Cannon.* Her prose is not terrible, but the book is poorly organized and edited, curious or lurid stories crammed in without evident logical links or broader resonance. It's humbler than Neil Fleishman's, but is yet another narcissistic enterprise masquerading—even to itself—as something greater.

Fleishman and Holt fooled themselves that they could make their own stories intelligible, whereas Del, Harvey and Phillip knew they needed a writer to make their grab for immortality. (*He was making his pitch to me,* said Malcolm, *no less intent on "using" me than I was intent on "using" him.*)

She uses people the way I use water, said Lucille about Del, but isn't that how subjects try to use a writer, to reflect them as they saw themselves? *I am like water,* after all.

Rebecca Solnit says *we are all the heroes of our own stories and one of the arts of perspective is to see yourself small on the stage of another's story,* but almost none of us thinks that way.

"Del would be glad that you're writing this," Lorraine told me, making me happy until she added, "as long as there's nothing unflattering!" This, I couldn't guarantee, not that I knew what was or wasn't flattering: people are proud of the strangest things and ashamed of things I don't find shameful at all.

I was bothered by the tone of my initial emails to Harvey, which are, like Del's to Simma Holt, not insincere but not wholly candid either. I didn't see a way around that. It would have been wrong on so many levels to tell him the things I'd heard and read about him, for instance.

Malcolm, too, wrote that she disliked the *fundamental falseness* of her letters to her subject—*the falseness that is built into the writer-subject relationship, and about which nothing can be done. Unlike other relationships that have a purpose beyond themselves and are clearly delineated as such, the writer-subject relationship seems to depend for its life on a kind of fuzziness and murkiness, if not utter covertness, of purpose.*

Harvey, too, as subject, was engaging in a rhetorical pas de deux, never letting more than a couple of days pass without writing to me, but always in that haughty, affected tone.

The writer isn't alone in his anxiety, says Malcolm. *Even as he is worriedly striving to keep the subject talking, the subject is worriedly striving to keep the writer listening.*

If the writer got to write the story and the subject got written about, though, was the covertness a problem? Yes, it was, because *the majority of stories told to journalists fail of their object. The writer ultimately tires of the subject's self-serving story, and substitutes a story of his own.*

But are we not doing that to one another all the time? What are others to us, if not their stories? They're a hug, a joke, a brief fog of breath. They are simultaneously a canoe trip ten years ago and lunch in a couple of weeks. What are we to them, if not their stories? We are major players or supporting cast (sometimes both, in different acts) or, in very rare instances, *the writer,* the writer of their lives.

Out of the triad of Phillip, Del and Harvey, it transpired that Harvey was the one with whom I had most in common, owing to my own past in development work and activism. With Sue Mitchell, his partner when he moved to Nicaragua, he had co-founded Tools for Peace, an ambitious program to assist Nicaraguan farmers early in the Sandinista era. Through my twenties, I often worked with people involved in that organization's Edmonton branch.

It was unexpected to find Harvey transforming before my eyes from a monstrous caricature into a credible, even sympathetic person. I preferred it, even though it called details of Phillip's telling into serious question. Was the family really ejected from Cuba for Harvey's racist attitudes, for example? In his memoirs-would-be-too-grand-a-word, Harvey took pains to demonstrate his long-time antiracism.

Forced to drop out of university for lack of money, he went to work in northern Manitoba, where he met First Nations people who, he said, *traveled great distances via dog-teams and snowshoes and did not speak either English or French but only Cree. I saw Indians as very few people have seen them.* The *bit of racism* he said he recalled wasn't something he flagged as such: when he tried the dried caribou meat that they carried in little buckskin bags to eat while running behind their dog teams, the rig foreman took him aside to say, *"Harvey you shouldn't eat that. It is not clean."* His reply was that these people had been eating it for thousands of years and it hadn't killed them yet.

This nascent consciousness of injustice grew. In BC, he wrote, *I made the acquaintance of many people on the reserve. The women made some of the best baskets on the Pacific Coast. They were roundly belittled by the whites for what? Having the ability to do it or was it because they could do something extremely well that the whites had no ideas how to even start doing? The realization of what terrible things the Europeans had done to the other peoples of the earth probably started here but did not come to full acceptance until years later, with a hope that when the darker skinned people came into their rightful place in the world's society, they should treat us more kindly than we ever had treated them.*

This was a favourite refrain—that Black and brown people should learn from their mistreatment and someday do better toward whites. It marked him as a man of his time, just as an experience he had while living in Grenada implied he "didn't see race." *The population was 95% black. It was natural after awhile to expect to see only black faces. I have never been a person that has much use for mirrors. I was in the bathroom one morning and for some reason happened to glance in the mirror and was startled to see that I had a white face.*

Statement upon statement belied Del's account of their departure from Cuba, as well as the reason Phillip gave for Harvey's having sent him to a shrink. Why had Phillip been sent to therapy? Maybe I'd be able to ask Harvey.

When Sue and Harvey deplaned on being evacuated from Grenada after Reagan's invasion, it made the Canadian national news. Practically everyone in Canada saw the footage; Lucille phoned Phillip from Ontario and told him to turn on the TV.

Soon after, the couple appeared on a Vancouver talk show run by Jack Webster, a confrontational Scottish-Canadian broadcaster with an outsize brogue. The episode is still available on YouTube: Harvey wore a crew-neck sweater in silver-brown, matching his short beard and untamed hair. Sue was in a royal blue blazer and scarf. Her eyes glittered.

They were gorgeous and fierce, appearing on *Webster!* to say that what the Americans called a coup was an internal problem the Grenadians should have been allowed to work out; that what the US had called "assassinations" were accidents; that all these misrepresentations were manufactured, excuses for the Yanks to yank a leftist thorn out of their capitalist-hegemonic side. Webster provoked them; they spoke truth to power, appearing to convince the host in real time.

As I realized that Harvey was credible, I started to read his papers differently. Perhaps simply hearing his story in his own words automatically made him less monstrous? He talked about more than justice and injustice. He was an inventor and innovator—I skimmed past more information about garlic breeding, refrigeration mechanics, cassava milling and nutmeg drying than anyone could possibly absorb—and a raconteur, with observations on co-workers and fellow travellers, as well as on culture and books, world history, natural history.

I saw ptarmigan in their winter white colours, he wrote, speaking of a time working on the Canadian Shield, *and caribou, that being the southern limit of their winter migration. On a sunny day it was not unusual to see four or five hundred in various flocks. I recall one spot where there was a big flat sloping rock. It was highly polished from the caribou sliding down it on their butts to the lake then running around up to the top again and down again as playful as goats.*

In early February 2014, while I was still making my way through his memoir, Harvey sent an alarming email: *I do not mean to interrupt your thought processes but certain things have happened that indicate that if you still wish face to face that such should take place as soon as reasonably possible.* I agreed to come for a short visit, sooner than I had planned, but made it contingent on an explanation. He revealed that he had suffered *two mini-strokes* which had left his *mind and communication abilities* intact. It was confidential: he seemed to be saying the strokes' effects were externally undetectable and was particularly concerned about not causing Vivia *ineffectual fretting.*

When I asked about location and logistics, he said the only convenient place for me to stay would be with him, in the house he shared with Vivia, an hour outside of Managua.

My family wasn't thrilled about my staying with a man who'd been accused of physical violence toward women. I wasn't worried about my physical safety—I figured I could fend off an eighty-six-year-old stroke victim if I needed to—but obliged them by advising the Canadian consulate about my trip.

On the phone, the consular representative responded with warmth, describing Harvey as a *charming old gentleman* with interesting stories to tell about his life in Nicaragua. Vivia wrote a friendly email asking about food preferences and whether they might take me out for a day trip.

And Harvey's emails, though still occasionally blustery, impatient or condescending, became warmer. Increasingly, I was prepared to like him, which was uncomfortable, given the pain he had caused and was still causing Phillip.

I couldn't not go. It was the only way to get answers to my remaining questions. And Phillip never suggested otherwise.

But a strange tension developed and intensified between my friend and me.

The night before I left, I phoned him, as he had asked me to do. I had previously discussed any and all research findings with Phillip, and initially forwarded Harvey's emails, as well, but he'd noticed I had stopped doing that. He said he wanted them for clues as to Harvey's state of mind, but the emotional tenor of emails is difficult to read even in the case of people who are verbally agile on the page, which Harvey was not.

Phillip could tell I was holding back and wanted to know why. I didn't mean to shut him out, but the story's shifts, and my unexpected role in those shifts, had made me crave some distance. I explained this as tactfully as I could.

"But that won't be the case when you come back, right?' he asked. I had no answer.

His voice was tight with wariness, or need, maybe jealousy or possessiveness: he was the child not chosen and I was his friend first.

Sitting in the airport, waiting to board my flight, I worked through all this in my diary: *When I told him I wanted to write this and said I'd give him whatever I found, did I relinquish some kind of writerly authority I would need?* Just as the version of Del that Phillip believed was overturned by Simma Holt's archives, Phillip's version of Harvey was likely to be disputed by Harvey himself. I needed to be open to all possibilities. Phillip himself acknowledged this and yet I felt crowded by his eagerness to participate.

I might not be able to give him a blow-by-blow, I concluded. What, then, could I give him—what was he owed, and could this trip benefit him in any way?

Harvey met me at the Managua airport. My first thought, a cliché, was that he looked like a homeless person: scruffy white beard, unkempt hair under a baseball cap, faded baggy clothes, outdated glasses. Really, he looked more like a farmer in the middle of his workday, which is pretty much what he was.

My second thought was how much he looked like Phillip. One of the last things Phillip said to me before I left was "Maybe he thinks I'm not really his son." Seeing Harvey cleared up that doubt, although the longer I spent with him, the more Phillip vanished and Harvey came into focus. ("I have some photos," Harvey would tell me while I was there, "and my father, my grandfather and myself, we look like the same person." Phillip's resemblance wasn't quite as strong as that, but Phillip's older brothers look nothing like Harvey, whereas no one would doubt Phillip's paternity.)

Harvey led me briskly to his truck. On the drive, he was affable, genuine, pointing things out, my guide to Managua. We passed horse carts and drink advertisements painted on walls as we left the city behind. When he stopped the truck on the dirt road to get out and open a bougainvillea-hooded driveway gate, his pretty Rottweiler, Titan, ran out and jumped up against the side of the truck to wiggle his eyebrows at me through the window.

But almost as soon as we entered the house, Harvey said, "Okay, we need to talk. We need to have an understanding. Yes. Sit you down." It was so abrupt I was alarmed. The door let onto the front room, a large airy space with a tiled floor and high corner shelves holding terracotta tchotchkes. We took seats at a small table. "I want to know if you have

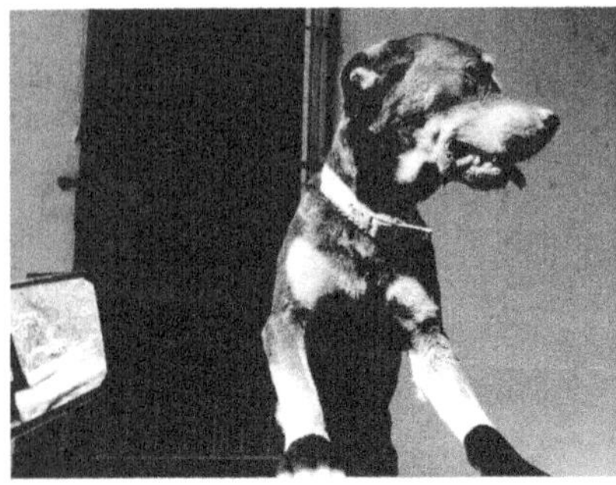

come here because of false information."

"False information?"

"Yes. I still don't know why you have come here, what your interest is in this biography."

"Now, hang on," I said, "it's not a biography."

"Well, what is it?"

"I haven't decided what I'm going to write," I hedged. "I don't want to write the answers before I ask the questions."

"Well," he leaned on his cane, which stood between his knees, "what do you imagine to be my story?"

I laughed.

"Why are you laughing? It's not funny."

I wasn't sure why I was laughing—nerves?—and sobered up.

"You sent me a hundred and fifty pages of your recollections," I said, "so whatever I thought I knew has been, to some extent, overwritten by what I've now read. But what the book will consist of, I still don't know. One thing I'm learning is that every turn in the research contains new revelations. And I'm still doing research."

He seemed content with this response and suggested we start.

Given that Harvey had hedged on whether I could quote from his memoirs, saying I needed Vivia's permission, and since there was so much in them that was unclear, I asked him to begin again at the beginning. I had few questions about his early life but a number about his marriage to Lucille. He had nothing good to say about her, described her as a grasping, lazy hypochondriac.

Later, Phillip decisively disputed the characterization of his mother as lazy. "She was forever doing laundry, bathing us in a tub on the kitchen floor. Heating the water on the stove. She darned, she knitted, patched all our clothes. No, Mother was not a lazy person."

In fairness, Harvey was reluctant, when we met, to talk about Lucille, since he said his sons "would strongly disagree with my assessment of their mother." I convinced him to go on by saying he didn't know what they would say or think, and that I wanted to hear his version.

Phillip had said that his mother was in and out of hospital the whole time he was small, theorizing that it was to escape Harvey. This didn't contradict the events Harvey describes, just their import. He told me Lucille manufactured complaints to avoid work. "She was a yo-yo in and out of the hospital. When it was necessary for me to work elsewhere, which was frequently the case as work was scarce, the boys were bounced around hither and yon."

So he mustered leverage—"I did some digging, and found out Lucille had already been married when we married"—and kicked her out.

I asked whether he'd had any concerns about separating the boys from their mother. He replied that she was not taking care of them, so he had no compunction about that. "This is her own children that she was abusing by her hypochondria."

Phillip's own recollection of his early childhood ends on his sole good memory of his father, who was then working on the railroads and took Phillip out with him one weekend. Three-year-old Phillip was terrified of the engine noise, so Harvey sat him on his knee and let him sound the horn.

Because he had no memories at all of the following two years and because Harvey was "an evil prick" forever afterwards, Phillip suspected that the trip had some traumatic aspect, that Harvey, as Phillip put it, "did something to me on that trip and couldn't live with himself."

Some people go to therapists to recover memories and achieve greater self-knowledge. Phillip goes to psychics. One of these mediums confirmed for Phillip that Harvey had harmed him in some way on that trip, though the details were hazy.

Now I learned from Harvey that, when Phillip was three, Harvey moved out because Lucille had fallen in love with a neighbour. They drew up a formal separation agreement, but, after two years apart, decided to give it another go. The marriage lasted just one more year.

Phillip had no recollection of his parents' separation, but after the outing with his dad, all warmth and fun, he had no memories at all for exactly the period of Harvey's absence. My suspicion was that his memory gap might indeed have a traumatic source: his father's absence.

When I later mentioned to him what I'd learned from Harvey, Phillip was taken aback. "I was really young. I don't remember those things. But whether mother was a trollop or not . . ."

I was shocked. "A trollop? Is that your word?"

"That's my word," he said. Every now and again, he would show this sort of prudishness, always to my surprise, usually in relation to women.

"Imagine she's unhappily married to Harvey and meets someone sweet," I suggested, tentatively. "Everyone who has an affair is not a trollop. It was a long-term affair, not a fling or repeated flings . . . Anyway, I don't like that label."

Even Harvey hadn't characterized her that way. But why had Phillip speculated on whether Harvey might question his son's paternity? Maybe here, too, notions lurked, shadowy figures behind frosted panes, windows on doors Phillip would rather not open.

I had arrived in Nicaragua mid-morning and we had gotten right to talking, my computer and recorder both set up on the cluttered desk in Harvey's room. Now I suggested a break. Mid-afternoon light filtered dimly through a single window high above the desk; there was a narrow twin bed, a filing cabinet and a small, crowded bookshelf. The room connected via the house's single bathroom to Vivia's bedroom, where I would sleep on a pallet they'd made up on the floor.

Harvey was spry, but his sternum domed out dramatically beneath his beard and his breathing was raspy, perhaps a consequence of a severe mining accident he'd suffered when Phillip was tiny. Regardless, it gave the impression that talking cost him effort.

Vivia was working long days that week as an interpreter for a tour group, but she had left guacamole and a tomato-cucumber salad. Harvey also offered me Wisconsin cheeses, bread, some mildly citrusy juice. As we lunched, he talked about Vivia, how she was the only one of his three stepdaughters to pursue higher education, though he'd offered to pay for all of them. "The other girls are doing nothing." He offered me a banana from one of several stalks lying in a corner of the kitchen.

We ate in the front room, where there was a large empty cage, calling to mind a parrot he'd mentioned in his recollections. Before I could ask, Harvey told me he had given the bird away because it started pulling out its feathers from loneliness.

I wondered if we should do a little more work and then perhaps go for a walk—he had wanted to show me his property.

He looked at the clock and said we should go for a walk sooner than later. Also that he had to feed the animals.

"What animals?"

"The kinkajous," he said. The cage I had thought was empty housed a baby, about seven months old, concealed in a sort of a reed hammock, shaped like a muff and hung over a branch. Noises I'd heard during our interview, which I thought were coming from outside, were in fact coming from the next room, which I now saw had a built-in wall-to-wall cage filled with kinkajous—Central American mammals with big eyes, small ears, prehensile tails and dexterous little paw-hands like raccoons'.

He fixed a plate of bananas, sprinkled it with fuchsia vitamin powder. "It's all legal," he told me, not that I had doubted that, or even thought about it. "I have a licence."

I followed as he went into the room to feed them and snapped pictures from the narrow corridor left by the cage. Several kinkajous were curious about my phone; Amigo, an older male, hissed at me.

"Territorial," said Harvey, "trying to let you know this is his place."

We walked out into his garden, which stretched back about fifty yards behind the house. Leaning on his walking stick, he pointed out mango, avocado, citrus. He cultivated bananas and referred to the varieties and hybrids by their lab names. He had 150 trees. Neighbours would come and cut stalks. He advised them on growing their own, just as Allan Toop had projected.

"A person who doesn't have anything to do curls up and dies," he said. "That's what I was doing in Managua. That's why I moved out here."

"Yes," I responded from beneath the great leafy canopy of his creation, "but there's a world of difference between not having anything to do and maintaining a hundred and fifty banana trees." Beyond his garden wall, a dusty horizon.

We went back into the house and tried to find spots for our water glasses on his desk. We unpacked the slide viewer he'd asked me to bring, to let him show me pictures of his trips, his inventions, the health-and-wellness presentations that became Sue Mitchell's primary vocation during their jaunts in the developing world.

I noted in my diary: *You have the feeling that if he encounters any practical problem, any practical task, he will succeed.* Harvey, it would appear, was winning me over.

Following Lucille's final departure, Harvey trained in steam and refrigeration technology, and moved to Chilliwack for a job. He found the Fraser Valley stultifying, conservative and religious, everything he hated. *I had also to try to find a mate to help raise the boys. My efforts in that area were mostly a dismal failure.*

Which perhaps is what made him vulnerable to the charms of an escaped parolee: *About 1965 by chance I became acquainted with a woman who had been close to Fidel Castro—she said. When I met her she was a parole violator from a bank robbery conviction for which she said she was not guilty.* I had seen hints of this in the Holt file—that Del claimed not to have robbed the Burnaby bank. Lorraine eventually told me, "She admitted to having robbed banks, just not that particular one."

I believed her for some years, Harvey wrote. *Interpol was looking for this person.* Clearly, he, too, thought she'd been a bigger deal than she was.

Harvey's version of the Cuba trip, repeated for me in our conversations, followed the rough contours of Phillip's, but was salted with details the kids wouldn't have known. On their voyage through California, for example, they stopped in San Francisco, working Del's contacts to try to figure out how to get across the border into Mexico. "Unfortunately, the place we had to go for the information was a homosexual gay bar and women were not allowed. So I had to enter this place: a den of thieves and I'm the lonely little petunia in the onion patch."

He said they bought off the chief of police in Ciudad Juárez to get Del into Mexico. "By today's standards he was cheap," Harvey said, with a laugh. "Three hundred Canadian. I don't think three hundred dollars gets you very much corruption in Ciudad Juárez today!"

He and the boys met up with Del in Mexico City and perpetrated the passport scam, an idea for which he took credit. Otherwise, little in his account of their month in Cuba contradicted Phillip's, until he got to why they couldn't stay:

"She had a lot of hazy stories with a lot of fantasy in them, but it seems certain that Fidel knew her, better than myself, in fact, in that we were asked to leave Cuba after one month."

Their translator regretfully conveyed a message to the family, direct from Fidel: Get out now.

"Even though I had been approached to work in refrigeration in the agricultural sector," Harvey recounted, still indignant. "They didn't have any refrigeration technicians. But that didn't cut any ice." So to speak. *"No, no: out, right now, out."*

Phillip would later agree that this made a certain sense: Castro seems to have been glad enough to shelter infamous criminals of conscience, but why would he make an enemy of the Canadian government over a small-potatoes bank robber?

In his memoirs, Harvey delivered a brief but complex portrait of the pre-Castro corruption and inequality suffered by the Cuban people, and of some of the goals and triumphs of the revolution: land reform; progressive mental health care; the elimination of the sex trade in favour of sugar as the basis of the economy. He also explained one salient feature of his personal style:

Many people do not understand the part of the beard in relation to the revolution and revolutionaries in Cuba. The men in the montañas with Fidel grew beards because they lacked the facilities to shave. However when finally they got to Habana, this then became instantly a mark of status and particularly as Cubans did not wear beards at that time they were easy to spot on the streets. Any man who grew a beard who had not been in the montaña would be shunned as pretentious. It was from this time on my return to Canada that I grew a beard and have wore it ever since in Solidarity with Cuba. Note that, not being Cuban, I did not/do not think that the prohibition applies to me.

Before I went to Nicaragua, I'd anxiously consulted with my agent and with writer friends about how to conduct myself in my interviews with Harvey. I'd done interviews before, but never like this.

"It's easy when you are speaking to someone to get sucked into their point of view," a veteran Canadian journalist warned me. "Then you get on the airplane and you return to your more objective space. It's important not to be seduced by what they're saying, and not to appear seduced, so that they don't feel hugely betrayed by how the story turns out when you write it."

What gives journalism its authenticity and vitality is the tension between the subject's blind self-absorption and the journalist's skepticism, says Janet Malcolm. *Journalists who swallow the subject's account whole and publish it are not journalists but publicists.*

I strongly support this attitude in journalistic writing about public figures. And I know instinctively how to evoke this tension in fiction, the use of a narrator, seen or unseen, to give the reader a slight ironic distance from a character. I may have been slightly conflicted, though, about how to write, or even think, journalistically about real people on otherwise private trajectories.

At bottom, Malcolm advises, *no subject is naïve. Every subject of writing knows on some level what is in store for him, and remains in the relationship anyway, impelled by something stronger than his reason. The reader of a work of journalism can only imagine how the writer got the subject to make such a spectacle of himself.*

I was impressed by the degree to which Harvey lived in accord with his principles; I liked how he spoke of Sue (with whom he had parted amicably) and of Vivia. But he had nothing good to say about any of the four women he married—Lucille, Del, Joan and Vivia's mother, Adilia. He even accused Joan of trapping him into marriage with a faulty IUD, leading to the birth of that last son I'd forgotten about. And Phillip and his brothers were strikingly absent from his written recollections, except for pejoratives and paranoid conjurings: *My natural sons have the idea that I suffer mental problems or some such to rouse myself in defense of the downtrodden although each would be only too eager to get their fingers into what they probably imagine as the honey-pot of my mythical bank accounts at my death. I have taken steps to prevent their being able to do so . . .*

I asked him what his sons were like in childhood.

"Something that I have noticed repeatedly in people," he started, speaking slowly, ponderously, "is that if you look at a child, middle-aged, old, it's the same person. What Phillip is now, he was when he was a child, and he was at twenty years old. What Rob was as a child, he was when he was twenty, and he's going to be now. Vivia, too. I'm not saying that when they were six years old, you could predict what the life of each of them was going to be, but you can look back at it and you can certainly say they have not changed."

This is not inconceivable, but Harvey hadn't had close contact with Phillip for forty-five years. How did he know which innate strains of his child's personality ultimately developed and which had withered?

"If you say Phillip hasn't changed," I asked, "how would you describe him, as a child?"

"He was a deceitful kid. When he was a teenager, he started being a con man; and he's still a con man." He switched to talking about Mary Lloyd, mentioning various people she fooled. "That's what con men are. They are very, very persuasive. They can talk you into ridiculous things."

I listened anxiously: the world of the book was shifting again. A couple of times that day, I had tried to send Phillip photos of Harvey but was stopped by a weak signal. Clearly, I wanted, on some fundamental level, to share this experience with him. Now, I was reminded again of my need to hear and weigh Harvey's perspective without Phillip's input.

Did Harvey have stories illustrating how Phillip was a con man, I asked.

"When we left Kitamat, we left Phillip and Rob. They had to finish school. We had the apartment paid for; they had a paper route, and they were supposed to come down when school was out. Our home was practically a Volkswagen until we found somewhere to live in Chilliwack. And who shows up but Phillip, with a wild story that Rob stole the money from the paper route. I was taken aback; it didn't ring true. Well, it turned out the money had been stolen: Phillip stole the money from Rob and told us just exactly the opposite. He was consistently that type of a person."

That was a long time ago, I said. Were there other more recent incidents that made him feel he couldn't trust Phillip?

"It was more a feeling you got," Harvey said. "I don't remember the particular instances. See, not too long after that,

Phillip got very friendly with Mary Lloyd. I'm not sure if pedophilia played a part or not. I think it did."

I started trembling. "Whose pedophilia?"

"Mary Lloyd. Mary Lloyd and Phillip."

"So you thought they were involved?"

"I thought they were involved."

I was stunned. But perhaps this presumption was inevitable: when I told others the story, I always said, "Eventually, Phillip and Del ran away together. That is, as mother and son." Their actions necessitated a clarification clause, which Harvey had never received.

I was pretty sure Harvey's belief was false, but I later asked Phillip about it explicitly, and he affirmed, "There was nothing between us."

"Nothing sexual," I clarified.

"Nothing sexual."

But he did think Del was beautiful and glamorous. He bought her a red rose every week, for Christ's sake. I got him to admit that it might have looked like, might even have felt like, infatuation, and surely Harvey sensed their connection acutely as his marriage broke down.

In Nicaragua, though, I was unprepared for this, so I decided to deke around the topic until I could give it some thought.

I tried to continue drawing Harvey out on fatherhood, on his sons, but didn't get too far. When I asked if he had expectations or hopes for his kids, he said no, that he hadn't done anything worth copying. When I asked about Rob, Harvey said he was driving a truck.

In our next break, I texted Geoff: *OMG, OMG. Harvey thinks Phillip and Del were sleeping together. Doesn't know Phillip's gay, I guess?! Can I out him?*

Geoff responded, *Tell Harvey. Phillip would be fine with it.*

Of course, I had to. The question was how. No: the question, as with so many things, was how to find the guts.

How conveniently literary: a real-life Oedipal drama.

In fact, though, neither *Oedipus Rex* nor the Oedipus complex provides a key that slips in smoothly to unlock the mystery of Harvey and Phillip's estrangement.

Phillip guessed that a childhood sexual transgression was perpetrated on him by his father. Harvey, conversely, guessed that an Oedipal sexual transgression was perpetrated on him by his son. Both injuries in fact involved transgressive sex—Lucille's affair; Phillip's homosexuality—that the wronged party lacked the means to discern.

The problem was the result: abandonment. Harvey left Phillip when Phillip was three. Phillip left Harvey when he was sixteen. And the resulting rage and pain and bewilderment conjured explanations to answer the unanswered *why*.

The truth *can* be devastating, but it isn't always. In these cases, the truth was less wounding than what the injured party imagined.

Why? It's the first question a child asks that parents cannot properly answer, the first question that only begets more questions. *Why? Why? Why?* The toddler's dawning recognition of the world's true vastness and its essential incomprehensibility—exciting and inviting, or threatening in the extreme, depending on the child and the family.

Not for the first time, I compared my own family with Harvey's.

Our first child threw horrific tantrums until he was four, his face purpling as he issued inhuman screams. Geoff and I, novice parents and overachievers, took his fits personally; reduced to tears ourselves, we each accused the other of incompetence. We asked our son, *Why? Why are you doing this?* Stupid question: if he could answer it, he might not have been throwing a fit.

But in between these episodes, we talked to him and to each other. We stuck with the conversations until our son learned to tell us what was wrong and came to hear from us about—or see for himself—our own foibles. We all had to forgive each other, and, in the heat of this labour, the tantrums were melted into the mosaic of our family lore.

I read somewhere when my kids were tiny that the toddler and teenage stages were parallel; in my demonstrably unreliable memory, this article said there was some hormonal equivalence between these stages. Famed child psychoanalyst D. W. Winnicott refers, in one essay, to a boy *at the height of his sex wave (at the toddler age and at puberty)*, but he doesn't explain this term or use it anywhere else and internet searches turn up little but junk. Medical evidence aside, though, these are—observably—delicate, unstable, revealing years, when the child makes a leap into independence, feeling fear and acting defiant, even resentful, but incapable of pinpointing the sources of these large emotions. The parent inevitably feels bewildered and angry: at the child for the outbursts, and at herself—that would be me—for her inadequacy as a responder.

So, on some level I was anticipating it in 2020, when we had another crisis—teenage stuff, exacerbated by the pandemic. Anticipation didn't lessen the difficulty, though: it was again excruciating in ways I'd never imagined. And again, once the conflict's acute phase passed, conversation and an assiduously built reservoir of goodwill rescued us, at least for the time being. Heating, cooling, annealing.

I tend, in conflicts with my loved ones, to lose all sense of future possibility: I'm fatally susceptible to the idea that the way a person is, or appears to me, in that moment, is how they are and always will be. Time and again, I experience my errors in this regard as a relief: my loved ones are much more than I can see; they are continually changing; governed by *that which unites everything on earth, the ongoing possibility of metamorphosis.*

Conversation, after tempers have ebbed, is the opportunity for multiple readings of my combatants, the people I love most in the world and who are most interesting to me. I want not to be trapped, tragically, by underinterpretation. But that can only happen if we keep the book of our relationship open between us. Harvey had shut that book with his son and was refusing, still, to reopen it.

Vivia came home, exhausted from her fourteen-hour day as a tour guide for an American school group. Her manner was self-contained, though friendly and seemingly candid. Her English was perfect: she had gotten a degree in Canada and stayed on for some years, before returning to Nicaragua because that was where her life was, her mother and sisters, and Harvey, whom she referred to as her dad. He had told her to stay in Canada. She said he needed her.

Harvey had gone to bed; she and I were getting ready to sleep in our shared room. She asked me how our interviews had gone. I said they'd gone well but that she and Harvey needed to decide whether I could quote from his written recollections. If I couldn't, I would need Harvey to repeat much of what was in them, which I was reluctant to do unnecessarily (particularly given the state of his health, which I couldn't mention—he still hadn't told her about the strokes). He'd been repeating a fair amount, regardless, but I'd only specifically been asking him to clarify things I didn't understand. Vivia wondered whether the clarifications would be enough, but I said that would leave me without the centre of the story, only the elaboration. It wasn't clear why she was hesitant to give me permission to quote from the document he had created for her. I guessed that there wasn't any specific reason, or not yet: Harvey had created the need for a decision by saying it was up to her; I just thought she wasn't someone who took any decision lightly.

"Anyway," I said, "please think about it."

I went to bed desperately tired myself and wondering if I should get up when Vivia did: she had to be out the door at six. When the doorbell rang for her, though, instead of waking, I dreamt that one of her sisters came and stood over me, telling me

I needed to answer the door, that it was an ambulance coming for Harvey, that he was in a bad way: the distillation of all my rising fears about what my remaining questions about Phillip and Del might do to him.

At a more decent hour, as we were getting ready to recommence, I mentioned to Harvey that I still didn't know if he and Vivia would give me permission to use the recollections, and that we would have to do extra recording if not. He said I needed to let things develop between her and me, take it slow, become friends, and then ask.

"Are you okay with it if she is?" I asked.

"Yes, sure, it's no problem for me."

"Why would it be a problem for her?" I asked.

"The same reason Amigo out there is hissing at you—this is her territory."

It was a plausible explanation and a good real-world metaphor. Yet I had begun to wonder about Harvey's understanding of human nature. He made much of his study of psychology, but he seemed to diagnose everyone in his life as "paranoid."

Of Del, for example, he said, "She was a destructive paranoid. There are constructive and destructive paranoids. Constructive paranoids are people that you just can't stop. They go, go, go and really do things. If you speak of famous men in history, the probability is that you're speaking of paranoids, but constructive ones. Destructive paranoids are just the opposite. There's no reasoning with these people."

At a certain point, he even referred to me that way, not pejoratively, but as if he were taking it for granted that it was simply a matter of scale: "I don't know how paranoid you are yet," he said. "I haven't had a chance to study you."

I couldn't figure out what "paranoia," as it's commonly understood, had to do with what he was talking about. (By contrast, Harvey himself exhibited some characteristics that seemed more in line with that DSM category.)

Although he felt there were turning points in his life that changed him in fundamental ways, his assessments of others were static and oversimplified. His politics didn't admit much nuance, either. His judgmental confidence and monomania seemed reflective of the truly revolutionary-progressive mind, a sort that has always interested and fatigued me.

He did portray a few people in complex or nuanced terms—his mother, Vivia. "My mother was a contradictory person," he said. "I never saw her reach out to a neighbour. Yet she would talk socialism to we children: *You have to look after each other.*"

I recalled that Allan Toop had said that Harvey would never deny a neighbour anything. "In Allan's view you maybe lived more according to what your mother said than what she did," I suggested.

I was shocked to see him tear up. "That's true," he said, wiping his eyes. "So let's pass to something else."

It was the second of my three days in Nicaragua. I was preoccupied with the obligation to confront Harvey on Phillip's sexuality.

I started by asking about his split with Del, and how she ended up back in jail.

"I can't help you on that. I don't think I ever knew just why she was arrested. Many people thought I had turned her in, but I had no intention of turning her in. Going back to jail would never cure, if you like, a person as sick as she was."

After learning Del had been reincarcerated, he went to see Del's mother. He found Phillip there. "I asked, What has taken place here? Because I had no information."

Phillip had told me this story. In his telling, Harvey beat him up. In Harvey's telling, a family friend there called the police, "for what reason I have no idea."

He learned Del was in Matsqui and went to visit her, but wasn't allowed in.

"Was there physical violence between you, in your marriage?" I asked.

"No."

"You never hit her?"

"Oh. Oh, yeah. In Kitamat. I don't know. We were both drunk." This had to be the New Year's Day broken coffee pot story. "She had a way of getting at you. We had a go. She was hitting me, too. Then she made out that she was a bleeder and had to go to the hospital. Another funky story."

"And that was the only time there was physical violence between you, just that one time in Kitamat?" On the recording, I don't wait for an answer. "Did you hit your kids? Regularly?"

"I don't think so."

I reminded him of a time he said Del left with the kids.

"She took the children to some hostel of some sort, for battered women in Hope," Harvey affirmed.

"Yes, that's why I was asking about the violence."

"No, no," he objected. "She was a con person, con man. What she told them to get into this battered women place, I have no idea, but because of the story she told, there was no way I could even approach the children. I suppose some sort of an order was out against me."

That sounded a lot like a restraining order, so Del must have been convincing. "Rob eventually came back home but Phillip never did?" I asked.

"That's right. What motivated that"—Del's leaving—"I have no idea. What made her think she could survive in the outside, dodge the parole officers, I have no idea."

He seemed to be implying that their marriage was protecting her from this fate, that she made herself vulnerable by leaving. I couldn't tell how different this was from what Holt and others had suggested: that he blackmailed her into staying the way a neighbourhood boss demands protection money.

"What made people think that you had turned her in?"

"I have no idea. There's no way I'd do that."

I asked why they got married in the US—he said it was her idea—and about a trip Phillip had directed me to ask about, when Harvey and Del went to the coast.

"Del said the reason you went to the coast was that you had the idea of checking yourself into a mental hospital," I told him. I had forgotten that Lucille had also said something in one of her letters about Del having driven him "to a psychiatric," which sounded metaphoric but could have been literal.

But Harvey shook his head, saying it had been nothing more than a job inquiry. "There's probably going to be a lot of these stories."

"Okay." On the recording, I sound relieved, which strikes me now as a deferment of the problem.

I moved on to the divorce, spiralling closer to the most sensitive topics. Although I don't know that I would do it any differently now, it's odd, at this distance, to retrace my strategy, or whatever you'd call it. Listening, I can feel my own squeamishness all over again. At various points, my recording is punctuated by animal shrieks, whether birds outside or kinkajous in the next room, I'm not certain. When Harvey pauses to think, the sound of his breathing, a deep, raspy whistle, fills the recording, but when he speaks, his voice is strong and steady.

"She's in the stand," Harvey recalled of the divorce hearing, "and the story she gave was horrible, was perjury."

"What sorts of things did she accuse you of?"

"I don't remember, but of a nature that I was really a blackguard."

"What was the settlement out of the divorce?"

"There was no settlement. It was a case of fifty-fifty split on the property at Peters Road." The place they called Strawberry Mountain.

"And did she buy you out?

"I don't remember."

"Phillip said she cheated you out of that property."

"I'm not going to argue with that. At the time, I was so sick of her and of that property that if they offered me peanuts, I would have taken it."

"And you took custody of Rob and Del took custody of Phillip?"

"No. How could Del get custody of anybody? The Parole Board would not give her custody of her daughter. This was why her husband's family had custody of the daughter."

This sounded wrong: What would the Parole Board have to do with child custody? And Holt and Del's letters make it appear that Del gave the children up when she went to jail and never tried to get them back.

"Welfare sent me some sort of official notice that I had to support Phillip," Harvey went on, "living with her. I was furious." This sounded like a child support order, which implies there was a formal custody arrangement, but when I challenged Harvey, I gained no traction. "I told them: *I have a perfectly good home, where he's welcome to be if he's acting in a reasonable manner.* So that thing collapsed. That's the only time any official thing came in about her supposedly having custody."

"Did you try in any way to make Phillip come back?"

"No, no, no. He was so under her influence. And he himself of course was very paranoid. Reasoning was impossible."

The time had arrived: if Harvey thought Phillip stole his wife, his anger and resentment, which had looked irrational, might suddenly seem proportional.

"But you also believed at that time that he and Del were living together as lovers, not as mother and son."

"I think so. I think so."

"On what evidence were you believing that?"

"He didn't have any girlfriends, so that's what I believed. Rob I think was the one who first glommed on to that idea. I think he actually accosted Phillip with it, *What are you doing sleeping with that old woman?*"

"What was Phillip's response?"

"I don't recall. Probably nothing. That would be the paranoid way out of it. You don't engage in that conversation if you can't win it. You see?"

Blood was pounding in my ears. "Phillip is gay. Phillip is homosexual."

"Hm," he responded, and added something I can't make out on the recording—either "Was he different back then?" or "Was he driven to that by Del?"

"I don't know how sexually active he was at fifteen," I said. "But can you imagine that this would be another reason he didn't have girlfriends?"

"The one that initiated this idea was Rob, and I imagine he would have a better understanding of this than myself."

"Okay. That's fine. I felt nervous to bring it up."

"Him being gay? That doesn't matter to me."

"I wondered if it would change your ideas of what happened then."

"No."

"When was the last time you spoke to Phillip?"

"It's many, many years ago."

"And yet you said to me, what Phillip was as a child, he is today. What do you know about who Phillip is today? What are you basing this on?"

"I have some information there that I'd sooner not divulge."

"So it's for reasons you won't divulge that you have no interest in seeing Phillip? It's been forty years. He has an interest in reconciliation."

"I'd have to think a long time about it, is all I can say. I don't think I care to discuss it anymore."

"All right. I don't mean to upset you. As I said, he told me to tell you that if you hadn't been the man you were, he wouldn't be the man he is, a person I find admirable—the intelligence, the curiosity, he's a reader . . ."

Harvey interrupted me forcefully. "Do you want me to be very truthful with you? I cannot discard the idea that you are . . . what's the word? You have been taken in by a con man. I have seen con people working, and they are so persuasive. I don't just speak of Mary Lloyd. He learned his trade from Mary Lloyd. And I have contacted people that have been in contact with him recently. These people knew him when he was younger. And they say there's no change. So thank you for your effort, but let's move on."

"Would these people be willing to talk to me?" On the recording, I sound eager and afraid. "Would I be able to interview those people?"

"I don't know. I will ask them."

I said I'd be grateful if he could.

Why would I believe anything Harvey said about Phillip? It's not that I believed, exactly, but that I was willing to.

What kind of a friend did this make me? Well, in this moment, I was trying not to be a friend. I was trying to be a writer, open, unbiased. I see now in my notes that the veteran Canadian journalist I consulted had not only warned me about how I went into my conversations with Harvey but also about my relationship to Phillip. *Make sure that you don't, by being too chummy with him, give over to his p.o.v.,* I'd scribbled as we spoke.

I didn't remember that she'd said that, but I'd instinctively felt the need to pull out of Phillip's orbit as I approached this trip. I didn't think Harvey was right, exactly, but I was intrigued by the possibility that there was more to Phillip than I could discern from my limited view of him.

In time, I would ask both Sue, whom I interviewed in Toronto, and Vivia, each of whom had known Harvey for decades, whether he had a frightening temper or was ever physically violent. Both not only denied this but seemed bewildered by the suggestion, as though it was too out of character for them to even contemplate.

That night, Vivia worked late. I fixed supper for Harvey and me: sautéing garlic and onions, mixing in beans, making rice. Harvey advised me to remove the skins from the garlic cloves by crushing them with the side of the knife. I got defensive—I had been given that tip before but never did it. Now, I always do it that way and think of Harvey when I do.

He sat on a chair in the kitchen as I cooked, in his characteristic posture—leaning on his walking stick as it stood between his knees—and chatted, about communism, about India, about fiction. "The thing you miss most, living in a place like this," he said at one point, "is intelligent conversation. I don't wear my hearing aid much because I don't need it to hear myself."

He kept busy with his garden and he had some books, but there was no library nearby, nor like-minded people apart from Vivia, who was in her twenties and had her own life.

His Spanish was only functional. I had brought him some novels in English, including my own, which he started greedily consuming the first night. Now he asked about a reference in my second novel to the attacks on Sikhs following Indira Gandhi's assassination. When I used the term "pogrom," he remarked that he had always wondered how to pronounce that word—a common problem among isolated but avid readers, one I'd experienced myself, knowing words but not how they sound.

During our breaks, in my days as his guest, as I reviewed notes and planned for our next session, he would knock on my door, saying, "I don't mean to disturb, but . . ." and ask my opinion on some matter of world history or human progress. *Just now,* my diary recounts, he came by to talk about Will Durant's proposal that *there were originally two western cultures: Greek—infertile soil, food shortages, wars rare, homosexuality accepted—and Israeli—fertile soil, lots of food, much embattled, homosexuality/nonprocreative sexuality not accepted. Now, he says, with world population reaching excessive levels, homosexuality will stage a major comeback.*

Sometimes he asked if I knew about something and was shocked that I didn't. If ever I corrected him on a factlet, he was taken aback and interested. But he assumed that his own knowledge was greater than mine, often starting on a topic by saying, "You probably don't know about this . . ." or "you'll find it surprising that . . ." I thought it a habit likely to alienate others.

He is tougher and smarter than most people, I wrote in my journal, *and that must be a difficult burden, except that he thinks it's everyone else's burden, not his.*

Harvey had offered to let his ex-partner Sue Mitchell know that I was working on the book, in hopes that I might interview her, and when we were finished dinner, he called her. From my bedroom, I could hear the warmth in his voice, which rose occasionally into laughter.

He and Sue met through activist circles as his marriage to Joan was dissolving, and moved in together, lived quietly, growing garlic and grapes. He worked throughout as a refrigeration technician at a local dairy.

Sue's energy and inventiveness still impressed him. "Have you ever heard of Cossack asparagus? It's cattails, just when spring has come. Sue read about this in one of her hippie cooking books. She came back one night—her arms were mud up to here. This is a city girl," he marvelled, and enumerated her other accomplishments: municipal recycling, Tools for Peace, third-world organizing and education.

"Do you think it made a difference to the tone of your relationship that you made an agreement not to get married?" I asked.

"She was a much different person," Harvey replied, gruff and brief as he always was in response to personal questions. I tried to press, but he wouldn't or couldn't go further.

I knew other progressive men of Harvey's generation whose ideas about women never fully adjusted as feminism moved into the mainstream. My suspicion was that when he married a woman, he cast her in a defined role. A wife could only fall short of those pre-existing standards.

Eventually, Sue, who was twenty years younger, returned to Canada to work in documentary film, while Harvey remained behind. From there, she wrote tender letters trying to parse the reasons for the separation and her feelings following it. Gradually, these shaded away into friendly exchanges on work and mutual acquaintances, and then on financial and legal matters that drew Harvey back north on occasion.

I can speak about all this because Harvey gave me multiple files of personal correspondence as well as papers related to his various inventions and innovations. He told me to take them with me. "Who else is going to want them?" he shrugged.

Incredulous, I asked, "Vivia, maybe?"

"She wouldn't know what to do with them."

I felt weird. "I want to tell her I'm taking them, and that I will return them to her or give them to an archive, according to her wishes."

"That's a better idea, sure."

When I further worried that the letters might be too private, he merely expressed surprise that "the personal stuff" interested me. I'm not sure if this was because he didn't think his personal history revealing of his identity, or if it was because he wanted to be remembered by his accomplishments, rather than, in effect, by his failings. Either way, it seemed he was still misunderstanding my project, though the project itself seemed to shift focus daily, either moving its centre or growing more diffuse.

After Sue's departure from Nicaragua, Harvey was at something of a loss in his work, particularly "so far as raising female status in Nicaragua was concerned." A friend in Canada, a woman, suggested he "concentrate on the particular instead of the general.

You have an *empleada*"—a maid, Adilia—"with three little girls, why don't you think about that?"

He didn't quite agree with the way she framed the idea. *It could not be the solution for the problems of all the women of Nicaragua.* Obviously. But he did it anyway.

("He married his housekeeper again?" Geoff asked.)

Not that I believe in marriage per se, Harvey says in his writings, *but I thought it better for her protection. It was never meant to be a Barbie Doll–made in Heaven marriage, but strictly one of convenience, her to raise a family and for me help a few years hence when I would be old and possibly in need of it.* I could understand: marriage has historically been more practical than romantic. *While some internationalistas adopted a child, one could say that I adopted a family.*

Having done this, he says he did his best to conduct the marriage along progressive lines, trying to cure Adilia of the sexist conditioning that, he felt, had damaged her confidence and self-esteem. Their early years were happy, *chummy, with mutual respect and regard for each other.* He further insisted that her daughters go to *the best schools that we could gain access to.*

But he says all this is in part to argue against an eventual accusation from Adilia: that he bought her intimacy. *She had been removing herself from whatever closeness existed causing conditions between us to become ever more strained. At what I thought was an indication from her that she saw where our relationship was going and wished to turn it around, we two went to Managua to buy household appliances. Following this by a few days I tried to have a conversation with Adilia in which I suggested getting our relationship back on a more acceptable basis. I was surprised to say the least with the venomousity with which she told me that my buying those appliances was nothing more than an attempt to prostitute her.*

He is appalled: he finds prostitution abhorrent; his actions show goodwill toward Adilia; he could easily have taken sexual advantage but didn't; he married her in order to safeguard her and her daughters' future.

None of this, to me, contradicted a fundamental idea that she was a "kept woman."

And, when I asked, Harvey affirmed the terms of Del's employment.

"Was there a presumed intimacy of some kind?" I asked about her and the other women he hired back in Chilliwack.

"Oh, yes, there was presumed intimacy."

"So that was part of the job."

"Uh-huh."

Harvey was outraged by Adilia's accusation that he would ever take advantage of a vulnerable woman, for sex or otherwise. There was something complicated and unresolvable here—a failure to acknowledge the inequality historically inherent in the institution Sue and he had avoided.

In *The Dialectic of Sex*, revolutionary feminist Shulamith Firestone says, *Engels has observed that within the family the husband is the bourgeois and the wife and children are the proletariat. But Engels has been given too much credit for these scattered recognitions of the oppression of women as a class. In fact he acknowledged the sexual class system only where it overlapped and illuminated his economic construct. Engels didn't do so well even in this respect. But Marx was worse.*

I humbly submit that Harvey, a petrified Marxist, was not great, either. He didn't recognize that the politics operational in the dynamics of his own home could be a microcosm of those that preoccupied him in the wide world. Loyal to Fidel's revolution (when Castro died, he wrote to me, "I think history has absolved him"), he apparently could justify, rationalize or ignore the oppressions baked into that regime, as with those in his domestic arrangements. Just as Daniel Ortega's progressive government in Nicaragua was by now suppressing political opposition and free speech—revolution in senescence collapses toward the conditions of its birth—Harvey started each marriage high on idealism and ended trying furiously to keep wife and kids under his thumb.

"He's very dictatorial," Phillip had told me. "One time, in the period of the fights leading up to the butcher knife, Del called him 'Hitler.' He fucking flipped his chicken."

Vivia's tour guide contract was over. She spent my second-to-last morning there cleaning house—nesting after a busy work time, an impulse I recognized—while Harvey and I went through his papers: correspondence, slides, plans for his inventions and other projects.

Our conversations started to wind down as we approached the present moment. He talked to me about the legal status of his current property, which he wanted to deed to Vivia with the provision that he could remain in it until his death. "Just in case Vivia for some reason gets ornery and we have some kind of a falling out. I need to protect myself that way."

That seemed smart, considering his history. The process was held up in bureaucracy, though, and when I asked for details, he said, "I'll show you!" He limped over to a filing cabinet and pulled out a handgun instead. "Hm," he said, sounding mildly perplexed. "It's cocked."

"Harvey is showing me a cocked handgun," I informed my recording, partly to preserve the scene, partly in case anything happened.

He held it up as I winced. "It's a forty-five. It makes a big bang."

I asked why the gun was cocked.

"I don't know why it was cocked. I left it that way, I guess."

"Does that mean the safety is off?"

"It's not loaded. Oh, no."

I exhaled. "Oh, okay. You just load it to fire it?"

"Put a shell in and *whoom!*" He and Vivia had bought it after some locals broke into their house. "I took a shot and Vivia took a shot, just to let people know there's a gun around."

I was reaching the end of my questions. I clarified a few last matters and suggested we might be finished. When I stopped the tape, however, Harvey said: "I probably shouldn't ask you this, but on what basis are you and Phillip friends?"

I told him how Phillip and I met, and how the story of their getting into Cuba started me thinking about a book on Del, a bank-robbing communist.

Harvey laughed. "A bank-robbing communist? No, she might have said Fidel was robbing banks to finance the revolution and used that to justify robbing banks herself, but she wasn't a communist. She was totally apolitical."

"Simma Holt told me Mary Lloyd could have been a great lady," I said, "except that she was oppressed by the men in her life."

"Which men?"

"All the men."

Harvey weighed this a little, and then asked, "What do you know about what happened to her first husband?"

"You mean Lew Lloyd?" I restarted the recorder and told Harvey what I knew: "At a certain point, Lew says to his roommate, *My wife's in town.* The roommate says, *Okay, go have a good time.* Then Lew's body was found in a ditch, shot." I rambled a little while longer before stumbling to a halt. "Was that what you were asking me?"

"No. What happened to her first husband is she shot him."

There's a momentary silence on the recording. "Del told you that?" I ask.

"She told me that."

"She told you that she shot him herself?"

"She told me exactly where she shot him."

"Really." On the recording, I sound as though I'm having trouble catching my breath, and I feel that way again, listening.

"Where did she shoot him?"

"On a bridge somewhere in Edmonton."

"On a bridge in Edmonton. When did she tell you this?"

"I can't really put a date on that."

"If not a date, then, in what phase of your relationship did she tell you that?"

"I would say we were a couple or three years into it."

"How did you feel when she told you that? Why would she tell you that?"

"I'm trying to piece it together. She was trying to justify something else. Now, at this moment, I have to admit that maybe she was deluding me. Somebody else was accused of this murder, and she was going to confess to it if the other guy was convicted."

This had to have been Kempster, who was acquitted.

"This was her yap-yap to me." He shrugged. "Whether it was true or not, I don't know. And she said that she had left some lights burning or something in her house in Vancouver so the neighbours would think she was occupied in the house, and she went off to Edmonton to kill him. Whether there's truth in it or not . . ."

"Did she say why she killed him, though?"

"I don't recall if she told me, I doubt if she told me, and if she told me, she probably told me a lie anyway."

"Was it a threat?"

"I think there was that aspect there. Like, *Don't cross me or that's what will happen to you.* Lloyd's sister, from Dawson Creek, told me that they knew that Mary had killed him, but there was nothing they could do about it."

"But how could they know? They weren't there."

"Well, no, you have a point there. Maybe something that Lew had said. I have no idea. But they figured that Mary Lloyd had killed him."

"Lots of people have feelings that turn out to be incorrect," I pointed out.

"True, true, true," he admitted. "So, I don't know. That was the story she told me."

"Wow." I was flabbergasted. "But if she told you that, and you believed it at the time, did you not want to turn her in?"

"It would do no good."

I was mystified. "She was a dangerous person . . ."

"What would you turn her in for? What evidence did they have against her? This is long after whatever happened to Lew was buried. If I went to the police and said to them, *Look, Mary Lloyd told me that she . . .* This is not evidence. This is only hearsay. It doesn't hold up anywhere."

"Because she would have denied that she said this to you."

"Of course. I couldn't have proven it. I didn't see anything. And how do I know that she's telling the truth? You see? It evaporates."

"You felt there was no point."

"The relationship was deteriorating rapidly at that time anyway."

"Mary Lloyd told Phillip she was robbing banks to fund the revolution. Did she talk to you about other banks she had robbed?"

The recording makes it sound as though Harvey is laughing and muttering through this, finding it ridiculous, but he could just be breathing strangely or coughing.

I repeated the question.

"People were robbing banks to fund the revolution," he repeated, "but she was no communist. She was no socialist. She had no ulterior motives for doing this except gain."

(When I asked Lorraine why Del robbed banks, she replied, "Money. I don't think it's too difficult to figure out.")

Harvey had said in his memoirs that Del claimed she was innocent. "What kind of innocent?" I asked. "Was she or wasn't she driving the getaway car?"

"I can't say. It was bits and pieces and I can't fit it together. It was too long ago. And then at some point, she admitted that she had robbed this bank. I know the building that was robbed, it was no longer a bank then, and . . . Well, you probably want to find something more interesting to talk about."

What did he think I was writing about? "No, actually, that's a big part of what I want to talk about," I told him. "You asked where I started with this book. Well, it started with Phillip's version. And you say that Phillip learned from Del how to con."

"No, he furthered his education. He was a con man before."

"So you don't think he was conned by Del?"

"A con man can be conned."

"And you think he eventually figured it out, and that's how he learned?"

"No. You see, he would watch her conning somebody else, and that's how he would learn, not realizing that he himself was being conned."

"Do you think it's possible Del believed her lies as she was telling them?"

"I can't answer your question," he said, but then he described what he termed "the inner workings of the paranoid mind" with reference to a kind of gaslighting I know from others. "They will be arguing one point of view. And when you come up with irrefutable proof that this is a lie, they are over here, not even talking about that. They will not even mention that again," but instead make other unrelated assertions about the same subject, including mistaken ones.

Is that what it would have been like to talk to Del? My ideas on each player in this drama owed at least as much to others' accounts as they did to direct interactions, as though I was drawing them based on their reflections in multiple mirrors. This story would eventually land me in just the situation Harvey described, though obviously not with Del.

As I thought through this, he moved on to talk about some paranoid neighbours, a convoluted history I couldn't follow.

"Getting back to Mary Lloyd," he said, now that my head was spinning. "She died? Did she get shot?"

That evening, my second to last, Vivia suggested dinner in Granada, a historic seaside town. Earlier that day, Harvey had asked her if she would be okay with my quoting his written recollections. She consented but asked me to ask her before I quoted anything. I agreed, and additionally asked about taking Harvey's papers with me, as he had offered. She said she was okay with that. And when I was done?

"I want them," she said.

"Of course you do!" I responded.

I was amused by the dynamic between her and Harvey. Sometimes, when he said something interesting or impressive, I would look at Vivia and she would raise her eyebrows as if to affirm my reaction. But when he spoke directly to her, she didn't make eye contact, remaining almost affectless, responding in single syllables. At first, I thought she was sullen, but I came to see her rather as someone who only speaks when she needs to and only says what she means. Harvey would twinkle at her, fond and teasing, trying to draw her out.

On the way to Granada, we stopped to get the car washed. As we sat and waited on the gas-station benches, Harvey said, "Vivia," in a tone I'd heard him use earlier, his signal that he wanted her to pay attention. "Vivia," he said, "I need to talk to you about something and now seems as good a time as any. As you know I have four sons, three from my first marriage and one from my second. I'm estranged from all of them, each for a different reason."

Vivia remained stone-faced as he went on.

"And this young lady," he indicated me, "somehow made the acquaintance of my youngest son from my first marriage, and so learned some pretty romantic stories about me. Now she's here to do research and is learning some more romantic stories about me and she's going to put it all together and try to find some kind of truth."

So, for all my vagueness, Harvey understood exactly what I was doing. I don't know if I could have described my own project any better.

My final day, we took some last looks through slides and documents as Vivia slept in. Harvey seemed contented to have passed on the story of his own evolution. "It's an ill wind that blows no good," he conceded, speaking of Del. "Had I not been talked into going to Cuba, my life would probably be a lot different. Probably a lot lesser. It was a hard way to learn, but Cuba really woke me up."

When Vivia awoke, we had a day out. She drove us to a favourite beach, where we paused at the entrance to choose a big red fish for lunch. We parked on a pad behind a palm-thatched shelter that gave onto the ocean, with a table set akilter in the sand and a hammock hooked into rough beams.

Harvey waited while Vivia and I frolicked in the waves. We took turns lying in the hammock and chatting. The fish was delivered, grilled and staring, with a cucumber-tomato salad, rice and juice. I took a picture of Harvey and Vivia smiling, the great fish between them on a platter atop a floral tablecloth.

Harvey and I had a postprandial stroll while Vivia took a last swim. He cautioned me again about Phillip and how I was being deceived, and I assured him I would proceed carefully.

When I got home and told Geoff about Harvey's accusations, he scoffed. "Phillip is not a con artist." Yes, it sounded outrageous, but it wasn't as though my social circles and Phillip's overlapped in any way that permitted me independently to confirm or deny Harvey's accusations. On what basis was Geoff so sure? He'd barely spent any time with Phillip. When I asked, he said he trusted my feelings, so that was hardly an independent corroboration.

But what had Harvey thought Phillip was conning me out of? My affection and regard? I'd given those pretty freely.

When I had challenged Harvey on this, during our stroll at the beach, he said something to the effect of *Some people con just to be conning; Mary Lloyd would lie just to lie.* It was her nature, he suggested, like she was the scorpion from the famous parable.

A journalist—according to my limited understanding—would be obliged to query Phillip on what Harvey said. It was not only a matter of good faith: I myself, in Phillip's position, would want to have the chance to respond to such accusations.

I phoned Phillip as soon as I could. Anxiety squirmed in my belly as I dialed, but then stilled with the first note of his voice: not only did its very timbre calm me, it made it lightning-clear that my distrust was unwarranted. Dear old friend, lovely old friend. I was flooded with relief, the sense of rushing back to his side, back onto his side.

I talked him through much of what Harvey had said. In some cases, he agreed that Harvey's version made sense. In other cases, he quibbled with details. I mentioned Harvey was having difficulty with his hearing aid. Phillip wanted to get him a better one.

I thought I heard a little tightness lingering in his voice. He asked if I had taken pictures of Harvey and asked me to send them.

When we hung up, I sent a couple: Harvey with his dog in the garden. Harvey sitting in his room, cane between his knees, frowning. (At one point, Harvey had shown me his five Nicaraguan passports; he aged through them in time-lapse, but his frown was as unchanging as though carved.) His beard and hair are long and white—a grumpy Old Testament prophet in a blue golf shirt and those square plastic seventies glasses that are maybe hip again.

Five minutes later, Phillip emailed back: *seeing those, thats why I dont want to see that fn prick again*

The note was ambiguous to me, its syntax and timing. I would try to give a close reading here of what I understood from it and what I didn't, except I honestly didn't think about it for very long. My second book had just come out and I was swamped, running around: kids, teaching, imminent travel. I would be going to the west coast on my book tour and Phillip had set up a reading for me at his favourite Victoria bookstore. Soon enough, he and I would be together again.

When I arrived at Phillip's home in Victoria, right away he asked, "How were things in Nicaragua?" The abruptness reminded me of Harvey, as so many things about him now did. Among Harvey's children, Phillip had turned out the most like him: a reader, thinker, observer.

Although I'd recounted most of it to him already, we started talking through it again.

"That photo brought back a lot of pain for you," I said, somewhat cautiously.

Yes. He told me that when he had confronted Harvey's face, he'd had a realization. "I thought, *I don't give a sweet flying fuck what you think.* He was a miserable prick back then, and he's a miserable prick now. When I'm that age, I don't want to be a miserable-looking prick like that. I want to have a smile on my face, kindness in my eyes, something good to give. Does he still breathe that way, make that sound when he breathes?"

I affirmed that he did and was glad to know someone else thought it was strange. When I'd asked Vivia about it—Was it a condition from his mining accident?—she looked at me like she didn't know what I was talking about.

"Oh, it used to terrify me," Phillip said. "You'd hear him coming, hear him at night, that breathing."

We talked about Vivia, how she cared for Harvey, how she said she'd never seen him behave the way Phillip described, no rage, no beatings.

"Could you put the difference down to the thirty-year gap?"

I asked. Harvey was a lot older when he married Vivia's mother—maybe his temper had faded with testosterone loss.

Phillip thought it might also be attributed to Vivia's being a girl. "You get a little girl, she's going to tug at your heartstrings. With boys, with that farmer mindset, he would have been different: *beat the crap out of them and keep 'em in line.*"

He also still wondered about his memory gap from age three to six. He was willing to entertain my theory that it was because Harvey left, but unwilling to renounce the possibility that there was something more sinister—an act, not an absence—that he had blocked out.

There were incidents on which he accepted Harvey's version over Del's. He no longer believed they left Cuba because of Harvey's racism, for example. But he disputed other facets of Harvey's narrative, such as the custody question. As for Harvey thinking he and Del were lovers, he found it "kind of comical," but also understandable: "She and I were joined. We clicked right away, from the minute she moved in, more so than a normal stepchild would have done with a parent. So I can see where he would have construed that."

I worked my way up to Harvey's accusations that Phillip was a con man, intent on deceiving me. Why would he think that? Phillip couldn't really come up with an explanation.

When I probed a little more, though, he burst out, angrily, "Harvey was abusive to me, and now it's as though he is expecting an apology."

Yes, exactly—this was why, in Nicaragua, I had offered Phillip's appreciation to Harvey but hadn't been able to bring myself to say, as Phillip has asked me to, that he wanted to *let bygones be bygones*. Phillip was offering forgiveness, but neither of them wanted to be forgiven. If anything, Phillip wanted to forgive. I couldn't yet tell what Harvey wanted.

Phillip made reference to a short essay I had recently published that mentioned an *extraordinarily beautiful young man* who had ridden past me slowly on a horse in Nicaragua, staring into my eyes as I rode the other way in Harvey's truck: *Yet another person I will never*

ever know anything else about, I'd thought, though I'd written about it in the third person:

The writer had thought the same thing before, but rarely recalled the thought after, and so forgot the people who inspired it. And even now, writing it, she thinks how differently you, the reader, will imagine "extraordinarily" and "beautiful" and "young." Imagining what you might imagine, she pictures a very different young man on the horse from the one she recalled, so that now she has two images of young men on horseback, and indeed several young men passed her that afternoon in Nicaragua, so maybe she's recalling one of the others or maybe she's making them both up.

Phillip led, predictably, with a lusty comment about young men on horses. But he connected with my search for meaning in misunderstanding. "With your power of words," he said, "it all sort of flows out. Like even this conversation could be part of the book."

All right, I thought again, *he gets it.*

But our conversation moved quickly forward.

"Harvey doesn't seem to have the gist of life," he said. "You're supposed to enjoy life."

I confessed my fear that Phillip would expect me, as his friend, to take his side in all things. "I think I need to try to stay impartial, for the sake of the book, but also I'm interested in both of your perspectives. I think both of you are giving me your best truths."

Phillip responded to the effect that the book seemed to be composed of various truths.

"Exactly," I said, "but many friends would feel betrayed by that. So I'm trying to make sure everyone knows what I know, so no one feels betrayed."

"Yeah," he said, his eyes hooded. "I don't want to come out of the whole thing feeling bruised."

"That's legitimate," I said. "I've had concerns all the way through. I don't want to drop the project now; I'm too deep into it. But you could opt not to know things anymore."

"Did Harvey enjoy your visit?" he asked, again a little abrupt.

"Was it good for him?"

"Yes, I think so," I answered cautiously, saying we'd had nice conversations, about literature, about history. Harvey had clearly welcomed the chance to talk about himself, his inventions and convictions.

"Good," Phillip said with a reflective air, and his efforts to be *good*, to *do* good, seemed to me in that moment almost holy. I'm not going to say a sunbeam struck him there in his kitchen, the thick hands cradling the porcelain cup, the lines in his face making him appear wise and vulnerable, but, in such moments, I thought I saw the whole of him, from the long past to now, the great effort he'd made.

"That's what I was saying," he continued. "There's no good reason for Harvey to be made to confront anything now in a way that's painful."

I wasn't convinced of this, but I appreciated him for thinking it.

I was trying to navigate the brackish waters between treating Phillip as a friend and treating him as a subject, but I was not being fully honest, with him or with myself: the fact was, I favoured Phillip. I believed him more than I believed Harvey. I should have told him that. I underestimated what he needed, what any of us need: affirmation, ongoing declarations of love.

Instead, I said I'd continue to advocate for him with his father, if he wanted, and to mediate in some fashion, according to his wishes. He didn't really respond. He still wanted to send Harvey a new hearing aid.

In the six weeks since I'd seen Harvey, he had continued writing to me, sometimes three letters a day, mostly about himself, but also still insisting that I was being fooled by Phillip.

Now I wrote him back: *I have tried to see myself as naive and potentially deceived by him, but I am having a very hard time finding anything Phillip has told me that doesn't hold water. He has told me so many stories so consistently for so many years; anything that I could corroborate has turned out to be true; and he has never tried to take any kind of advantage, financial or otherwise, in all the many years I have known him. He has only ever been sweet and giving. Are you sure we're speaking of the same person?*

Harvey started to come around. *I can but say that possibly I am misjudging Philip after all these years,* he wrote. *My bad reports re his actions all precede your experience so I have to concede the possibility of change.*

I responded by once more describing Phillip's earnest and honourable nature, his generous actions, saying I could see no evidence of deviousness, rather the opposite.

Harvey finally capitulated. *So you are a very convincing lady. It is possible that my informants were not as observant as I assumed. Perhaps they saw what they had assumed was there. I put a lot of thought into it this morning on awakening and decided that you can tell Philip that he can communicate with me but his justifications will have to be very very convincing.*

I responded that Phillip had no justifications beyond wanting reconciliation, but it seemed the time had come to let Phillip speak for himself.

I told Phillip what Harvey had said, asked if he wanted to see Harvey's emails or wanted my help with writing to him.

Ever since Phillip first started emailing me, his notes had been cryptic, though I see, looking back now, that there were lots of them. Mostly small exclamations, messages of affection, and jokes, unevenly cobbled with phonetic spelling and random punctuation. My offer to help Phillip write to Harvey was motivated in part by concern that his writing wasn't up to the task. Also, I was in the middle of their relationship, whether I liked it or not, and wanted them to have any help I could give.

About a week after I returned from Victoria, I called him.

"Hi," I said, when he picked up. "How are you?"

For the first time ever, he said, "Not good." I thought I had misheard. He was so relentlessly positive.

I said, "What's wrong?"

"This has opened up one motherfucking can of worms. When you said that about Harvey, it just wrecked me. I never want to see that motherfucking, cocksucking prick again. I thought I made that clear that first day we talked."

I was staggered. He hadn't made that clear. Or had I not wanted to hear it? I said it was up to him how or whether he wanted to proceed with making contact with Harvey; I only said I would broker it if he did.

"I'm sixty years old. I told you it took me a long time to put all that away. It took me a long time. I don't need this shit in my life."

I apologized profusely for having misunderstood but pointed out (hesitantly, because I didn't even want to say Harvey's name) that a few months ago, he had been ready to come to Nicaragua with me.

"When all this started," he said, "Harvey wasn't even in the picture."

"It's true," I said. The sound of his voice, it's painful to describe: taut, torn. He'd put things away and sat on the lid, but they'd gotten out now and were ravaging him.

I asked if there was anything I could do.

No, he said. It would take time, that was all. "G'night, darlin'," he said, but he sounded hard, not affectionate.

I could wait. It wasn't surprising that he needed time.

That week, I had a big professional commitment—the scarily prolific and, simply, scary writer Joyce Carol Oates would be a guest of our creative writing program; I was hip-deep in her novels, preparing to do a Q&A.

Phillip and his story migrated to the rim of my concerns. Beyond the dim halo of my perceptions, though, the story, and perhaps Phillip himself, had begun to fracture and fray.

A few nights later, I was leaving the hot, crowded hall where

Joyce Carol Oates had read—a successful event. Geoff was beside me; the evening air cooled my face. I opened my emails as we walked, checking what I'd missed. A long day.

There was an empty email from Phillip, consisting only of a subject line:

I will have nothing further to do with your book or you you are not to contact me under any circumstances.

A TRAIL OF ROSES

ALMOST EVERY ROOM OF my house contains treasure sent by Phillip. In the bedroom, three rustic bottles, in three sizes, three earthen hues, stand atop the piano. Behind them, hanging on the wall, an old wooden washboard with glass ridges.

In the living-room alcove hangs a whimsical piece of folk art: a paper dress on a homemade wire hanger. Its neck and hem are decorated with red and blue stripes like an airmail envelope; the bodice reads PAR AVION/VIA AIRMAIL; the skirt is franked *Paris France Poste 1937* and addressed in a fancy hand to *Eiffel Tower, Champ de Mars*. It was a gift to our daughter; that year, Phillip gave our son a vintage set of whittling knives. Beside the alcove, on an erstwhile terrarium stand currently bearing our *Oxford English Dictionary*, leans a rough-hewn saw: one side of its blade is painted with a Canadian lake view in oils, the other with a train cutting through a prairie foreground, the Rocky Mountains traversing the blue distance beyond.

My study is painted chartreuse, a fact I'm pretty sure Phillip didn't know when he sent me the chartreuse-and-gold tea set—curved and curlicued as if bodied forth by John Tenniel—that now sits chartreusely on my shelf. A fanciful oilcan that would have done the Tin Man proud rests on a curved corner shelf. On my desk, a postcard of a Remington typewriter, cut to the shape of the machine: *I trust this card finds you and the family well,* its handwritten message reads. *Tis a change to recieve a post. When you gase at this on a shelf remember we're thinking of you.*

It was one of his mannerisms to refer to himself in the plural but only now do I see that he crossed out *I'm* and wrote *we're* instead. Was it merely a comical verbal tic, as I'd always thought, or some indication of his spiritual practice, the idea that he was never alone? What else had I missed? The gifts tickled me but were also a little embarrassing: I was ever anxious to reciprocate but I'm not good at material objects. The only thing I've ever confidently selected for someone else is a book.

Also, Phillip's gifts occasionally felt as random as they seemed thoughtful. Who was he thinking of when he sent me a ponderously realistic Edith Lansdowne sculpture of a spruce grouse? I went into the bedroom to examine it just now, its head cocked quizzically at me as though we don't get each other.

In our kitchen are several more practical items. Not only a carved laundry beater that rolls around idly on its curved end, but a wooden mortar and pestle and a paddle-shaped cutting board. I reserve that board for onions and garlic, using it daily and thinking of him every time I do.

The week he quit me, I sent him a package of gifts. Perhaps a cutting board? He collects them and I have bought several from an artisanal board maker who vends at our farmers' market.

At some point, I sent him some vintage linen napkins: whenever I stayed with him, a French pastry-maker friend of his would cater. A beribboned stack of boxes, each containing a rich delicious meal, would sit on Phillip's counter when I arrived. He would have set the table with fine china, selected a cutting board on which to arrange between us the quiches, brioche, vegetarian sausage rolls. But he didn't have cloth napkins and I'd teased him that paper towels spoiled the effect.

At some point, I sent him a mug from our co-op; I sent him a couple of printed tea towels from an Ozarks maker. I'm pretty sure

I got him another mug in Brazil. He collects bookshop tee-shirts, and I sent him one from our town's legendary used bookseller, Dickson Street Bookshop, whose jumbled shelves spread arterially within a half-city-block of low sprawl.

I don't know what I enclosed that spring of 2014. I only remember that, on returning from my book tour, I'd bought a few things to send as a thanks for hosting me and organizing my reading, but—busy week—hadn't gotten around to sending them yet before his email arrived.

Now, I put them in the mail with a thank-you card and responded to Phillip's email. My subject line: *I love you. I'm dropping the book.*

I kept my email brief and apologetic: *I don't want or need to write this book, if it will cause you such anguish. I'm really sorry for being so slow on the uptake about your change of heart.*

I was doing as I'd been advised. It didn't feel like a choice, though it was a close call.

"It's the trauma speaking," said my publisher, when I called to tell her what had happened. She'd been my sounding board and confidante throughout the years I'd been thinking about this book. "You need to drop it. You will feel shitty, there's no way around that." She sympathized—I'd invested so much in the project—but she said I wouldn't be able to write it. "Any writing you do would be so surrounded by caveats and worries that you'd never free yourself into it." She was speaking both as a former journalist and as a long-time editor. "All this may or may not become grist for something else in future, possibly something fictional. But, for now, you just have to set it aside and wait."

I knew she was right, though I wished she weren't: I wanted to be Janet Malcolm, Joan Didion, clear, ruthless. But, apparently, I'm not.

That weekend, Geoff and I had spontaneous drinks with our neighbours: dear friends, former New Yorkers, finance people with finely tuned personal and cultural sensibilities.

"It's *your* book," Canem informed me as though this was all I needed to know.

Michael, her husband, ventured to say Phillip was being manipulative, even if he might not be aware of it.

"I don't know." I shrugged. I wanted the impossible: to feel secure in my decision. "Maybe I shouldn't be writing about someone who's so isolated and vulnerable."

"What about all the other Phillips out there who might be benefited by this story?" Michael asked. "I can't imagine there are many, but . . ."

Canem broke in. "What if he has other long-term relationships? People like you he's not telling you about?"

Geoff frowned and shook his head.

"I worry that I was just pursuing it out of ego," I said, flattered by their faith in me, their eagerness for the book, even if it was just because they were my friends.

"Maybe you're quitting because it supports your egotistical image of yourself as a good person," said Michael. He sipped his beer like he was toasting his own rhetoric, but his look for me was kind.

"It's your book," Canem repeated. "You need to protect your craft. I don't know Phillip, and I have no allegiance to him. I have to stand up for my friend Padma's book."

It was the same fierce partisanship I had failed to offer Phillip, the unbridled enthusiasm Geoff had failed to offer me, all valuable but not actionable. I filed it away.

My family had reacted variously, my mother outraged, my father wounded on my behalf, but they all wanted me to drop the book. Geoff was more sympathetic to Phillip than most of the other people in my life, but he also couldn't see how the project was worth the distress, especially now that I was getting it from another source as well.

Phillip had broken with me about a month after I returned from Nicaragua. Until that point, my correspondence with Harvey had been cordial, even warm: full of chat on books and politics and that spring's earthquake (he, Vivia, Titan and the kinkajous were all fine), good wishes, good faith, mutual admiration.

Harvey had, because of my insistence on Phillip's good nature, softened toward his son, even speculating on his own failings as a parent, though he rapidly backtracked: *Did I expect too much of them too soon? Did I lack the necessary patience to allow them to bloom? I came to the decision many years ago that to waste time and energy fretting about it would serve nothing because their characters are already solidified.*

As soon as I started to challenge his version of any story about Phillip, though, he lashed out, insisting that Phillip was lying about everything, all the time.

Example: Phillip's threat to shoot him. Phillip had said that he had been pushed to the brink by Harvey's cutting off the power and water when Phillip and Del were living in a trailer on Strawberry Mountain. He'd grabbed a gun and started out toward Harvey, before cooling off and giving up.

Harvey disputed all this, with some decent counter-arguments: Phillip said the police confiscated the gun, for example, but Harvey asked whether *as a parolee, wouldn't Del have been sent to jail for firearms possession*? The main thing Harvey kept insisting, though, was that he was living too far away for Phillip to walk.

"But Phillip never said he arrived," I repeated. "He was a hotheaded sixteen-year-old. He quit after half an hour, sat down by the side of the road, and then went home."

Somehow, though, Harvey couldn't hear this and hammered on it more than half a dozen times over the next two years: *It's too far. She couldn't have had a gun.* Unless I would accept Phillip's version as false, Harvey thought we had nothing to say to each other. And yet he continued to write. As did I.

Some of his objections were more objective, if objectively wrong. He asked me why I kept spelling "Philip's" name with two l's, that "Phillips" was a surname, not a given name. When I said this was how Phillip spelled it, he said it was a lie typical of this sort of person and that he would be proven right by Phillip's birth certificate. He didn't respond when I said I had seen letters from Lucille spelling it as Phillip did. (I'd considered asking Phillip if I could see his birth certificate when I visited him, but it seemed a bridge too far.)

It felt like a glimpse of what Harvey himself had termed *the inner workings of the paranoid mind. They will be arguing one point of view. And when you come up with irrefutable proof that this is a lie, they are over here, not even talking about that. They will not even mention that again.*

He would repeat angrily that he wasn't lying, even though, as I reminded him, I never said he deliberately lied, just that he was mistaken.

He insisted that Del had only one daughter. Instead of citing Phillip, or Simma Holt, or Del's own letters—all sources Harvey would discredit—I said that that the newspaper reports on the robbery always mentioned two daughters. He wrote back, *I have found you rely on periodicals almost as a source of incontestable truth whereas I have found them to be exactly the opposite.*

He recounted a time a Vancouver journalist came to Nicaragua on a reporting trip and wrote a story where she made things up. *See?* Newspapers are unreliable.

He went on to surmise that Phillip had directed me to the "periodicals" I referred to. By contrast, he cited his own reliability as the reason I should believe him: *Without your acceptance of Philips carbon copy of Mary Lloyds approach to life/truth/whatever it is very difficult to put my words into a context that you can/will appreciate.*

I lost my temper. *Since you condescend to instruct me on basic points of media literacy,* I wrote, *allow me to condescend to instruct you on a basic point of logic: this is called a tautology.* Phillip had withdrawn and I was feeling reckless. Harvey had cost me this project; I had nothing else to lose.

A barrage of emails ensued. I pictured him as Yosemite Sam, jumping up and down and screaming, whiskers standing out horizontally: *I would like to point out to you,* he spat, *that as of this moment, you, unlike myself, have never seen a con artist, so you may get the idea once again that I am lecturing you.*

What did he know of my life? Nothing. And he occasionally simply seemed confused. I had started to wonder whether his cognitive function was impaired. He said he'd had strokes. Maybe I was causing him one right now.

He never produced those other sources he'd alluded to when we met. Ultimately, there was only one such informant he directed me to, and a follow-up interview was unnecessary: *One of the persons who told me as much about Philip of the last 40 years without realizing they were doing so is yourself,* he wrote—to me. *In your account of Philips stories I did not even need to close my eyes to hear Mary Lloyd speaking.*

I don't think I need to describe my reaction.

The angrier he got, the more ungainly his prose. His ugly, misshapen phrases, *like sledgehammer strokes*, sometimes physically nauseated me. And yet: I'd told Phillip I was quitting but didn't tell Harvey that. Why?

I had dropped the book. And I was still working on it.

It was a different kind of bifurcation. For the literary writer, all of life is material. I never know what observation, event, physical sensation might come in useful. I record it all.

So, I made notes on everything my friends and family told me. I kept writing to Harvey. I kept thinking about it all, turning it over, *saving it up*. It was my habit.

The only boring passage I have ever encountered in a Hans Christian Andersen tale comes in the middle of "The Snow Queen," right after Gerda awakes from her trance in the garden. In a panic, uncertain of how long she's been out, she starts asking the flowers if any of them knows anything about Kai.

The lily responds with a story of a Hindu woman committing sati: random. The morning glory tells a story of a young girl leaning over a high balcony and pining for someone. Is it referring to Kai?

Each flower tells a story that sounds allegorical, but that, when Gerda tries to parse it for guidance, turns out to have nothing to do with her or Kai. "I'm only telling you my story, my dream," they respond blithely, one after another, as my eyes start to cross, recalling what Kai said to Gerda earlier about a snowflake's icy, engineered perfection: *"Much more interesting than real flowers."* Apparently, it doesn't take much.

As Gerda heads out, the narcissus trips her, exclaiming, *"I can see myself! I can see myself!"* It tells a story of a little dancer, standing first on one leg, then on two. *"She's just an illusion. She pours water from the teapot onto a piece of cloth. Cleanliness is good! The white dress hangs on a hook. She puts it on. I can see myself!"*

Gerda, the very soul of forbearance, loses her shit: *I don't care to see or hear about you! What kind of a silly story is that?*

Harvey had seemed, briefly, lucid on my project. Now he was increasingly infuriated that I was discussing his ex-wife and ex-kid instead of his innovations in mace drying or the reprocessing of industrial by-products into cattle feed, and he was equally enraged by my refusals to swallow his bizarre contortions wholesale.

I reasoned with him on the first point, saying I had no need to grill him on his agricultural expertise. That was not in dispute, whereas his characterizations of his family members were.

When I told him that Phillip would not be contacting him after all, he said his son had *fallen into his appropriate slot quite awhile ago*, so he had been expecting what he had received. *It is yourself that should look more closely*, he wrote. *The "nitty gritty of the problem" is that I recognize that Philip/Phillip has matured into an adult phase of what showed early on. You, like so many were with Mary Lloyd before the truth could no longer be ignored, are convinced that his tales are true. Fine. That is your fall about to happen at some future date.*

He started saying he was reconsidering his decision to participate in my project. *Your story will be far more colourful if it includes his fantasies but I do not have any wish to be involved and decided awhile ago it's time to pull my prick out of this party.* This choice expression, he told me, was one of Del's favourites.

And yet he continued to write to me, emails with attachments of six, twelve, eighteen pages, saying Del was a liar and manipulator and that Phillip was, too.

"He's a crazy old man," Geoff pleaded, refusing to read a letter I had written back. "You're not going to convince him."

It's one of my biggest faults, as my husband and my mother will attest: I find it very hard to drop an argument.

But my own fury, too, came from a deeper place than reason. Poking holes in his logic was almost too easy. My ire was raised because I was doing battle on behalf of his child. Harvey called himself a defender of the downtrodden, but, as with many progressives, he didn't like any suggestion that, in some situations, he was the downtreader.

One of my most provocative salvos was suggesting to Harvey that Phillip had learned deceptiveness not from Del but from Harvey himself.

Harvey had offered instances of minor childhood crimes as evidence of Phillip's fundamentally deceptive nature—stealing Rob's newspaper money, padding the bottom of his berry baskets to make it appear he had picked more than he had—but stealing was a salient facet of Harvey's own adult life. He was proud of it. In our interviews, he snickered as he told me how he stole diesel oil from the railroad when his job was maintaining a tank of the stuff, how he helped other employees to help themselves. He stole meat from his meat-packing plant. He stole gold from his mine. All this was quite apart from the cattle rustling and bootlegging, for which his sons were requisitioned labour. Wasn't it possible,

I asked Harvey, that Phillip's childhood thefts were a version of following in his father's footsteps?

Predictably, Harvey took exception. *While I made alcohol, I never bootlegged nor did he "help" me.* He neatly justified the cattle rustling: *There was pound law at Peters Road but the neighbours did not respect it and their cattle damaged our gardens for most of the summer. So in the fall they paid their debts for pasturage*—his hands were clean.

Ditto the corporate theft. On stealing the gold out of the mine, Harvey fumed, *Philip, of course, was not even born at that time, so any thing he says is pure supposition.* (Not quite: Phillip recounted to me what he'd heard, as a child—Harvey made no secret of it—and everything he told me was accurate according to what Harvey himself put in his recollections.)

There were eleven miners killed in the eighteen months preceding my accident, he e-shouted, *and according to the mine, it was always the miners' own fault!!!!!!!*

I didn't judge Harvey negatively for high-grading. The mines' management, he said, had no clue how much quality gold they had—even the engineers sent down to instruct the miners couldn't recognize it—and they were using and discarding miners. They had it coming.

But it wasn't a stretch to think that a child of Harvey's—made to work all the time under threats of a beating, never a kind word for his efforts—might think of padding a berry basket as a way of sticking it to the man.

Assigning such defiance to Phillip, though, might just be wishful thinking on my part. Remember that, while he admitted to many of the minor childhood offences, Phillip had no recollection of ever feeling rebellious. Long after these exchanges with Harvey, I read D. W. Winnicott's essay "Stealing and Telling Lies," where I encountered a more heartbreaking possible explanation of petty thieving.

In an ordinary household, quite a lot of stealing goes on, Winnicott says, *only it is not called stealing. Little children quite regularly take pennies out of their mothers' handbags. Usually there is no problem here whatever. A child goes into the larder and takes a bun or two, or helps himself to a lump of sugar out of the cupboard. In a good home no one calls the child who does this a thief. It may be necessary for parents to make rules; life in a household to some extent consists in the working out of the relation between parents and the children in these and similar terms.*

But a child who, say, regularly goes and steals apples, and quickly gives them away without himself enjoying them, can be called a thief. He will not know why he has done what he has done and if pressed for a reason he will become a liar. The thing is, what is this boy doing? The thief is not looking for the object that he takes. He is looking for his own mother, only he does not know this, for the person from whom he has a right to steal; in fact, he seeks the person from whom he can take things, just as, as an infant and a little child of one or two years old, he took things from his mother simply because she was his mother, and because he had rights over her.

I can never read Winnicott as a writer or scholar, only ever as a mother; reading this, I recognize how our kids transgressed this way all the time, knowing, I suppose (I never thought about it before) that if they were caught, I'd either remind them of the limits and bring them in line, or find their naughtiness amusing. (In the latter instances, I moaned that they were weakening me with their *evil powers of cuteness*, and they erupted with devilish glee.)

What Phillip did or didn't do as a child is lost to time, and such blunt analytic instruments are a violation of the complicated web of his psyche. But Winnicott's wisdom filled me all over again with rage at Harvey (presumably *fucked up in his turn*), who failed his small son so badly, driving away his mother and condemning him—for life—when he acted out.

Note to self: it's *my* character flaw that Harvey's illogic so inflamed me. Especially since my challenges were only the proximate cause of his rage. His deeper anger was spurred by my turning the focus repeatedly to others when what he wanted was for me to write about him, his story, his thoughts on his world, his version of himself. He was infuriated that I was designing a snowflake instead of repeating his narcissistic prattle, *tiring of his self-serving story, and substituting a story of my own.*

But look again at that last phrase: *a story of my own.* Does this mean a story I would write, or the story I had lived?

When this whole thing started, said Phillip, *Harvey wasn't even in the picture.* But neither was I.

I knew that if ever I had the chance to write this, I would not have the ethical leisure to mask my own role. Truman Capote kept himself—dishonestly—out of *In Cold Blood's* frame while Walter Kirn put himself at the centre of *Blood Will Out.* This was the new true crime. From the first moment, I was an actor, a character. Phillip and Harvey had made it explicit that they wanted to be in the book. But had I consented? Were the things I'd said, thought, and lived on the record? Since when?

Gary Saul Morson, in the list of 163 Tolstoyan Conclusions that ends his study of *Anna Karenina,* says *each person is a natural egoist who sees the world as if it were a novel in which he or she were the hero or heroine. But morality begins when a person can see the world as if he or she were a minor character in someone else's novel.*

What is morality, though, when you're not only a minor character but the writer of that book?

Maybe my problems stemmed from amateurishness; maybe a veteran journalist, reading this story, would say that with proper training I never would have fallen into these psychological potholes. Or maybe the problem is some sort of mental or ethical flabbiness that goes beyond professional inexperience.

Many writers concur with Dorothy Gallagher, that *the writer's business is to find the shape in unruly life and to serve her story. Not, you may note, to serve her family, or to serve the truth, but to serve the story. This is an attitude that some have characterized as ruthless: that cold detachment, that remove, that allows writers to make a commodity of the lives of others. But a writer who cannot separate herself from her characters and see them within the full spectrum of their human qualities loses everything in a haze of nostalgia and sentimentality. Bathos would do no honor to my subjects nor, most important, bring them to literary life, which is the only way they could live in the world again.*

This doesn't answer the questions of why, whether or how they want to live in the world again or the writer's ethical helix: giving the subject's story new life in a form they don't recognize and even disavow. *Bathos would do no honor to my subjects*, says Gallagher, implying that our writing is meant to honour them, which I honestly wanted to do, though surely that is not our role, either.

Whenever Janet Malcolm got a letter from McGinniss's subject, she said, *I would put off reading it—the writing was unrelievedly windy—but when I finally read it something unexpected would happen. I would find myself shaken and moved. Nevertheless, once I began writing this chronicle, I lost my desire to correspond with him. He had (once again) become a character in a text, and his existence as a real person grew dim for me.*

My exchanges with Harvey would soon slacken. I didn't think I'd uncover many more facts on Del. And I was gambling that if I killed the book, I could still preserve my friendship with Phillip.

And yet.

I wanted to rub what I'd learned between moistened fingers, separating its tissue-thin pages.

When, that spring, a writer friend asked me if I knew what drove me toward this story, my blurted response was a reference to some family drama of my own, the details of which she knew, but which I won't disclose here. (No one, myself included, has consented to go on the record with that one.)

I wanted—as Nathalie Léger says in *Suite for Barbara Loden*, her book about a low-level actress who made a film about a low-level criminal, both used by the men in their lives—*to link my present with the history of certain emotions experienced by other people.*

I had quit the book, in all sincerity, and yet woke up every morning thinking about this story. I would go to my desk to write, but I had no other book under way, so I would make notes on this one.

In the parable of the scorpion and the frog, a scorpion needs to cross a river. She promises a frog that if it takes her across, she won't bite it, but, halfway across, she bites it anyway. *Now we'll both die,* cries the frog. *Why did you do that?*

I can't help it, the scorpion responds with her dying breath. *It's my nature.*

Writers gonna write.

In real life, we cannot be severed from our shadows. They are always right there with us, sometimes bigger and scarier, sometimes shrimpier or paler. Even in Hans Christian Andersen's story, in fact, the scholar grows a new shadow after his original one leaves, just by going out in the sun. And when the old, now-independent shadow comes back, the new shadow curls up like a poodle at its feet, watching keenly, silently, taking notes.

I was not only a character in this saga. In common with every other character, I was preoccupied with my own story: my distress, what I needed from this book.

It was as though the book had become a door, said Rebecca Solnit, meaning that people came through her book to meet her. But when I said to Phillip, *I'm dropping the book,* a trapdoor opened under me. I didn't need to look down. I hadn't seen the abyss beneath it for a long time, but I remembered it well enough.

When I was twenty, my brain shoved me over some unseen cliff into what felt, literally if subjectively, like a cavern. I knew, in a way, that the cavern existed only in my mind and yet it was so tangible that I had trouble believing it was my own creation. Some part of me was in the objective world, but I was perceiving it from a slight visual and auditory remove, through some transparent yet muffling membrane. The cavern was my new reality. Red streaks glowed hot up its high charcoal-grey walls. I crouched at the bottom. The opening, if there was one, was so far above me that I couldn't see it. There was obviously no point in trying to get out.

This is how I experience depression—not as a sadness but rather a burial. That first breakdown hit in the last month of my BA, my first year away from home. A dear friend, whose family tree was riven with bipolar disorder and who recognized my symptoms, sorted me out sufficiently that I could finish the year. I went home and recovered.

Before my crash, I'd been rampantly energetic. I loved to spread myself too thin—so many interests, so little time! I entered university at sixteen and switched my major every year, convinced with each switch that I had found my life's calling. On graduating, I took a job in research, the natural extension of my degree in sociology. In my free time, I studied French and worked on social justice initiatives. A year later, I went to India to give my time to a rural community, but I turned out to have no skills they could use, so I was forced to spend a summer in stillness: watching, waiting, listening. My neurology wasn't wired for the softer impulses. I imploded again.

I returned a wreck. Gradually, I re-immersed myself in my activities, building up a sense of purpose and identity, clawing my way up out of the cavern. A year after that, seemingly recovered and reconnected, I went abroad again, this time to Europe, and again was confronted with my essential impotence in the wider world. Once more, I tumbled over the cliff, like Psyche's mean sister, bumping and scratching until I hit the bottom. Each time, the depression lasted longer; each time, I was more self-destructive.

My poor distraught mother convinced me to see therapists: a blithe suburbanite who had me hang over a pommel horse and scream; a massage therapist who would search out points of extreme tension and work those until I screamed; a chilly Englishwoman in a huge wingback chair whose tone of voice and facial expression never varied, making me want to scream. (I'm not maligning all therapists—later in life, I found a great one. But a bad therapist is at best ridiculous and at worst parasitic.)

My mother, terrified of losing me to suicide but resistant to anti-depressants, searched out a psychiatrist who'd lost his licence for prescribing amino acids as depression treatment, an alternative that has now gained some currency. I went along indifferently with the program, and suspect it helped quite a bit with my neurochemistry, whose role I wasn't acknowledging.

I was convinced that I knew the source of my problems: my worthlessness. To my frustration, no one who knew me would affirm this. A big part of me thought I was the only one who really knew what was going on; a small part admitted I was clueless. Clearly, those two parts needed to talk, but how and where could they get together?

I began to keep a journal. One of the therapists may have suggested it, or it may have been a practice whose time in my life had finally arrived. I began by writing about how stupid and unaccomplished I was. Getting it down on paper gave it a cast of objectivity—it was in writing and so it had to be true on some level.

I further bolstered my case by writing about how focused and brilliant everyone else was. Seeing ink fill a blank page is its own pleasure, a quick and easy sense of accomplishment. Perhaps because this was what I needed, I continued.

I took notes on my housemates (I was by this time living in a co-operative full of outsize characters), co-workers, books, films, and strangers: fragments of overheard conversations; facial expressions meant for times when no one was looking.

As Patricia Hampl put it, *the self-absorption that seems to be the impetus and embarrassment of autobiography turns into (or perhaps always was) a hunger for the world.*

Getting these observations down on paper made it impossible to hold to my superficial notions. My jottings made me acutely aware of others' struggles, their imperfections, the ways they didn't know themselves. I was less and less able to elevate them merely to bolster my bad opinion of myself. I also found myself shaping my own narrative, choosing interesting ways to describe myself, if only to keep myself interested. The page gave me the distance to read myself as though I were a character.

Perhaps I found, in this distance, compassion.

In this time, I joined a theatre company as an apprentice. Per my modus, I wanted to do everything, so they let me direct, act, do community outreach, and join the novice playwrights' circle. My one-act comedy, *House of Sacred Cows*, was set in an exaggerated version of the co-operative house where I'd lived. I drafted it in a single sitting and felt something I'd never felt before—a defining, comprehensive emotion; a stillness that announced itself momentously, like the angels in *Angels in America.*

É arrivato! My métier.

We tell ourselves stories in order to live, but some of us take that more literally than others. I understood then that writing was a lifeline I'd dropped down to the bottom of the cavern and used to pull myself up. If my depression's main symptom was the belief that my life was without meaning or purpose, writing gave it both, a receptacle for everything I saw or felt. Every joke, every insult, every injury given or received, every sublime interior moment had a label now: *material.*

Was I the scorpion, following my nature to my own destruction, or a spider, spinning my own lifeline?

The spider's tale is different. As Ovid tells us, Arachne wove a tapestry to rival the goddess Athena's. Athena's tableau depicted divine beings in their majesty, all chilly royal perfection, while Arachne's showed them disporting amorously, giggling and jiggling.

The goddess, enraged by her rival's insouciance (it's not clear whether she's more offended by Arachne's skill or her subject matter), destroys her work. Arachne tries to hang herself, but the goddess loosens her noose and changes her into a spider.

Arachne lives on and weaves: abstract, geometric works that show her technical prowess but omit all the rest of what she knows, *unthinkable things,* as the shadow calls the fruits of his spying, *what no person should know, but everyone would like to know.* And so we are the poorer.

I needed to write. I had quit this book and now my thoughts on it were drying up. I started scrabbling for other ideas. At a party in Montreal, I met Seagram heiress Phyllis Lambert. Fascinating: Could I write a novel inspired by her? On a drive from Calgary to Banff, I heard a CBC radio report on human-Neanderthal mating. Fascinating: Could I write a novel inspired by them? None of the ideas stuck.

I was swinging above the abyss, starting to panic. Then, at the end of May, I received a terrible shock. At a party near his home in Minnesota, my cousin Koushik had had a heart attack in a swimming pool and was in a coma. He was the son of my father's brother, which made him, in our community's parlance, my brother.

Out of twenty first cousins on that side, three of us became professors. I was the youngest of the three. All three of us had been beset by demons of self-destruction. The eldest, Raju, had drowned under dubious circumstances and now Koushik had done the same.

Sontag says melancholy was once thought of *as the artist's disease.*

Raju was an economist and poet, twenty years my senior, interesting but distant. Koushik, less than two years older than me, was a brother of my heart. He grew up in India, but on summer visits when we were kids, he would tease me and pull pranks, just like a real brother. Our lives took parallel tracks on opposite sides of the earth, and, in our teens and twenties, we grew close on common grounds: books, ideas, ambitions of travel. A decade later: failed first marriages. His was far more tragic, a bitter split, a daughter he hardly ever got to see, a devastation that healed and reopened, healed and reopened. He accumulated debts, health problems, a tenure denial, maybe a drinking habit?

W. G. Sebald, in *The Rings of Saturn*, a book motivated by his own nervous prostration, describes a fellow professor at Norwich who works surrounded by floods, mountains, drifts of her papers, so that she is *reduced to working from an easy chair drawn more or less into the middle of her room where, if one passed her door, which was always ajar, she could be seen bent almost double scribbling on a pad on her knees or sometimes just lost in thought, like the angel in* Dürer's Melancholia, *steadfast among the instruments of destruction.*

Destruction? Hardly. Dürer's personification of melancholy, according to Wikipedia's quite elegant entry, *stares past an area*

strewn with symbols and tools associated with craft and carpentry, including an hourglass, weighing scales, a hand plane, a claw hammer and a saw.

That Nathalie Léger quote I mentioned earlier? It comes up when she finds herself alone in a Connecticut motel: *I was reminded that only in unfamiliar bedrooms do we perceive with such clarity the true nature of our existence. What had I come here for? All I wanted to do was to collect some images; I was looking for something tangible to express uncertainty. I wanted to link my present with the history of certain emotions experienced by other people. With nothing better to do, I emptied out the contents of my incredibly cluttered toilet bag and started to arrange the tubes, jars, and pencils, laying them out one by one, unsure as to whether I should organize everything by category, size, or. . . . So there I was. I looked at myself in the mirror, like Dürer's angel of melancholia dubiously contemplating the tools of her paltry knowledge, or like the woman in the Hopper painting, sitting alone on the bed in a hotel room, bent over a book in her lap, leaning over the abyss.*

Tools of paltry knowledge vs. craft and carpentry vs. instruments of destruction. *Melancholia,* said Joseph Leo Koerner, *is an occasion for thought . . . designed to generate multiple and contradictory readings. Interpreting the engraving itself becomes a detour to self-reflection.*

Here's what I see in Dürer's print: the angel of melancholy appears at first to be paused in writing—she holds what could be a pen; there's a book in her lap. She rests her chin in her hand, directing a sardonic look beyond the frame.

A closer look shows she's holding a compass: she might have wanted to write but, with the tool to hand, she can literally only go in circles. And the book in her lap, the one she is bent over, is closed.

To her right and above her, however, sits a cherub, absorbed and unconcerned as he scribbles in his own book. She is the angel of melancholy, but he is the angel of her.

What is the angel of the angel of melancholy? A writer.

Koushik had healed his life: he had a second marriage, to an insightful, accomplished, even-keeled woman; they had a wonderful son together; he secured a prestigious post at a premier American research university. He was becoming all he was meant to be, my brother. Reader, thinker, cook, father, joker, bon vivant. (I can still hear his voice.)

Now, May 2014, a heart attack in a pool. My father and I flew to Minneapolis. Koushik's sisters were beside themselves. They had lost their mother to a heart attack in their teens; their father had died just a few years prior.

Koushik lay in his hospital bed, not still and picturesque like in a movie coma, but restless and gleaming, eyelids twitching, right hand jumpy. What was he looking at? Did his hand want a pen?

That night, all night, amid the red and blue and blinking lights, I sat up in the room where he lay, talking and listening and writing. *I was reminded that only in unfamiliar bedrooms do we perceive with such clarity the true nature of our existence.*

Five days later, the doctors had a conference with all of us—there were a lot of people there by this point; Koushik had a talent for love and our family sticks together. There was no reason for optimism. His wife allowed them to remove the tubes.

In those same five days, I was taken over, inappropriately but ineluctably, by a new novel idea, about mixed-race twins, one raised in India by their birth mother, the other adopted into Canada. I scribbled notes between making soups, taking turns helping out with all our kids, meeting Koushik's erstwhile and current graduate students, colleagues, neighbours and friends—so many people who loved him, so many people he cooked for, joked to, taught, husbanded, fathered, brothered—and organizing for the memorial, which was raucous and maudlin, on the back porch of his dream house, in the heart of Saint Paul.

What good is intelligence, if you cannot discover a useful melancholy? Writing transformed my useless melancholy into a useful one.

I would never get Koushik back. And Phillip, my rogue angel, another brother from another mother—would he ever return to me?

That same week, Phillip wrote to me from beyond his billowing dead silence.

Phillip had sent another empty email but with a very different subject line: *alls good alls well am taking a bit of time*

On our way home from Koushik's memorial, my parents, husband, kids and I paused for three days in a cabin beside a lake. There was no Wi-Fi and cell service was poor. We could send texts or short emails from the porch, but mostly stayed offline.

Our second day there, my phone rang: Phillip. I was scared to take the call and stressed about it dropping if I did. I let it go to a message and listened to it when we got back to civilization a day or two later.

Phillip's voice was normal again, cautious, but warm. He wanted to talk. I called him back, opening my computer to take notes.

"Well, we should clear the air," he said, without preamble. "I don't think you should give up the book. You've put so much work in on it."

"I was just so angry at myself for not anticipating the return of your trauma." I started crying. "I've been so worried."

"You shouldn't worry for me that way." His voice was cedar bark and tender leaves, warmed in his hands, a balm.

"I want to know what set you off," I said, "but it's okay if you need time."

He enumerated the factors. He was offended that I could, even briefly, wonder if what Harvey said about him was true. "That threw me for a loop. You've known me for twenty years, so if you don't understand who I am, then I don't want anything to do with that. *Fuck it,*" he'd thought, *"I don't sell myself based on my words, you look at my deeds, and how I live, and if that's not enough, well."*

To my mind, I didn't really have his deeds, only his words: our friendship had very little context. I didn't say that; again, reason had nothing to do with the truth of this situation.

"And then there was the stuff with Harvey," he went on. "Like, when I read that first email from him to you, where he said he would be willing to meet and talk with you but that I'm not welcome, I thought, *he's scared*. He doesn't want to face me, because of the shit that went on before."

He consulted a psychic. She reinforced his suspicions.

"She said, *he's ashamed*. I said, *That's what I thought, but I don't like to be judgmental*."

Which was why he had asked me to tell Harvey, *No hard feelings, see you on the other side*.

"There's no way to overcome it on this side—too much prejudice and digging heels in."

It made sense—he was right—and I was chagrined again not to have been able to perceive either the futility of attempting reconciliation or his desire to desist. "Because having that pushed down my throat again, I thought, *no way. Not a chance, Jack*. I'm an old man, I'm not going to have that in my life."

In one swift stroke, he let me know why I'd misunderstood and would never fully understand: "Unless a person has gone through stuff along those lines"—abuse—"all the talking, all the reading, is not going to let you know what it's like. When negative stuff gets in, it takes a while to clear the air. So I needed time, to clean house, get myself in order, remind myself of how I want to live and be in the world. Which is also why I wanted to call you, not take too long. If you don't, things can harden, and then you can't go back, eh? It becomes permanent."

He suggested we meet.

That summer, by coincidence, my family and I were going to western Canada on a road trip and planned to spend a week on the island of Lasqueti, the very place Phillip had gone to get off heroin. One of my oldest friends had moved there years earlier and built a house, including a guest cabin, entirely out of driftwood—logs that got away from the logging industry. It was off the grid, restful. Phillip hadn't been back in the intervening years, had lost touch with the people who had befriended him there. He thought he might look them up.

Six weeks later, I stood on the ferry dock on Lasqueti. My family and I had arrived a few days earlier and spent the time cycling to the beach, exploring tide pools, cooking dinners that lasted through long evenings.

The ferry hove into view, neared. I made out Phillip's profile as he peered out over the water. Gladness swelled my heart a little and I moved forward. Stiffly upright in freshly washed jeans, a checked shirt, a blue jacket, clean-shaven, fresh haircut, mouth set in a downward arc. The sea's light glinted off his bifocals. Briefly, so still and absorbed in the horizon, unaware of being watched, he looked hyperreal, like an Evan Penny sculpture. I was certain I perceived the light that had always drawn me. Maybe it was too late for me to see him otherwise; maybe I'd always had the power to descry it, *because it was he, because it was I.*

Phillip had contacted his old friends, Kathy and Lawrence, who would host him. They were onshore waiting for him, too, but the small crowd contained a high proportion of earthy-looking folks with long grey hair, so I didn't know which they were until he alighted.

Lawrence, an escapee from the British titled classes, was taciturn; Kathy, who would have been a bonny Canadian lass back in the day, loquacious. The next day, we met up at the farmers' market. All three bubbled with delight at their unexpected reunion.

"We only knew him for this long." Kathy showed me an inch or so between thumb and finger. "And we've thought about him ever since, wondered where he was and what happened to him. So I said to Lawrence, *Let's put it out to the universe, to find out.* And here he is."

This was some west coast logic, but I got it.

"I wouldn't have known him," she went on. "I saw him coming across on the ferry, looking really uptight and conservative, and I thought, *Who's that guy?*" It'd been almost forty years, and Phillip didn't recognize them either, for what it was worth: he'd walked right past them on his way to hug me. "But then this morning, I saw him without his glasses and he was twinkling—twinkling!—and I said, *Oh, yes. You're Phillip.*"

They had seen it, too, Phillip's heart-light, and still did.

"We loved him. Some people." Kathy shook her head. "This morning, as we were having coffee, he took hold of my foot and said, *I'm going to do your feet.* Oh!" She looked heavenward with a euphoric expression, as though her feet were still tingling. "That's the kind of person he is."

They were perhaps five years older than Phillip, and had trusted him to babysit, even though they knew he'd come to the island get off junk. Their fellow islanders said they were crazy. "He was this flaming gay guy"—hippies were hardly immune to the homophobia of the era, so perhaps that was part of the objection—"looking after our daughter. We'd come home and he'd have Neil Diamond blaring and they'd be dancing." The child adored him. "He was a mess when he was here, though. I'm sure he had some dark periods."

That afternoon, my family made their own plans while Phillip and I walked the island's biggest road. It's unpaved, with footpaths dissolving into forest on either side. The ferry doesn't run on Tuesdays, a measure to prevent Lasqueti from becoming a yuppie commuter suburb. Although we occasionally moved over to let a truck pass, it felt like strolling in the woods.

"So," I licked my lips, a little dry from the dust of the road, "how are things between us, and what's your thinking on my project?"

"It's all good," he said, that well-worn phrase, "between us. And my feeling on your project is that it would be a shame for you to abandon it. It would be a fascinating story. And you've done so much work for it."

"So you're fine with the project," I clarified, needing to take this point by point, "but you don't want any part of reconciling with Harvey?"

"Yes, that's right."

"I hope you understand that I was confused because you said you did at first."

He nodded.

"I was slow to grasp the change in your feelings."

"Yes," he said, "it was when I saw the picture. That's when it changed."

"And you were hurt that I suspected you, that I'd been swayed by Harvey."

"Yeah, when we met to talk, I felt like you were looking at me like you wondered if I was lying."

"I wasn't," I said. "I was telling you what Harvey said. I felt bound to consider every side."

He picked up a fallen fir bough, twirled it like it was a quill. "I just felt, if you could believe that, you don't know me. I'm glad we're having this talk, though," he shone his eyes at me, "to get it all out."

"If I were to continue, would you still be willing to participate? To let me ask about matters that conflict with your accounts, to ask about your own biography?" I picked up my own fir bough and sniffed the bright-smelling sap. "You don't need to answer this now."

"I'm not going to answer it now," he returned, so quickly that it sounded like he was just trying to go along with me. Then he told me anyway that he would. "I will answer all your questions. It's my project to be true to the book and be myself and it's your project to be true to the book and write it."

"Okay," I said. "I'm going to think about it." If he could take time to think, so could I. "I'm going to wait a year. If you still feel the same way, I'll consider restarting. But if I do, I won't stop. I can't go through this again."

He said he understood. I followed up by putting it all in writing.

A year later, I recommenced.

STONES UNTURNED

When Del was put back in Matsqui, Simma Holt arranged for her sister Hannah, a graphologist, to analyze Del's handwriting, possibly as part of the process of trying to prove Del worthy of release.

There is repression and anxiety in this letter, Hannah wrote to Del. (Genius: Del was writing to her from jail.)

You are an excellent home-maker but from what Simma tells me, you picked the wrong person with whom to set up house. A very good imagination and originality show in your writing as well as a very keen intuition . . . a warm, kind, thoughtful, intuitive person, who would do no harm to anyone.

You are very secretive and sensitive, Hannah observed, however, *and it would help you so much if you could really talk things over.*

I could easily believe Del to be imaginative and intuitive but not that she would *do no harm to anyone*. Rather, her imagination, charm and intuition seemed part of *what was going for her at the time*: talents and forms of intelligence she could use to harm or to help, as well as for other ends known only to her.

You have some really high ideals, Hannah told her subject. *Do not let anyone kill these lovely qualities in your writing.* I find it hilarious that, for Hannah, writing is interchangeable with character, as if preserving certain qualities in the handwriting will safeguard them in the personality as well.

Del replied that she found Hannah's reading accurate except for one thing: she didn't see herself as secretive. Rather the opposite: she tended to talk too much. Also, she wrote that she had *trusted people more in the past four years than ever before in my life.*

Beyond this, she testified to how much she owed the Kingston P4W staff, and to feeling terrible for disappointing them by violating the conditions of her parole. *I could not adjust,* she wrote, though it took a while for her to understand why: *I had and still have a very great need to be independent. Believe me I now know how to handle it.*

I bet she did. And I'm sure she had no trouble speaking to people about herself, but what did she say? Almost none of their Chilliwack friends or neighbours knew about her criminal past.

Del's assertion of her *very great need to be independent* strikes me as possibly one of the truest things she says. The problem was *how.* How to live as a free individual when everyone wants you defined relationally, when *good woman* is synonymous with *good wife and mother?*

"She was brilliant," her daughter Lorraine told me. "She was a very talented artist. She would write poetry, send me poems."

Harvey attested that he had set up an art studio for her and Phillip told me that she had paid Neil Fleishman with a mask she had carved. "She found a long piece of wood with part of it rotted out, so it already had the beginnings of a face. She shaped it and gave it eyes." Fleishman's bill had come to "something like $15,000." When the mask was done, she and Phillip dressed up, hitchhiked to Vancouver, and presented it. Fleishman complimented Del effusively, immediately had the mask hung in his office, and, most surprisingly, accepted it as full payment.

Where is that mask? Lost, as with so much else. Phillip's account of it brought to mind Michael Ondaatje's novel *Anil's Ghost*: over the course of the book, a temple sculptor carves an enormous face of Buddha, saving for last the eyes. In the book's final scene, he carves them wide open.

Del's letters—not her handwriting, her actual writing—have verve and expressive talent. She had told Simma Holt that she was planning to write her life story. *The Fairy Tale of My Life.* If she had written it, what would it have said? Who did she think of as her readership—her daughters? Holt? the Canadian public at large?

Harvey said that Del *sometimes told the truth although often when she did she would then start to enlarge upon it so the end product was a great distortion. Other times it was as is said "made of the whole cloth."*

Oscar Wilde suggested that the art of lying was an endangered métier: *People have a careless way of talking about a "born liar," just as they talk about a "born poet,"* he says in "The Decay of Lying." *But in both cases they are wrong. Lying and poetry are arts—arts not unconnected with each other—and they require the most careful study, the most disinterested devotion.*

Harvey, along with Norman Lee and others, thought Del was an evil, manipulative liar. Simma Holt and Del's other champions believed her to be noble, truthful. Neither side was very interested in a more slippery possibility, that she was an artist of the self, inventing personas the way Harvey invented machines.

"Del was so perceptive," Lorraine had said—able to sense what people wanted to hear. Another word for that is empathy, a much-touted quality these days.

Unlike bullshit, empathy is socially sanctioned. It's a necessary quality in both writers and con artists. We manipulate: another word for turning something around to show its various facets and possibilities, what I'm doing here now, with you.

Really: you have no idea how much I have bullshitted to bring you this story.

I have fuzzed timelines, to present information in a logical and digestible manner.

I have withheld or compressed details, quotes, minor contradictions, interviews and informants, to allow the story to cohere.

I have pulled quotes from other writers even when I disagreed with much of what they said in the books I was quoting from. I could write a long essay disputing Alexander Nehamas's readings of friendship in film and literature, detailing the ways that unexamined anti-feminism and homophobia periodically narrow his vision and, in a couple of cases, fatally undermine his arguments. Instead, I used the bits that worked for me.

But most intellectuals bullshit to some extent, and it's common, in books about ideas, to find bullshit statements in between great insights.

I have the sense at times of the world tidying itself up for consumption, of a meaning delivered like meat already cut, strangeness of a sudden making sense—Garth Greenwell, speaking of something else entirely in a way that appears exactly relevant to what I'm talking about now.

Sometimes, as in Derrida's *Spurs/Éperons*, a book supposedly on Nietzsche's style but largely a collection of spurious (haha) statements on "woman," a book's contents are both bullshit on the page and true in what they demonstrate—for example, that women are often treated as objects in philosophy while men are subjects.

Harry G. Frankfurt's *On Bullshit* bullshits. But it also presents real, original truths.

Telling a lie, says Frankfurt, *requires a degree of craftsmanship, in which the teller of the lie submits to objective constraints imposed by what he takes to be the truth.* Bullshit, by contrast, is *panoramic rather than particular.* He writes, *The mode of creativity upon which it relies is less analytical and less deliberative, more expansive and independent, with more spacious opportunities for improvisation, color, and imaginative play. This is less a matter of craft than of art.*

As far as I can tell, omission, overstatement and a degree of inventive flair may be the only routes to argumentative or narrative truths. Not scientific or historical truths—those are meant to be replicable, verifiable—but unique, non-replicable truths, which can perhaps only arise in the spacious ground fertilized by bullshit.

Derrida says, paraphrasing Nietzsche: *From the beginning, nothing has been more foreign, incompatible, antagonistic to woman than truth—her great art is the lie. Her greatest purpose is appearance, beauty.* This is what Del was up against. So she *used what was going for her at the moment.*

I'm not going to shake the world, she said, *hell, no woman is ever going to shake the world. I thought I was going to once, but no more.*

Del wasn't a master manipulator. She was a bullshit artist, an amateur. But she might have been a great one.

When I restarted this project, I recorded Phillip's history properly, systematically, over several visits to his house, as I had done with Harvey: asking questions, filling in gaps.

Through this same period, my relationship with Harvey deteriorated. *Authority wants to replace the world with itself.*

Harvey quit me, multiple times. *I WILL HAVE NO PART OF THIS CACA,* he would say, and then, unable to resist, send pages upon pages arguing his points, defending himself, his own caca mixed in with credible bits and pieces. I would thank him for the valuable parts, challenge him on the illogical ones. He would withdraw just briefly enough to draw breath and then blast me again. His bullying and bluster brought Phillip and me closer, tacitly confirming his portrait of his father. Eventually, Harvey and I stopped writing.

In March of 2018, an old friend of his forwarded me his obituary. He had died in his sleep at ninety, the previous December, in a care home but with Vivia by his side. I offered to call his sons—Phillip hadn't heard, so I thought the others must not have either—but when I reached Ben, the oldest, he told me Vivia had called and told him. I had put Ben and Harvey back in touch, and they had been friendly, but now Ben told me that Harvey had stipulated that no one was to inform Phillip or Rob when he died.

"Why?" I asked. "What harm could come to Harvey at this point?"

"No, none. I think it's just the satisfaction of keeping that information from them," Ben said.

If Harvey was the atheist he claimed to be, why would he think there was to be any satisfaction in punishing Phillip after he died?

It was as though he wanted to constrain his own ghost.

However skewed his views on human psychology were, he clearly understood one thing: even if the truth can be devastating, not knowing can make life unbearable.

Anyway, his wish was contravened, and maybe that was his soul rebelling, shucking its bitterness as it crossed over, rinsing it away in that narrow river, and sending Phillip the news through me.

Mary Lloyd would occasionally enter a pensive mood in which she almost expressed remorse for things she had done, Harvey wrote me on one occasion. *These came at odd moments. An example is when she spoke of the surprised look on Lloyd's face as she fired the shot on some bridge in Edmonton.*

It was the last big remaining question: What happened to Lew Lloyd? I believed I knew: Kempster. I had more information than the jury—Norman Lee's "eavesdropping" transcripts had been inadmissible at trial. But knowing who did it and even why didn't tell me how, nor did it help me reconcile the things Harvey had told me that had caused me to doubt my conclusion.

Two journalist friends in Fayetteville had advised me at various points. Now, at a dinner, one of them, Matt, asked how it stood. I told him that I was making what would be my final research trip west, to interview Phillip and visit archives, and that it was going to be frustrating to be so near to Kempster and not be able to talk to him.

He insisted that I had to go to Kempster's house. When I objected that the man had said he wouldn't talk to me, Matt said it didn't matter.

"What does he like?" he asked.

"What?"

"What is he into? You need to take a gift. Show up at his house carrying a gift."

"He's into dogs," I said, recalling his Facebook picture.

"Great," he said. "Take him gourmet doggie biscuits." He smiled and nodded, like, problem solved.

My other local consultant, Bret, concurred: "You have to go." His manner was as resigned and rueful as Matt's was full of the spirit of adventure.

The big surprise was that Geoff agreed, too. "You need to go talk to him," he said, as though he hadn't been pushing back against all of this for years.

"So I need to talk to the murderer," I repeated.

"I could go with you."

"No! What?"

"I'm not really afraid that anything might happen to you. Are you?"

"No," I said. "I'm nervous. But not of that."

"Whatever my reservations about the project," Geoff said, "I think you need to see it through. Go ask Kempster what happened. What have you got to lose?"

Dear Mr. Kempster, I wrote the next day, worried that if I waited, I'd wait forever.

What does it mean to be a good person? This is the question at the heart of the book I am writing, a look at lives touched by Mary Lloyd—a mysterious and complex lady, to say the least. I know that talking about Mary means revisiting a painful time in your life and I understand you not wanting to reopen the topic. But I was so struck, in our brief conversation, by the emotion in your voice when you talked about her daughters. I'm not surprised to know you are long-married and a father. Your younger self strikes me as earnest, dedicated and passionate—all the qualities a person would need for a good and steady life.

I said he could set whatever limits he wanted on our conversation. We could stay off criminal matters, for instance: I was interested to hear from him on other topics, too, such how he'd achieved his current life, and what he thought of Mary from a distance of sixty years.

On the other hand, perhaps it would be a weight off of you, after all these years, to set the record straight on the events of 1956.

I had already confirmed with a lawyer that there was no legal risk to him. I let him know this and, also, that unless he told me otherwise, I would knock at his door on a Saturday about three weeks from the day of mailing.

I enclosed a copy of one of my books and sent it to the address listed with the phone number that had got me through to him two years earlier.

The days ticked away without a response. I felt I had trapped myself into going, and maybe that was what I needed to do.

I would stay a half-hour drive northeast of Deroche, at the Harrison Hot Springs Resort, where Phillip had worked and Del had partied—scenic research into others' memories, others' lives.

I checked in on the Friday afternoon, briefly distracted by the lobby's stuffed grizzly bear in a Mountie suit, the carpeted restaurant full of Russians. I had a second-floor room overlooking the hot pools, one for families and one adults only, so close I could eavesdrop from my window.

Saturday morning, I woke at five after a restless night of Kempster dreams, his glowering face, his angry eyes. On my way to Deroche, I stopped to buy a pie. I'd called a friend for ballast the night before and fretted that gourmet doggie biscuits might make me look like a stalker. She said, "Find a bakery—buy something still warm."

Geoff had said he was not concerned, and yet he was tracking me on his phone as I drove to Deroche. Black cliffs on one side, Fraser River to the other: it was pretty, but I was so anxious it was all I could do to focus on the road. The penultimate turn on my

GPS led me toward what looked like empty fields. On my right was a rough-looking compound, a diner and a bar, little more than conjoined shacks. I drove up to it and went in. The place smelled of old grease and cigarette smoke; the woman behind the cash looked worn and hostile. I was procrastinating, yes, but I also, predictably, needed to use the washroom, and she let me.

Exiting the gravel parking lot, I took the next right and there it was: a row of bushes had hidden the low, white, clapboard house, a sign that said KEMPSTER, two cars in the long driveway, with garden ornaments, bird feeders, and wind chimes all around.

I texted Geoff, *Here!*

He texted back, *I know!*

And James Stanley Kempster pulled up next to me in a white Jeep.

I could hear his dogs barking. He smiled at me, ambiguously, from behind the wheel. Clutching my phone in one hand, I grabbed the pie off the back seat. His dogs had tumbled out of the car—two tiny, and one huge—scampering and barking as I introduced myself.

His face turned watery. "Oh."

"Did you receive my letter?" I asked.

"Yes," he said, closing the car door and standing up straight, a plastic carry bag over one arm. "Did you receive mine?"

"No," I said. No. Yikes. *Damn you, Canada Post.* "Did you tell me not to come?" It would turn out later that I had turned on my recording app in my nervousness, so all of this is on audio. "I'm so sorry. I wouldn't have come if I'd received it."

"Well, why don't you come in," he said, turning toward the house. "We'll talk for a moment."

Yes, I thought. *Yes, yes!*

"My wife's away, at a ladies' retreat," he said as he went around the side and unlocked the kitchen door.

Yes. Serendipity.

As the dogs continued bucking and romping and scrambling, he made us tea in the tiny kitchen. "So, how did you come?" he asked.

I described my route and he commented on it, a favourite pastime of his generation.

I carried the tea into the small living room and he slid a child gate shut between us and the dogs. I looked for a place to set our cups down amid tchotchkes and doilies and a multitude of framed photos of children.

"You've got a lot of grandchildren," I remarked.

"We've got two children and eight grandchildren, so we've done very well," he agreed. His house was on his son-in-law's dairy farm—Kempster and his wife had moved here after a trucking business he started with their son went belly up. Before that, he had spent thirty-five years as a medical lab technician, a profession he trained for after getting out of jail.

He mentioned that he had reciprocally sent me a book along with his letter. "I just happened to be reading a book by a Pole jailed for Christianity. You mentioned your book has to do with the Air India disaster. This has to do with another disaster, an ongoing disaster. A Christian doesn't even get fair treatment in what we call a Christian country of Canada. You can have a protest or parade in Vancouver for practically anything, but if a Christian tries to do it . . .! We know that, as far as the numbers go, places like Indonesia, or Rhodesia or places in Africa, Christians are getting killed by the hundreds and it's not reported."

Having discovered I was recording, I belatedly asked if I could record.

"Oh, is that what you're doing?" he asked, looking at my gadget.

"No," I responded. "I wouldn't do that without permission." Except by accident, of course. Anyway, he said it was fine.

We started by talking about the robbery. "It was just a stupid thing I did when I was young," he said. "I was young and behaving stupidly."

He was tender and measured in the way he spoke about Mary. She used people, he agreed, but she had suffered with her first husband, the one before Lew, which "probably affected her quite a bit. But I know very little about her. I didn't know half a dozen people she was associated with. And from talking to her husband, I presume that there was a problem she had with drugs to some extent."

"From talking to Lew Lloyd?" I had never heard about a drug problem.

"Yeah. When I was with her, he said to keep her away from drugs, as a protective measure."

"So he left and asked you to look after her?" This was unexpected.

"Well, I broke up the marriage, I would say, by having an affair with her," he responded. "But he was still involved. This was his family, so he was very concerned."

Kempster made the robbery seem like an accommodation that both he and Lew made to Mary, "on another one of her flings," as he put it. "We would have never gotten into any trouble if it hadn't been for her."

"You and Lew?" I asked, mystified at his seeming alliance with the man I thought he had killed.

"Yeah."

"The robbery was her idea?"

"Yeah. She got us into a very precarious situation and then she made the suggestion. It was a spur-of-the-moment thing. But not for her: she had it all planned, but us, we knew nothing about it."

So it *was* Mary's play; Kempster and Lew were her puppets. Did Kempster have the impression she had robbed banks before?

He didn't know anything about that, he said, though she'd shoplifted, maybe for the thrill. He gave the impression that he didn't know anything about Del's leftist leanings, but I doubt he would have been particularly sympathetic, so she had likely hidden such inclinations from him.

I backed up a little, asking whether Kempster and Mary met through Kempster's sister, as the preliminary trial transcripts indicated.

"Yes, that's right," he answered. "She was a friend of my sister's. And I worked with Lew on a couple of occasions, on the docks."

"My friend, her stepson, said there was a lot of criminal activity around the docks," I said, "petty stuff."

"Oh, yeah. They had their own society. They had their ways of doing things. If they were loading, they would drop a case of liquor and break a bottle or something and would keep what was left."

I couldn't say it was relaxed between us, exactly—I wasn't relaxed—but his apparent openness was disarming. I went ahead and asked the question: "What do you think happened to Lew?"

"I don't know," Kempster said. To my chagrin, I believed him. He seemed candid, reflective, at ease. "There were associations from their past," he went on. "Lew had spent time in jail before. But I'm sure it was because of her. I'm sure it was something they had concocted, and he wound up taking the fall for it."

I kept fishing from different angles. "I interviewed Mary's ex-husband, who said she told him that she killed Lew Lloyd. I asked why he never reported her, and he said it was because she lied about everything. Does that make any sense to you?"

"She always had an agenda. She was manipulating people. So, how she got Lew and I into such a state that we went with her on that escapade, there was such an emotional circumstance, that morning."

"Just that morning?"

"Yes, that's right. All within an hour. She had us in such a state that we just went along with her."

"How did she get you in such a state?"

"I don't really want to discuss that part. But it was very serious. It was even life-threatening."

Later, I would regret not having pushed. Instead, I asked, "And why did Lew leave for Edmonton? For a fresh start or some other reason?"

"I think he went there to make a fresh start," Kempster said.

"He had a good friend that he was with."

"Did you ever think that Mary had something to do with his murder?"

"I don't know," he said again. "They had friends that I didn't know. Lew had his own friends and she had her associations from before."

"It also seemed to me that Mary was trying to mislead you about Lew," I prompted, "saying he was a bad person, which made me wonder if you in some way were trying to protect her and the children from him."

"I don't remember any of those things. I didn't know, most of us didn't know we were being manipulated."

What did he mean, *most of us?*

"There were other men in her past that she talked about. She still had very strong connections with all of these people: any of her previous partners, romantic partners, she still had them on the string. Even though some of them were married, she still had them on the string."

JAMES S. KEMPSTER, 35, of Vancouver, who was arrested at the coast on a charge of armed robbery by police investigating the slaying near Edmonton June 24 of Lewis Lloyd, 37, of 10332 116 St. The charge against Kempster is connected with a bank holdup in April in Vancouver, in which two men and a woman took part. Police state Kempster is being questioned in connection with the death of Lloyd, former Vancouver longshoreman.

I asked a little more about that, but he didn't offer any specifics, so I changed tack. "The judge, when you were acquitted for the murder, said, I'm sure you had something to do with this and that Mary Lloyd was behind it. How did you feel, hearing that?"

"I remember him telling me that I should be careful about my associations," Kempster said. "That's the only part I remember."

"And you felt that to be true?"

"Yeah, I knew it was true."

I started edging up again on the murder question. "People said you had gone to Calgary that weekend."

"Yeah, I had business in Calgary. So I wasn't here and I wasn't there."

Which meant he lied under oath. "What business did you have in Calgary?"

"It was personal business. I don't want to get into it. It wasn't related to the Lloyds."

It occurred to me in this moment that Mary might have tried to frame Kempster, but he didn't buy that.

"That never occurred to you?" I said.

He said it hadn't.

"Did you think that Lew Lloyd was essentially a good person, a well-meaning person?"

"Yes, yes," he said, not so much insistent as impatient, as though he took this for granted. "He was a good person. He just got into something, the same as I did." He sighed heavily.

Much of this came out in the first twenty minutes of our conversation but he didn't seem inclined to kick me out. He was alone for the weekend, only the dogs for company, and maybe I was a little more responsive than they were, though they were pretty demanding.

So I stayed for a couple of hours. He was prone to monologues that I found confusing. When I transcribed them, I could see why: they didn't make much sense. On a vague level, he was in favour of personal responsibility. On a granular level, I couldn't really tell what that meant. Every once in a while, I'd remember why I was there and ask a direct question, which he would answer without hesitation, willing and undefensive.

"I think you were in love with her," I said at one point.

"Oh, yes," he answered.

"You really were."

"Well, yes, that's the whole problem," he said. "It was a romantic, sexual thing."

"Honestly, until I came to see you, I thought that you had killed Lew."

"No," he said. What else could he say?

"I thought you had been manipulated into doing it. But now

it looks as though what she told my friend was closer to the truth: that it was their associations."

"Yeah. I don't know," he repeated. "Like I say, I was away at that time, too, so . . ."

It was the last answer I would get to my question, *the mystery to a solution*. Where could I even go from here? Eventually, I left him in his little white house and drove back to Harrison Hot Springs. I left my car at the hotel and walked out on the lakefront boardwalk, where I found a bench and called Geoff.

"He didn't do it," I told him. I felt stymied, but it was also a relief. I liked Kempster and I bet I would have liked Del. I liked their imperfections and I wanted them to have what remained of their privacy.

Kempster's letter and package had arrived at my house while I was at his house. Geoff had texted a photograph from our mailbox: Kempster had addressed it to Arizona instead of Arkansas, presumably what caused the delay. That, or serendipity.

I told Geoff that Kempster was writing a book, too.

"Oh, yeah? What about?"

"About winter driving."

He started laughing.

"I know. He told me about it at length. Winter driving. Apparently, there's a great need."

I spent the afternoon transcribing and then, stretching my arms and neck, walked out once more along the waterfront. This was where Del's ashes were scattered—the end of the line, for her and, it seemed, for me. If she knew what happened to Lew, she took it to her grave. But she might not have known, either—something else we would forever have in common.

In the following months, I would come again to feel that Kempster had to have been involved in Lew's death. Surely his affirming to Mary the accuracy of the truck photo, as he had in the jail when he thought they were alone, implied he knew more than he admitted. And what was he doing in Calgary and what didn't he want to tell me about the morning of the robbery? Could it be that upright Kempster, committed to protecting Mary, was still protecting her? Could he even have been responsible for the murder and forgotten?

That would be extreme, even compared with other failures of memory I had encountered in the course of this research: Phillip forgetting Harvey's absence; Harvey forgetting Mary's second daughter and Phillip's second "l." I never thought either of them was lying deliberately, and I found it hard to believe Kempster was either.

But it wasn't entirely beyond me to imagine that Kempster had been in some hormonal fugue state that led him to behave in ways unimaginable—unrecoverable—once he came to himself. And in any case, as William Maxwell tells us, *in talking about the past we lie with every breath we draw.*

I had advanced the drift until I blew out the last wall and came out blinking in the obliterating light, a brightness, like the blue at the end of *Thelma and Louise*, that hides whatever can no longer be known. No drifts remained to advance. Except, perhaps, Cuba.

CUBA RETURN

Phillip and I started talking about a trip to Cuba. He was eager, though I had to do all the planning, which turned out to be uncharacteristically difficult for me. Somehow, repeatedly, I failed properly to note or follow the few clues that might have brought us closer to the locations of Phillip's childhood sojourn. I forgot that Del had mentioned Santa Clara to Neil Fleishman. I literally couldn't find Oriente province—it turned out it hadn't been a province since 1976, but surely the internet could have mentioned that? Phillip said they'd visited a school in Varadero, but I kept coming up empty. By the time Geoff found an image from an old book that mentioned an international school there, Phillip had learned Varadero was now a holiday resort and told me in no uncertain terms that he wasn't interested in visiting it. The one extant place we knew for sure he had been was the Hotel Habana Libre, so we would start there.

He was optimistic that I would find something about Del in the Cuban archives, but that idea overwhelmed and bewildered me. So much of her history had disappeared even from Canadian caches. I never contacted Cuba's Archivo Nacional, never even looked it up until just now, to find out what it was called.

The idea was somehow to retrace his childhood journey, though increasingly I thought of it as a retracing more in spirit than in letter.

At some point, though, Phillip hinted that he was seeing this also as a bonding trip for the two of us, capping the metaphorical journey we'd undertaken, the journey of the book.

When one of his friends at work learned we were travelling together for almost ten days, he asked, "So are you going to be at each other's throats by the end?" I had no such fear, and Phillip was laughing when he passed the crack on. I think.

Phillip arrived in Havana twelve hours before me. In the middle of the night, after a gruelling journey, he was told our hotel was unpaid for. He disputed this and refused to pay. When I arrived early the next afternoon, I found him in a state: he'd sat in the lobby waiting for me that entire time. When I presumed it was an innocent error, he pointed to an entry in a guidebook I had bought him, noting that this exact con was common on the island. "You didn't read this very well, did you?"

I would eventually determine that it had been a misunderstanding, not a con, arising from difficulties I'd had booking this state-run facility. After hours of chasing down various staff members, receiving complimentary beverages as they kept us waiting, we extracted a belated apology and were given our keys.

It soured Phillip on the Habana Libre, which anyway looked nothing like the enchanted place of his youth. The pool was rebuilt and repositioned; there were no cabanas; and no one was serving the coconut pudding that would have returned him, like madeleines and linden tea, to that brief optimistic time.

Once he had freshened up, though, he started to enjoy himself. Cuba—it's hard not to like.

Early in the trip, when we were apart (he didn't go out on his own, but I did), I would start fretting about how little we had in common, the trip having made some of our differences stand out.

What would our friendship become without the book to work on?

But each time we reunited, I felt an immediate, molecular gladness: we would try some new fruit, enjoying each other's reactions; he spotted a balcony with a table for two over looking a piazza and figured out how to get us up there for lunch; I took us to a club where I danced salsa with locals while he grinned and blushed, surrounded by attentive ladies.

On some unconscious level, though, I must have known that the critical distance I needed to write the book was incompatible with the uncritical appreciation I feel for my friends, Phillip included, moment to moment.

When I fretted over being an amateur, I recalled that *amateur* is cognate to love. How to reconcile that with Malcolm's statement *that the masters*—not, you may note, the amateurs—*of the nonfiction genre achieve affection for the subject?*

McGinniss and his subject *clothed their complicated business in the mantle of friendship*, Malcolm said, implying what most of us believe, that love between friends is straightforward, simple, unlike familial love—complicated because it is required—or romantic love, which is complicated by pursuit, then by maintenance, or managing the end. In fact, *pace* Nehamas, friendship is *like every form of love*, complicated in its own particular ways.

Most writers who talk about the thorny matter of journalistic representation do it after the process is over and done. They distill it, make it clear, like gin or vodka. Let me attest here to what they omit: the emotional debris that remains as sediment on the still's surfaces, long after the writer decants the intoxicating draught of story.

What were we doing here? In my mind, it was like our trip to Chilliwack and his childhood home: I wanted to accompany Phillip back to this formative place, witness his reactions to whatever vestiges remained, and see Cuba for myself so I could render it in my own words. Scenic research: soft, unpredictable. I'd done it many times for fiction.

His idea, though I didn't properly realize it ahead of time, was more concrete. He wanted to fulfill the mission Del and Harvey had abandoned: helping the Cuban people.

When he was a kid, as they walked out onto the tarmac in Mexico City to board the plane to Cuba, some man in white coveralls appeared and, as Phillip put it, "slid a little box into Del's hand, and kept on walking."

On the plane, Del kept the box on her lap. "When they went around giving out declaration forms," Phillip said, "I looked at her and she gave me a look, shrugged, like, 'I don't know.'" She admitted as much to Cuban customs, who opened it. "There was a letter inside that said, *Please take this to Dr. So-and-so*. It was serum for elephantiasis. There was an outbreak in the swamplands."

On our trip, Phillip had toted along two fifty-pound bags of slightly out-of-date medical supplies from his workplace, wanting to donate them to a teaching hospital he had identified, eight blocks from our hotel. We hauled the bags there by cab, then spent two hours in an outdoor waiting room, looking at palm trees and listening to birds, before a polite gentleman called Carlo requested that we take them to the Ministry of Health. The hospital would fetch them from there.

Phillip was unhappy—he was deeply skeptical of government involvement. I thought that odd, considering that he was sympathetic to the revolution. Wasn't the point of communism that the state took care of everything? He shrugged, willing to be convinced.

As we walked away with the bags, though, Juanita, a woman employed in some ambiguous capacity at the hospital, caught up with us and offered to take them off our hands. Through me—she, like most people we'd met so far, spoke no English, and Phillip had no Spanish—Phillip accepted, then was forced to rescind when Carlo reappeared, running down a path toward us, begging us to follow protocol.

But that evening, Juanita and Carlo appeared together at our hotel to tell us the Ministry of Health had given us a special dispensation to donate directly. Two days later, we went back to the hospital.

I wondered what use the hospital had for two bags of random equipment. But Phillip intended the supplies to be a calling card: he wanted to establish a channel for a regular shipment that would be gradually refined to suit their needs. The hospital seemed to understand. We had a meeting with an upper-level administrator, along with an orthopaedic surgeon who spoke English and a few other people; then a tour, conducted by Juanita.

I was willing to believe that Phillip, peering about the hospital appraisingly and asking lots of questions, knew what he was doing. But I felt uncomfortable, gawking at Cuba's sick and at its beleaguered doctors working the underfurnished wards. When Juanita signalled to a doctor that Phillip had a question about some equipment, she came over; on learning Phillip was not a doctor, she rolled her eyes without answering and returned to her tasks.

Finally, we were done—free of the bags, free to amble through the city, to stay in beach-facing cottages at Meyer Lansky's old hotel on Isla de la Juventud, to birdwatch at an artists' co-operative turned eco-resort.

These were the activities I had planned, but Phillip had had other things in mind. He said he thought we might see farms and farmers, schools, factories; why didn't I visit a university, he asked. The hospital visit, which had so embarrassed me in my ignorance and helplessness, was exactly the sort of thing he'd hoped for: forging north-south partnerships. He hadn't said this ahead of time, though, and I was loath to arrange it now.

Perhaps I'm excessively skeptical about charity tourism. It's a common practice to take gifts of small luxury goods to Cuba; everyone we met was unsurprised and pleased at the baseballs, pens and barrettes that Phillip handed out. The hospital had ultimately appeared to take Phillip's donation seriously. Was my vague unease misplaced or exaggerated? I have a vague unease about almost everything, so maybe it's not for me to say.

Phillip appeared to love everything we did, but repeated, throughout our trip, his desire to see *regular people*. To me, with my experience of India and NGOs and well-meaning white missionary types who can't speak the language, that meant interrupting Cubans' lives and work to gawk at them. It was partly that feeling of being ignorant, taking up time without offering much back, that had precipitated my breakdown in India thirty years earlier.

But to Phillip, it meant being a cultural ambassador, and, as we toured Old Havana and the Malecón and the Moncada barracks, I suspect he felt mounting within him an inexpressible resistance.

I was distracted, that week, by two dramas, faraway yet very near to me: one of my best friends had had a long-awaited baby, and my darling grandmother was nearing death.

At the eco-resort, I found a Wi-Fi signal in an awkward corner. My friend Sheila had received the gifts I'd sent to her in Brazil: Margaret Wise Brown's *Runaway Bunny*, whose stalker-mommy I had played in countless reenactments with my daughter, together with a stuffed bunny. Sheila told me she called the stuffie Paulo Coelho, an extension of our running joke about this dubious author whose name means rabbit in Portuguese. I'd also enclosed two dressy outfits, one Indian, one Chinese, that belonged to our son when he was a baby. I save our kids' most excellent clothes to send as blessings; I'd held these ones back twelve years for her.

And, over FaceTime, I spoke to my grandmother, who was slipping in and out of lucidity in Edmonton. My mother's mother, she had lived in my uncle's house and helped to raise all of us grandkids, just as my parents had come to live with us when our first child was born and been part of our household ever since.

I'd gone that fall to help look after her, as had my sister and cousins; my mother and her sister were each staying there a month or more at a time. Now all of them were gathering. From Cuba, I joined a FaceTime with her and with Geoff and our kids in Arkansas; my mother asked her to bless the children.

When I'd visited, Grandma was terribly weak and tired, but otherwise still unchanged: funny, affectionate, peppering me with questions, large with opinions. Forced to quit school at twelve, she was a reader and a musician. She became a ferocious hockey fan after immigrating to Canada, the sort who wins arguments by citing stats. She watched Oilers games with a japa-mala in one hand, lips moving as she recited slokas to empower the players.

I didn't feel right cutting my time in Cuba short, but started researching flight changes, hoping I'd get to Edmonton in time.

One night, I tried, uncharacteristically, to tell Phillip some anecdote about Sheila, not about her baby, but maybe about our travels together, in India or Brazil. I recall my voice straining with awkward excess to bridge his silence. I felt from him a mild frisson—jealousy, maybe, or just an inchoate awareness of my life's benign, hidden dimensions.

One night in Havana, we shared a cab with a hip young Welsh couple. Phillip, in an expansive mood, dropped nuggets of his story and our relationship: his stepmother the bank robber, weird details about Mexico City. He never said why we were in Cuba. This was not an elevator pitch; it was gabble.

"We're writing a book," he further said, to my alarm, as the Welsh couple looked on unreadably. "We've been working on it for ten years. You should see what she's found"—he pointed his thumb at me—"a regular Sherlock!" He roared and they laughed along, but I was, once more, embarrassed.

I told him later that I didn't want to talk about the book until there was a book. This wasn't true, but how could I tell him the truth: that I hated hearing it the way he told it.

And what did he mean "we" were writing a book? On a hike

one afternoon, I worked my way around to asking him whether he thought we were co-writing or if that just how he talked?

"No, no," he said, flustered. "That's just how I talk. It's your book. I said that before and I mean it. You write it how you want." Whatever his dreams for its uses, whatever he thought might be inserted *verbatim*, he affirmed that this was my book.

He knew that I planned to give him a share if I made any money from it. I reaffirmed that now, but he cut me off, saying he hated to talk about money. Laying a hand on my arm, he said, "You're as honest as the day is long. I know you'll do the right thing."

Mutually assured, we moved on. I had recently learned he was in debt, presumably a combination of his antiques habit and a boyfriend he'd been supporting. I was surprised to hear it, and briefly wondered if that was part of his motivation for convincing me to return to the book.

Several nights in Cuba, I awakened in crisis. Part of it was my grandmother, but mostly it was a dawning understanding that I might have attempted the impossible, that there were barriers in the friendship I hadn't acknowledged, that the friendship might be cannibalized by the book. *Perhaps literature,* I wrote in my journal, *is as close a proxy as we can create to true intimacy, since it solves the irreconcilable problems at the root of intimacy, the fact that we are changing all the time and that we always see the beloved through the screen of our needs.*

One evening, in a limo en route to the improbably beautiful eco-resort, he marvelled, "Look at this. How did this ever happen, our friendship and this whole thing? With you, in your station in life, a real author, and me . . . I'm this dumb farm kid."

I was taken aback and protested. He was exceptionally curious and alert, and as good a reader as any middle-class person with humanist sympathies and his own idiosyncratic interests and biases. Plus he was fun. And sweet. Like my favourite cousins, though I never told him that. I'm not sure why I never told him that.

But I also knew, from my attempts to explain the book, that he couldn't grasp its concept—not a question of intelligence but specialization—and I was already starting to accept that I didn't owe it to him. His relationship to it was as model to painting: he didn't commission it, he didn't own it, and he wouldn't get to say how it went, even if he was its inspiration—a memorable figure that, if not for me, would be forgotten.

On the morning of our last day, Phillip told me he wanted to try to reconnect a last time with Juanita, the aggressively friendly woman from the hospital. I collapsed a little. I'd wanted to go the Museo Nacional de Bellas Artes, make last notes in my journal, see the famous Cuban National Ballet. (I had stood in line for tickets—Phillip's first ballet, prompting me to quote *Black Swan*: *Never seen ballet before? You're definitely not gay.*)

To meet with Juanita, he would need me to translate, and likely to take him to her—he was insecure about getting around on his own in Havana. Also, why her? Our interactions with her had been the murkiest of all, whereas the bag drop-off had ultimately been overseen by a high-level hospital administrator, who had told Phillip she would take charge of any further supplies or equipment he could send and had given him her email.

He conceded, coming with me to the art museum. At the door, though, he suddenly looked drastic: he wasn't interested in this highbrow stuff, he reminded me, but in real people. He made a gracious if quick exit and we met up in a few hours later, both of us well satisfied, I thought.

As Phillip and I walked through central Havana, trying to find a place for lunch, he growled and whirred with lust, making appreciative comments about men we passed, as he always had. I'd gotten used to it. This time, though, he interrupted himself, saying, "These people are so natural. To get them involved in that corruption, that smut, I just wouldn't."

"Are you saying that someone who's not really gay might go with you here because of the power differential, because you're a tourist? I mean, there are homosexuals here," I pointed out.

He was evasive, but eventually said, "You know when those people were dancing, and it was just this energy, their whole body, you know what I mean? How do you describe that? You can't."

I thought he'd done a pretty good job of describing it, but he hadn't answered my question.

It wasn't the first time his contradictory feelings about his sexuality had startled me. From our first meeting on, he'd been so gleeful and candid about his encounters that I assumed he celebrated his sexuality, but, as I learned over and over, it was complicated.

Trying to explain his views on karma, for example, he told me he probably did something bad in a past life to be reincarnated as a homosexual.

"You think being gay is a punishment?" I asked, alarmed.

"Well, that I would be reincarnated as an unhappy gay," he qualified. "After I stopped drinking, I started reading a lot of metaphysical stuff, souls talking. They say that, on the other side, we choose a difficult life because you learn more lessons that way."

I felt a flash of anger. His philosophy put the blame for suffering on the sufferer. But as he kept talking, I heard how these beliefs allowed him to cast himself not as a victim but as someone who embraces a challenge.

"I'm the person I am now because of all that stuff I had to go through," he said, a favourite refrain. He told me how, when he was young, any time he suspected he was going to get laid, he would feel a thump in his stomach, an intuition of something bad.

He finally understood it after consulting a particular psychic.

"She did her spiritual healing. When she does that, they talk through her, a totally different voice. The first time, it scared the shit out of me. There's this little old lady and then, all of a sudden, you hear this deep voice coming out of her."

I resisted the urge to comment as Barry White or Mickey Mouse.

When the seer exited her trance, she looked up a name in a book and said, *"They—"* Phillip pointed up at the ceiling *"—told me to give this to you."* It was a reference that led him, via two helpful librarians, to an article about a Dutch order of religious celibates. "I took this to mean that they up there were saying to me to abstain from sex, saying, *You shouldn't do that.*"

"That thump in your gut when you were young seems explicable without the intervention of Dutch celestial bodies," I said, impatiently defending him against himself. "Society all around you was saying that homosexuality was wrong."

"But the thing is, I didn't know the term 'homosexuality,'" Phillip plaintively insisted. "I didn't know the term 'fruit' or 'fag' or any of that."

I didn't believe him. "Concepts like that are buried so deep in the culture. You would hear an insult like 'fag' or 'nancy-boy' or whatever, but you're not effeminate, so you might not have ever twigged that those could apply to you, but how could you not have absorbed this idea?"

"When I was going to high school," he mused, "there was a boy on the bus, and I thought, *He might be one . . .* And years later, I was in a gay bar and saw that guy."

"So you did know about homosexuality!"

He made a droll face. "Well, the thing was, I really liked men."

Walking alongside him in Havana, I fell silent, recalling that exchange, and he changed the subject.

That morning, as we'd left our B&B, I'd watched him pack his pockets with three-peso bills. On the street, shortly after, he walked up to a man leaning on a crutch, maybe waiting for someone, and offered him a bill. Another man crossed the street ahead of us, with the see-saw gait of polio. Phillip walked after him, tapped him on the shoulder until he turned around, and pressed a bill into his hand. As Phillip turned back, the man made eye contact with me, bemused: *What the heck?*

But when beggars asked us for money, Phillip refused. A woman asked us to buy milk for her child; he refused. Okay, she may have been lying; she tried to lead us to what she said was a store—a con? Who knew.

Eventually, I asked him, "How do you choose who to go after and give money to?"

"Just their energy," he responded, with a gesture toward his heart.

It reminded me of his insistence on giving the medical supplies directly to the hospital instead of to the government, trusting his own instincts over pre-established channels.

As we finished lunch, I checked my emails and realized that I'd gotten the time of his flight the next morning wrong. It was two hours earlier than I'd said. Phillip panicked: he needed to get back to our rest house, to organize, pack, get his head together. I'm a practised and somewhat insouciant traveller; most people aren't. I respected his need to get himself in order, and felt badly for my error and his tension, but I regretted the loss of ceremony to mark our last day.

My flight was later than his, so I went to see *Swan Lake*. I'd hoped for better, but it was as expected: technical proficiency but a production that looked as though it had been recycled every year since the revolution, men in velvet brocade jackets, swans bourréeing in and out of knock-off Busby Berkeley formations.

I left at intermission. A tip from friends led me to a non-descript door on a quiet street. Inside, I found a tiny, brightly lit boîte called Patio de Egrem, that specialized in rhumba, just percussion and voice, very west African, with dance throw-downs and an audience of thirty or so who seemed mostly to be friends of the band. People were summoned up from time to time to guest on vocals. I was seated with a woman about my age, Marilene, who told me she came every Sunday.

"What do you want to eat?" she asked. "Drink?" She asked me for five pesos to look after it. I gave her ten, thinking she might get herself something as well, but, asking me to mind her purse, she put in the order and brought me the change.

The plantain tostones were the best I'd had. Another woman asked me to watch her purse while she went out for a smoke. I did, and drank my mojito and danced with Marilene, and then, around eleven, I walked home.

Weren't these *real people*, as real as when they were working a factory line or scything sugar cane or getting a blood pressure reading? They seemed as real while singing or dancing or sculpting as they might be while going about any daily business, *eating or opening a window or just walking dully along,* even if they were also, simultaneously, showing their *finest sides.*

I saw Phillip's light on when I got in and knocked to say good night. His manner was still odd—discombobulated and anxious, I thought. When I got up at four to see him off, he said to me, just before getting into the cab, "By the way, I wasn't *chasing people down to give them money.*"

I apologized for having misunderstood and hugged him goodbye, then sent him an email, apologizing again for my question but also saying that that wasn't exactly what I said. (It wasn't about what was said. It never is.) I also apologized for the ways the trip was perhaps not what he had hoped.

When I arrived at the airport seven hours later, I found him in the departure lounge, his plane delayed. He'd made a new friend, a snobby Cuban biologist. The three of us drank coffee, speaking in English except for when she didn't want him to understand: *How are you two friends?* she asked, implying I was wasting my time.

Estoy escribiendo un libro sobre su historia familiar, I responded, feeling hard toward her.

Phillip and I said goodbye again. He still seemed a little remote, but he didn't have a smartphone, so wouldn't have gotten my email yet.

Friendship, says Alexander Nehamas, *like every form of love, points ineluctably to the future.* I knew that when he got home and back in his comfort zones, when he read my email, things between us would return to normal.

LIKE EVERY FORM OF LOVE

By an unforeseen set of circumstances, I ended up writing this book in summer 2021, at the start of a year-long fellowship in the UK. It came quicker than any other book I've done, though it was exquisitely painful at times.

In London, I sat at a little desk before a floor-to-ceiling window that opened on a wrought-iron Juliet balcony through which climbing roses threaded. Beyond that, a T-intersection, a neighbourhood park, life's passing parade.

After two months of pounding on my computer keyboard like a writer in a movie (David Rakoff on ways to *broadcast creativity in a movie: sit at a typewriter, reading the page you've just written, realize that it's shit and tear it from the platen, and toss it behind you. Cut to wastepaper basket overflowing with crumpled paper*), I was nearly done.

It had otherwise been a fun summer: COVID-19 was ebbing, and after eighteen months confined in Arkansas, the quotidian liveliness of our north London neighbourhood was a tonic. I was damn proud to have occasioned this opportunity for our kids: a year abroad, afternoons choosing between the National Gallery and Regent's Park, all of a world capital's incidental delights.

Crossing Hampstead Heath one day alone, I experienced a curious realization. Not only had I been unusually free of self-loathing throughout these two months (I still, absent full-fledged depression, fell prey to that dreaded state and spent hours fighting free of it), I'd been inflated with the opposite: confidence, buoyancy. I was hanging out with successful writers, enjoying them without any residual psychological noise. I felt unusually accepting of my body. Whence this steadiness?

On a weekend trip to Paris just before I wrote this concluding section, Geoff and I were browsing the warrens of Shakespeare and Co. (as you do). I came upon him delighting in a book of Don Paterson aphorisms. He pointed to one custom-made for translators: *No sense steps into the same word twice.* On waking the next morning, though, I recalled the one I'd spotted just beneath it: *Self-loathing gets me out of bed in the morning, but for years it kept me in it.*

What makes Don Paterson hate himself? I ruminated. *He's so prolific, I'm not surprised he has trauma, but—*

A realization in the form of a memory broke into that train of thought: my seven-year-old self leaving for school, older kids passing through the walkway beside our house. *Dirty Paki!* they shout, sneer, snicker. I freeze. Worse epithets follow. I wait. There is nothing else to be done. I must have told my parents the first time it happened, because they told me to ignore them. That's what I'm doing now.

In the years of intermittent bullying that followed, I would tell my mother and father what was happening only two other times that I recall: once when I was getting physically beaten up each day on my way home from school and another time when they saw me come in the house after a kid spat on me. He'd been sucking on a pink gobstopper and his drool was bright against my favourite yellow jacket, hard to hide. In these cases, they invoked other authorities.

With adolescence, the bullying became more personal: alpha girls in the locker room ridiculing my training bra as I tried to change, or sticking a menstrual pad on the trophy case in the school atrium and using it to make leaden, persistent jokes about my name, what passes for wit among that type.

I was ten when I started seventh grade: short, skinny, brown, timid, unathletic and academically accelerated, the perfect victim.

I tried to pass for ditzy, until I realized that didn't fix the problem. When I came out again as smart, that precipitated other torments.

How could I not have realized this might be at the root of my shame? I'm ashamed all over again talking about it now. (No wonder I never wanted to write autobiographically.)

If I ever referred to these events in conversation, I skimmed through them matter-of-factly and, to the best of my ability, amusingly. It never occurred to me—until now—that there was any lingering effect. I was a middle-class kid with loving, competent parents, and I always had at least one or two loyal friends (who never ventured to defend me, but also carefully never mentioned the episodes they witnessed, and so spared me the repetition of my humiliation).

So what if I was intermittently taunted (and beaten up and spat on and isolated) during my formative years? Big deal. Worse things happen, kids can be cruel.

Now: behold my husband and kids, so gorgeous, brilliant, hilarious, responsive (also stubborn, obtuse, impatient and bossy, like me); behold the dream home I built my parents with money from my writing—a bespoke, light-filled apartment thirty feet from my kitchen door. I spend my days doing what I like best. My work has taken me around the world. I should be ashamed to be ashamed!

Yet I was. Until London.

Why?

This book was bringing me, too, toward the relief of this acknowledgement: what happens to us in childhood happens our whole lives, even *deepens like a coastal shelf.*

I have no reason to feel sorry for myself, but maybe I can finally feel sorry for the child I once was.

Among the many topics I haven't addressed here is the question of the origins of Phillip's sexuality. Homosexuals, like heterosexuals, like every shade in between, are both born and made. His father's absences and abuses were likely residual in the chalice of his sexuality, but who can ever parse that alchemy?

He was a working-class white man who could pass for straight. I am a middle-class brown woman and could never pass for anything else. But we both carried a sense that our greatest shames were also our greatest sources of knowledge, that our sufferings, in his words, *made us what we are.*

(Another brilliant friend, survivor of adolescent trauma that clouded her brain and impeded her potential, wondered to me once: *What kind of genius might I have been, had that not happened to me?* We only know what kind of genius she is in part *because* that happened to her.)

There was an imbalance between Phillip and me, I know. Whenever I won an award or whatever, and dutifully reported it to him, he would comment on how *lucky* I was—how, in his words, I must have *horseshoes up my ass.* Not wrong. Once, in Cuba, I said something about my feelings of insecurity. He looked at me uncomprehendingly. See above: gorgeous husband and kids, professorship, etc. He envied my life; I did not envy his.

And yet, as Adam Phillips puts it, *We should be more attentive to the affinities between people who have little in common; which would include the affinities we have with our selves.*

I flew from Havana straight to Edmonton, to find my grandmother no longer lucid. I stayed a week, taking shifts in her room along with my mother, her sister, her brother, her sister-in-law, and their kids. Grandma died a few days after I left. My cousin, a physician, ensured that it was painless.

Somewhere in this time, Phillip responded to my email, saying that he had been pretty upset when we parted and needed a break. I said to take whatever time he needed. I let him know about my grandmother.

A couple of weeks later, he emailed, saying he no longer wanted to be in the book. *I feel you have not collected the material in good faith.*

I forwarded the note to Geoff with a comment: *Fucking hell.*

How could Phillip accuse me of bad faith? I'd crossed every *t* and dotted every *i* in the word *faith*. I'd written the manual on good faith and I'd paid in the currency of pain. Right?

But, looking now on Wikipedia, I learn bad faith can include self-deception.

Taken that way, maybe I'd been in bad faith all along. But is it mere self-justification to suggest, in that case, that Phillip had been, too?

There is nothing in theory, and certainly nothing in experience, to support the extraordinary judgment that it is the truth about himself that is the easiest for a person to know, says Harry G. Frankfurt. *Facts about ourselves are not peculiarly solid. . . . Our natures are, indeed, elusively insubstantial—notoriously less stable and less inherent than the natures of other things.*

I wrote to Phillip. *I know you were upset on leaving Cuba, but I didn't know it had anything to do with the book.* I asked what had brought it on. *This is completely the opposite of what you've been saying for the last four years . . .*

No answer. I emailed again, subject line: "hurting. please call." *I'm in such pain and bewilderment over this. What's going on? What did I do?*

No answer.

I phoned.

"Hello?" He still had a landline, you won't be surprised to learn, with no caller ID.

"Phillip, it's Padma." At the sound of his voice, my heart had already risen, that familiar gladness.

"You can fuck right off," he said. "I don't want anything to do with you." He hung up.

We haven't spoken since. I sent him a birthday card, five months later, but never heard back.

I loved him. I love him still, with a force that surprises me.

GHOSTED

GHOSTING: OUR CONTEMPORARY TERM for abandonment, departure without explanation, when in fact what ghosts do is accompany us, stay with us even after death.

Had I enraged Phillip the same way I did Harvey, by confronting him with his own behaviour, for not seeing him as he saw himself?

Geoff suggested as much: "He Harveyed you," he said, after Phillip cut ties.

Alice Miller, in *The Drama of the Gifted Child*, says people often express gratitude to parents who brutally disciplined them. Phillip never denied the terrible harm Harvey had done him, but he admired Harvey's principles and insisted that, if Harvey hadn't treated him as he had, he himself *wouldn't be the man I am today*. I had privately dissented, but now thought he might be right, just not in the way he meant.

My sin against him and Harvey, though, went beyond refusing to passively reflect their self-images. I threatened to convert them into literary characters, but they already saw themselves that way. Just not as my characters.

Then again, perhaps that wasn't the crux of the problem at all. Perhaps it wasn't about how I saw Phillip but that he suddenly saw me: my judginess, hypocrisy, egotism. A couple of his other friendships ended during the years we knew each other.

Once I'd asked him why. "Sometimes friends get too close," he said. I had thought that meant that they'd become critical or bossy, but maybe it meant the opposite, that they suddenly came into focus for him and he couldn't stand what he saw.

Perhaps a shard of the mirror blew into his eye.

In the final section of Hans Christian Andersen's tale, Gerda finds Kai in the Snow Queen's palace, *arranging and rearranging pieces of ice into patterns. He called this the Game of Reason, and because of the splinters in his eyes, he thought that what he was doing was of great importance. . . . He wanted to put the pieces together in such a way that they formed a certain word, but he could not remember exactly what that word was. The word that he couldn't remember was eternity.*

The Snow Queen had said, "If you can make that shape for me, you'll be your own master, and I'll give you the whole world and a new pair of skates." But he couldn't do it.

On returning from Cuba, I finished a draft of this book.

It failed, as I said. I couldn't *put the pieces together, couldn't find the shape.*

"Why don't you write it as a novel?" Geoff asked, as exhausted as I was, or more—a loved one's suffering is often more painful than our own. "That's something you know how to do."

Reader, I tried.

That failed, too.

I couldn't get inside either Del's or Harvey's head to invent actions or motivations. Phillip's, yes, because we loved each other, and he'd given me permission, and I believed he had really bared himself to me. But shape Del into fiction? No. I knew enough to know it had been important to her to keep a part of herself unseen; making her into fiction would have meant stripping her of that screen. (And what would I do if I found myself in Harvey's head? Nothing but search desperately for a way out.) The ethics, essentially, were impossible.

I put the book aside, working instead on almost anything else, all the other projects I'd ginned up to keep me busy and sane.

The nights before and after Phillip's next birthday, I dreamt of him. By then, the COVID-19 pandemic was cresting. Phillip was an immunocompromised health-care worker in his sixties.

I kept checking west coast obituaries, full of dread, but, thank god, nothing turned up.

In that time, I got a new agent. She asked what I was working on: short fiction, the twins novel, translations, I answered, and maybe this story. She got excited when I mentioned it. If I had let it go, why did I mention it? Well, obviously, because I hadn't.

"It's failed twice," I warned her, direly. I'd been writing the same book for twenty-five years. Everyone I knew was sick of hearing about it.

Still, I heard its silent ticking.

Books are solitudes in which we meet, says Solnit, but this was one in which my friend and I had parted.

Not writing it wouldn't bring him back, though.

One may have to undergo the same realization, write the same notes in the margin, return to the same themes in one's work, relearn the same emotional truths, write the same book over and over again, says Maggie Nelson, *not because one is stupid or obstinate or incapable of change, but because such revisitations constitute a life.*

Phillip told me once that when Harvey broke with someone, it was for good: they were dead to him. By Harveying me, it turned out that Phillip had given me the distance I needed to *write it.*

So it was that, in spring 2021, I went on a writing retreat. Away from my family and isolated by the pandemic even from the one or two other writers at work there, I reread my transcripts, and secondary sources, and hundreds of pages of notes: Notes on Process, Notes on Story, Notes on Structure, Notes on Revision. I was digesting my research, my reflections, my history, like the caterpillar, eating the roses of memory, then cocooning and eating my own brain, to fuel this metamorphosis.

Because wasn't I, too, to be a butterfly for this story? Wasn't I, too, to have my colours spread and pinned?

A migraine came on, persisted, became unbearable; I went home a day earlier than planned. Plan be damned: the week following, I wrote the opening section, twenty pages, over five days, without revision or pause.

I emailed the pages to my mother and my agent. *Do you want more,* I asked? *If so, I'll continue. If not, I'm out.*

Yes, they said. *Continue.*

"I want to find out what comes next," my mother affirmed, "even though I know all too well what comes next."

I'd paused while waiting to hear back from my agent and my mother, a pause that now stretched to months. Vaccination levels were surging, allowing us to accept the fellowship in England, which precipitated paperwork and organizing; my parents, unable to come with us, would move back to Canada, perhaps permanently. It was exciting and wrenching and a logistical maze. Writing receded.

In this time, I got a text from a friend, Eve. We didn't know each other very well and I hadn't seen her in some years, but she was close with other friends of mine, and our sons were the same age. She'd had a dream about me, she said. Could we talk?

My friend Shana had already mentioned the dream to me.

"Eve is super psychic," she said. "I think it's relevant to your book."

I tried to keep my face neutral. I have dreams of random people all the time. Eve's dream might be amusing. *Relevant,* though? Unlikely.

Before we could meet one-on-one, Eve came to a party at our house. As she was leaving, I asked casually about the dream. I was listening as if her account was a trifle, until she got to the end, when the party scene around us, in my memory, grew muffled, dim, remote.

Eve had dreamt that I had a meeting with a man with whom I was going to be working very closely. He was an angry man, with a rough way of speaking. There was some male authority figure in the room, along with some other guides, all of whom were quite specific about how I should work with the angry man: he would make the work very difficult for me, they said, especially if I didn't follow their directions, but whenever he became irascible, I needed to ask him, *What do you want your legacy to be?* This would calm him and let us do the work. *What do you want your legacy to be?*

I asked Eve if I could come and see her.

Alone together, at her house, I asked if she knew anything about my current project.

"No," she said. "I'm just super psychic." She had trained for years, honing her abilities. "I'm pretty sure I had the dream because of Shana, because you're friends with her."

She'd been driving on Old Wire Road at the time, a place she often sees the dead—the old telegraph route: apparently ghosts like their jokes—and an image popped into her head: my grandmother, in a yellow sari. *I have been trying to get through to Padma but she hasn't been open.* She'd been trying to warn me, to protect me. She went through Shana because I wasn't listening.

Longing—*Grandma!*—and skepticism surged in me.

Phillip had talked about this sort of thing all the time, though never so convincingly.

I told Eve I couldn't get behind the idea of souls retaining anthropomorphic identities.

"No, no, no," she said. "They don't. But when they want to speak to us, they sometimes take that on, because it's easier for us."

I suggested it might be a fine line between being psychic and being sensitive and imaginative, but the more we talked the more unnecessary such distinctions seemed.

"Can I tell you what else your grandmother is saying?"

Grandma was still talking? Sure, I said.

"She wants to help you write this book," she said, "wants to collaborate," to offer a more sophisticated—*slippery* was the word that came to mind for Eve—understanding of this aspect of the book. "Your understanding of these matters is elementary."

Yep.

"She'll give you a richness of understanding. You need to be open to her, to have conversations with her."

By this point, I had moved past thinking about whether I believed, to feeling nervous about discussing my book with my grandma: our closeness, as with my mother, always made me self-protective when it came to my writing, my thoughts, my process.

"I'm resistant to that," I told Eve.

"It's your ego," she said. Grandma said not to worry: she herself had relinquished her ego. She wouldn't get in the way.

The next morning, I woke before dawn, sifting through recollections of the conversation, wondering if Grandma would appear to me, or what. I drifted back to sleep but was awakened by loud, awkward knocks on the bedroom door, like those noises generated spontaneously by old houses. Had I heard such knocks and creaks more often since starting work on the book again?

I opened the door to make sure it wasn't one of the kids, or my mother-in-law, who was also living with us: nope, no one there, or no one I could see. I opened my iPhone calendar to see what I had on for the day and found a reminder—an icon of a raised finger with a string tied around it—labelled *Grandma*.

There were no other reminders, in part because I don't even know how to use that function.

I texted my mother: *Is today some anniversary concerning grandma?*

Mom: *Not that I can think of!*

It was May 4. May the fourth be with me, I thought. She was a force, a force to be reckoned with.

A few weeks later, I went to see Eve once more and told her about the knocking, the reminder, a dozen other strange incidents. *Apophenia*: seeing connections between unrelated things.

"It's all her," Eve said.

It seemed almost caricature: knocking? Really?

"What an amazing twist," I said. My attitude toward Phillip's spiritual beliefs might have been, for him, one of the most frustrating things about me.

"That's the legacy he wants," Eve said. "Your grandmother's telling you: *that* is the legacy he wanted."

I'd never been skeptical of Phillip's own abilities—I totally believed he was capable of tonal resonance, for example, whatever it was, and that he brought a *deep soul learning* to his work.

But I had been dismissive of the information psychics gave him, and any reading he'd recommended to me turned out to be nonsense.

Eve didn't disagree: "Most new-age writing is terrible, and most of those writers never seem to have considered matters of appropriation or structural racism." This woman was literate, current. And she channelled ghosts. What else had I missed, out of intellectual hubris, emotional blindness, vanity, insecurity? Why was the lesson always, always, to *be humble?*

"And so that's going in the book?" she prompted.

I felt put on the spot. But hadn't I just said that?

Yes, I said, yes.

"Progressives discount all this," Eve went on. "It's a binary that goes back to Descartes's deal with the Pope. You know about that? Descartes and other scientists wanted to dissect bodies, to advance science, so the Pope said, okay, but leave the soul and spirit alone. Okay, said Descartes, and from that moment forward, western science ignored the spirit, the soul, energy." She said progressives needed to wake up if we were to advance our agenda.

Meantime, Grandma was standing by. Eve started laughing: Grandma had materialized an old telephone receiver, and was holding it, like, *call me up*. With her other hand, Eve said, she wrote WRITE in air, in smoke.

And she showed Eve a game, palanghuzhi, one of the few items she'd brought with her to Canada when she immigrated, two gourd-shaped pieces of wood hinged together to open, like a book, revealing seven carved cups in each half. She and I had played endless rounds, every day in summer when I was small, scooping up tamarind seeds or cowrie shells by the handful, dropping them one by one into the cups.

Where does a story begin? Rebecca Solnit asks. *The fiction is that they do, and end, rather than that the stuff of a story is just a cup of water scooped from the sea and poured back into it . . .*

Grandma's blue Noxzema container of those seeds, those shells, sits on my desk now, one of the few items I brought with me to London. Each morning of these months of writing, I have used them in invocation. *Call me up.*

And so I came to London, and sat at my desk looking out at the climbing roses, and started once more to write, galvanized by grief, not rendering my friend as noble or heroic or as though composed only of *his finest sides*, but rather loving him as I am loved.

Writing brought me to realize that perhaps what I'd feared had not in fact come to pass: Did the book cannibalize my friendship with Phillip or did the friendship merely run its course? It seems to have ended for the same reason as Phillip's other friendships: because we got too close. The book pressed the friendship to persist, then the friendship's dissolution made the book possible. They *moved together for a little while, like dancers*. Just because they couldn't coexist, it doesn't necessarily mean they killed each other.

At the end of "The Snow Queen," Gerda enters the castle to find Kai sitting before those befuddling pieces of ice, alone and thinking, thinking, alone.

She flings her arms around him, crying out his name, but he is stiff and cold, almost as though frozen to death. She bursts into tears, which thaw his heart, making him start to cry, too, hot tears of recognition and regret that wash the splinter from his eye. It's all so ridiculously great that even those pieces of ice start dancing with joy, and when they get tired, they lay themselves down to rest in exactly that pattern he'd been trying so hard to find, the pattern that spells *eternity*.

The friends wander out of the castle, holding hands, chatting about their grandmother—though they're not related, she somehow belongs equally to them both—reminiscing about the roses they shared across the bower. They retrace Gerda's long journey through wild northern lands, meeting again those who helped her, including my favourite character, a foul-mouthed little robber girl who comments to Kai, *I wonder if you really deserve to have someone running to the ends of the earth for your sake.* Gerda changes the subject.

Rose-tinted: what we say when a person sees things as better than they are. The price of regaining lost innocence is another kind of unseeing, but disenchantment, says Solnit, *is the blessing of becoming yourself.*

The friends return home, walking through the city and up the worn stairs to Grandmother's apartment. Nothing in it has changed, but *as they step through the door, they notice they have grown up.*

Along the bower, the roses are blooming. They have not been awaiting the friends; they are not a remedy for anything.

It is summer, and, in summer, blooming is what they do.

BOOK CLUB GUIDE

1. The title of this book is taken from a book, *On Friendship*, by the philosopher Alexander Nehamas. What did you initially think the title meant? How is friendship like or unlike other forms of love?

2. Padma says that her desire to write a book about Phillip might have meant she made an extra effort to keep the friendship going despite distance and differences in life circumstances. In other words, the book might have let the friendship take root. Sometimes proximity occasions friendships, say with neighbors or colleagues, despite little else in common; other times, a friendship chemistry ignites based on shared interests or perspectives. What do you think is most important as a basis for friendship? Do your friendships owe more to circumstances or other kinds of connection?

3. Telling—and learning—his own story was often painful for Phillip, to the point that, midway through the process, he quit. After a pause, though, he recommitted, saying, "It's my project to be true to the book and be myself..." and telling Padma, "and it's your project to be true to the book and write it." Why do you think Phillip wanted to participate in this book? Do you think his aims were fulfilled?

4. Harvey, for all his suspicion, also seemed quite interested in being written about. Del, also, said she wanted to write her life story. Why do so many of us want our stories told? And what about the exceptions—why do some people not want others to know their stories?

5. Throughout the book, Padma questions whether or how a writer can write about a loved one. Many writers write about family members and close friends, though it might be a bit more common to write about these relationships after they are over. (Ann Patchett wrote about her friend Lucy Grealy, after Grealy died; others write about deceased parents or ex-spouses.) Do you think Padma would have been able to write this book if Phillip had not ended their friendship? Is this more Padma's story or Phillip's?

6. While Del gave Phillip the affection and attention he craved as a young adolescent, and her daughter said that she tried to be a good person (for example, she was vegetarian), she also told many lies and the book never puts to rest the possibility that she had a hand in her husband Lew's death. How do you feel about Del? Was her lying was justified because of her circumstances? Or was she manipulative and pathological?

7. Harvey is high-minded—concerned with poverty and racism—but also rigid and maybe even abusive. He believes he has lived according to his principles and helped many people but he has also left a trail of hurt family members. Many people who have brought about good in the world, from Gandhi to Martin Luther King, Jr., have been criticized for their personal conduct. How do you weigh a person's principles and public commitments against bad personal behavior?

8. Padma retells three Hans Christian Andersen stories in the course of this book: "The Ugly Duckling" parallels Phillip's development; "The Shadow" is an allegory for the writer's split self; and "The Snow Queen" reflects and refracts her complicated friendship with Phillip, as well as their mutual disillusionment. How did the fairy tales make you see this story differently?

9. The book also makes many other references, to philosophy, myth and literature. What were some of your favorite external references or quotes? Why do you think Padma brought in so many other voices?

10. There are images interspersed throughout the book, some archival, some contemporary. Most of them aren't strictly necessary to the story and yet they seem integral. How did you connect with the pictures? How did they change the story for you?

ACKNOWLEDGEMENTS

First thanks go to "Phillip," the North Star of this project.

This book was generously supported by a grant from the Canada Council for the Arts and a residency at The Writers' Colony at Dairy Hollow.

For research assistance and information, I'm indebted to "Lorraine" (Del's daughter), Tony Brown, Linda Eversole, Simma Holt, Gabrielle Idlet, James Kempster, Marshall Lloyd, Sue Mitchell, "Ben" Totten, Harvey Totten, "Rob" Totten, "Vivia" Totten, and Cameron Willis.

Justin Anthony Barnum, with whom I taught a course on women criminals in life and literature, directed me to Erving Goffman's *The Presentation of Self in Everyday Life.* Thanks to the students in that class and in my two Boundaries of Nonfiction classes, for many useful insights and to Elizabeth DeMeo and Andrew Butler for their specific comments on this project.

Ravi Kumar and Shoba Kumar hosted and fed me in the course of my research, as did Sudha Seetharaman and Anand Kamalakar, and Amber Pikula and Reid Wilson.

For illuminating conversations, literary friendship and general encouragement I am grateful to Canem Arkan, Deena Aziz, Catherine Bush, Michael Cawthon, Matt Farwell, Carolyn Forde, Sylvia Fraser, Deborah Freedman, Alexander Freer, Kate Frohlich, Sugi Ganeshananthan, Padma Ghosh, Shana Gold, Shannon Haragan, Jean Hitchman, Arun Kumar, Kathy Kumar, Maya Kumar, Thara Kumar, Annabel Lyon, Tessa McWatt, Deepa Murthy, Vasantha Murthy, Timothy O'Grady, Alix Ohlin, Heather Rekhi, Sheila

Ribeiro, Meg Rosoff, Thomas Schlich, Bret Schulte, Stephanie Schulte, Shyam Selvadurai, Rebecca Solnit, Samanth Subramanian, Joan Silber, Jeni Tackett, Marina Warner, Lawrence Weschler, Bruce Westwood, Meg Wheeler, and Greg Wise.

Jonny Schremmer and Dave King gave me perspicacious and generous readings. Shelley Tepperman did all the above and advised me to buy baked goods. Eve Agee brought my grandma back.

My mentors and models Elizabeth Evans, D D Kugler, Howard Norman and Manil Suri have challenged me, directed me, and shown me not only how to make art from life, but how to make a life in art. I owe them.

Anne Collins of Random House Canada has been a stalwart companion to this project from its earliest days. Anjali Singh, of Ayesha Pande Literary, helped me see how to return to it after I'd quit and cheerled me through the culminating stages. This book likely wouldn't exist without them.

My parents, Bhuvana Viswanathan and S. P. Viswanathan, have been unreserved and unwavering in their support of my writing. They are my close advisors and guides.

My grandmother, Dhanam Kochoi, was and remains my literary beacon.

Big, big, big thanks to Geoff Brock, Mira Brock and Ravi Brock, for the best lines and the best laughs. You are my ballast and my joys.

My poor and unreliable memory is a subject in this book: I hope I have not forgotten to give gratitude wherever it is due.

NOTES AND CREDITS

In longer quotes, I have not always used ellipses and sometimes have moved sentences around, so that what appears here as a single statement might not have appeared that way in the original. To those who say this editing might make it appear that the writers meant something they didn't, I might say that sort of translation happens every time we read a book: *the truth—that thing I thought I was telling.*

On translations :

The Nathalie Léger quote from *Suite for Barbara Loden* was translated by Natasha Lehrer and Cécile Menon.

Otherwise, translations are mine. When I quote from Hans Christian Andersen's tales, I am mostly relying on Erik Christian Haugaard's translations, but I have consulted others, particularly Tiina Nunnally's, and then edited the English versions according to my own taste.

My husband, Geoff Brock, helped me considerably with the bits from Italo Calvino.

Attributions for the italicized lines I've borrowed that aren't already credited in the text :

Page 2: "the stern, brass-knuckled poetry of the dangerous classes"- Tobias Wolff, "A Bullet in the Brain"

Page 4: "In fairy tales the coming of a stepmother is never regarded as anything but a misfortune", William Maxwell, *So Long, See You Tomorrow*

Page 19: "life being, as Ortega y Gasset once remarked, in itself and forever shipwreck", William Maxwell, *So Long, See You Tomorrow*

Page 25: "the single maker of the song he sang, the single artificer of the world in which he sang", After Wallace Stevens, "The Idea of Order at Key West"

Page 60: "Fuck and run", Liz Phair, "Fuck and Run"

Page 195: "fucked up in his turn", Phillip Larkin, "This Be the Verse"

Page 201: "*É arrivato!*", Federico Fellini, *La Strada*

Page 201: "We tell ourselves stories in order to live." Joan Didion, *The White Album*

Page 215: "Authority wants to replace the world with itself." Adam Phillips, *Unforbidden Pleasures*

Page 225: "the mystery to a solution" John Irwin, *The Mystery to a Solution: Poe, Borges, and the Analytic Detective Story*

Page 239: "eating or opening a window or just walking dully along", W. H. Auden, "Musée des Beaux Arts"

Page 243: "deepens like a coastal shelf", Phillip Larkin, "This Be the Verse"

Page 260: "the truth—that thing I thought I was telling", John Ashbery, "A Sedentary Existence"

Credits for pieces published previously :

The essay referring to the boy on horseback in Nicaragua was published by the *National Post* in 2014, in their Afterword series.

Parts of the chapter describing my depression are taken from an essay called "A Hunger for the World," published in 2015 in *Event Magazine* 44/1, and republished in a collection of their Notes on Writing in 2021.

On names :

I have slightly changed the given names of these people: Phillip, his brothers Ben and Rob, Del's daughter Lorraine, Harvey's step daughter Vivia, and the accused pedophile Edwin Mingham. All other names and dates, as well as all quotes from interviews or archival materials, are accurate and confirmable, albeit in edited form.

The images:

Page 3: Heron, Paul Brennan, Pixabay

Page 9: Cover of *Edmonton Journal*, June 25, 1956

Page 10: Underwear advertisement, *Edmonton Journa*l June 28, 1956

Page 15: Mug shots of James Kempster and Mary Lloyd, *Vancouver Sun*, January 15, 1957

Page 74: Hans Christian Andersen papercut (ã Det Kongelige Bibliotek 2002)

Page 77: "Sun's Simma Holt," *Vancouver Sun*, July 4, 1956

Page 80: "Bank Holdup," *Vancouver Sun*, April 19, 1956

Page 84: Mary Lloyd reading, courtesy of Simma Holt file

Page 86: The Little Bungalow, "Not by Salads Alone,"https://publications.gc.ca/collections/collection_2017/sp-ps/JS94-1-4-3-eng.pdf *Federal Corrections*, Vol. 4, No. 3

Page 87: Isabel Macneill, courtesy of Holt file

Page 89: Portion of letter from Isabel Macneill to Simma Holt, courtesy of Holt file

Page 94: Portion of letter from Mary Lloyd to Simma Holt, courtesy of Holt file

Page 133: Harvey Totten Firearms License, courtesy of Harvey Totten

Page 144: Photo of Titan the rottweiler, courtesy of the author

Page 177: Photo of Harvey Totten, courtesy of the author

Page 203: Albrecht Dürer's "Melencolia"

Page 223: Photo of James Kempster, *Edmonton Journal*, July 5, 1956

ABOUT THE AUTHOR

Padma Viswanathan's fiction has been published in eight countries and shortlisted for the PEN USA Prize and the Scotiabank Giller Prize. Her stories, essays and short translations have appeared in *Granta, The Boston Review, BRICK*, and elsewhere. Her translation of the novel *São Bernardo*, by the Brazilian novelist Graciliano Ramos, was published in 2020 by New York Review Books. Originally from Edmonton, Alberta, she now divides her time between Montreal, Quebec, and Fayetteville, Arkansas, where she is Professor of Fiction at the University of Arkansas. She has served as fiction faculty at the Banff Centre, the Vermont Studio Center, Kundiman Asian-American Writers Retreat, Bread Loaf Writers' Conferences and the Low-Residency MFA of Fairleigh-Dickinson University. She is married to the poet and translator Geoffrey Brock.

7.1BOOKS

Made in United States
North Haven, CT
25 July 2024

55439097R00168